Gastronomy, Tourism and the Media

ASPECTS OF TOURISM

Series Editors: Chris Cooper, *Oxford Brookes University, UK*, C. Michael Hall, *University of Canterbury, New Zealand* and Dallen J. Timothy, *Arizona State University, USA*

Aspects of Tourism is an innovative, multifaceted series, which comprises authoritative reference handbooks on global tourism regions, research volumes, texts and monographs. It is designed to provide readers with the latest thinking on tourism worldwide and push back the frontiers of tourism knowledge. The volumes are authoritative, readable and user-friendly, providing accessible sources for further research. Books in the series are commissioned to probe the relationship between tourism and cognate subject areas such as strategy, development, retailing, sport and environmental studies.

Full details of all the books in this series and of all our other publications can be found on http://www.channelviewpublications.com, or by writing to Channel View Publications, St Nicholas House, 31–34 High Street, Bristol BS1 2AW, UK.

ASPECTS OF TOURISM: 74

Gastronomy, Tourism and the Media

Warwick Frost, Jennifer Laing, Gary Best, Kim Williams, Paul Strickland and Clare Lade

CHANNEL VIEW PUBLICATIONS
Bristol • Buffalo • Toronto

Library of Congress Cataloging in Publication Data
Names: Frost, Warwick, author.
Title: Gastronomy, Tourism and the Media/Warwick Frost, Jennifer Laing, Gary Best, Kim Williams, Paul Strickland and Clare Lade.
Description: Bristol, UK; Tonawanda, NY: Channel View Publications, [2016] | Series: Aspects of Tourism: 74 | Includes bibliographical references and index.
Identifiers: LCCN 2016011391 | ISBN 9781845415747 (hbk) | ISBN 9781845415730 (pbk) | ISBN 9781845415778 (kindle)
Subjects: LCSH: Food tourism. | Food in popular culture. | Mass media—Social aspects.
Classification: LCC TX631.F76 2016 | DDC 641.01/3—dc23 LC record available at https://lccn.loc.gov/2016011391

British Library Cataloguing in Publication Data
A catalogue entry for this book is available from the British Library.

ISBN-13: 978-1-84541-574-7 (hbk)
ISBN-13: 978-1-84541-573-0 (pbk)

Channel View Publications
UK: St. Nicholas House, 31–34 High Street, Bristol BS1 2AW, UK.
USA: UTP, 2250 Military Road, Tonawanda, NY 14150, USA.
Canada: UTP, 5201 Dufferin Street, North York, Ontario M3H 5T8, Canada.

Website: www.channelviewpublications.com
Twitter: Channel_View
Facebook: https://www.facebook.com/channelviewpublications
Blog: www.channelviewpublications.wordpress.com

The policy of Multilingual Matters/Channel View Publications is to use papers that are natural, renewable and recyclable products, made from wood grown in sustainable forests. In the manufacturing process of our books, and to further support our policy, preference is given to printers that have FSC and PEFC Chain of Custody certification. The FSC and/or PEFC logos will appear on those books where full certification has been granted to the printer concerned.

Typeset by Nova Techset Private Limited, Bengaluru and Chennai, India.
Printed and bound in Great Britain by Short Run Press Ltd.

Contents

Figures

Authors

Warwick Frost is an Associate Professor in Tourism, Hospitality and Events at La Trobe University, Melbourne, Australia. His research interests are in heritage, rural tourism, events and tourism, and the media. He is Editor of the Routledge Advances in Events Research series and a member of the organising committee for the biennial International Tourism and Media conference series.

Jennifer Laing is an Associate Professor in Management at La Trobe University, Melbourne, Australia. Her research interests include tourist narratives, heritage tourism and exploring extraordinary tourist experiences. She is Editor of the Routledge Advances in Events Research series, a member of the organising committee for the biennial International Tourism and Media conference series and a member of the Editorial Boards of *Journal of Travel Research, Tourism Analysis* and *Tourism Review International*.

Gary Best is an Honorary Associate of La Trobe University, Melbourne, Australia and an independent consultant and author whose writing focuses on cultural tourism, gastronomy and festival and event management. His research interests are diverse, but tend to focus on tourism and the media; automotive history, heritage and culture; travel writing; distinctive cultural interactions in touristic contexts; and the means by which all of the above operate in popular culture.

Kim Williams is a Lecturer in the Faculty of Higher Education at William Angliss Institute, Melbourne, Australia. Kim lectures in event management and human resources. Her research background is diverse, but tends to focus on human resources issues, with a prime emphasis on professional development and training. She is also interested in event management, gastronomy, fashion and wine tourism.

Paul Strickland is a Lecturer in Hospitality Management at La Trobe University, Melbourne, Australia. His research interests include ethnic restaurants, Bhutanese studies, space tourism, wine, fashion and business education simulations. He is a PhD candidate researching in the field of wine events and social media usage.

Clare Lade is a Lecturer in Tourism and Hospitality Management at La Trobe University, Melbourne, Australia. Clare completed her PhD in regional tourism development, concentrating on network development and competitiveness through business cluster theory along Australia's Murray River. Her primary research interests include gastronomy and regional festivals, regional tourism development and dark tourism.

Part 1

Foundations and Principles

1 Gastronomy and Tourism through the Media Lens

The Accidental Tourist (Anne Tyler, 1985)

Macon is the central character in this novel. Based in Baltimore, USA, he writes a successful series of guidebooks for Americans who are forced to travel overseas on business. The idea is that such 'accidental tourists' want familiarity and sameness rather than travel adventures:

> Accidental Tourist in France. Accidental Tourist in Germany. In Belgium. No author's name, just a logo: a winged armchair on the cover. He covered only the cities in these guides, for people taking business trips flew into cities and out again and didn't see the countryside at all. They didn't see the cities, for that matter. Their concern was how to pretend they had never left home. What hotels in Madrid boasted king-sized Beauty-rest mattresses. What restaurants in Tokyo offered Sweet'n'Low? Did Amsterdam have a McDonald's? Did Mexico City have a Taco Bell? Did any place in Rome serve Chef Boyardee ravioli? Other travellers hoped to discover distinctive local wines; Macon's readers searched for pasteurized and homogenized milk. (Tyler, 1985: 12)

Past Views of Travel and Food

Until quite recently, food was viewed as a necessary evil for most tourists. It was fuel, a convenience, a hygiene factor in the tourist experience – mainly noticeable if it was bad (Quan & Wang, 2004; Scarpato, 2002a). As Cohen argued, while most tourists were interested in sights, customs and cultures that were different, they were, 'able to enjoy the experience of change and novelty only from a strong base of familiarity, which enables them to feel secure enough to enjoy the strangeness of what they experience' (Cohen, 2004: 38). An *environmental bubble* of escorted group tours and international hotels allowed the visitor to venture out, but return to safety and

3

familiarity for comfortable and comforting dining. The epitome of such a view of travel was the ubiquity of *international cuisine,* a series of generic Western dishes that came to dominate global hospitality practices and training courses. The result of such standardisation was that tourists were not only assured that hotel chains offered the same standard accommodation and service, but they were furthermore provided with the same *safe* menus. However, with sameness came dissatisfaction. In introducing her groundbreaking *A Book of Mediterranean Food*, Elizabeth David assured her readers that it contained recipes for, 'honest cooking' as opposed to the 'sham *grande cuisine* of the International Palace Hotel' (David, 1951: 5).

Where more adventurous travel occurred, food was one of the risks. The more exotic the destination, the more likely it was that the intrepid visitor would succumb to an upset stomach or food poisoning. Such perils were a badge of honour. A good traveller was one with a *cast-iron stomach*. With the rising popularity of travel narratives from the 19th century onwards, a series of food-related tropes developed, and were in turn copied by those who followed. To illustrate, we consider one of the best-loved travel narratives of the Victorian era.

A Ride to Khiva (Fred Burnaby, 1877)

A captain in the British army, Fred Burnaby was looking for adventure in a time of peace. When he saw a newspaper item that the Russians had forbidden British travellers to enter Central Asian territory under Russian control, he was outraged. He resolved to publicly flout this restriction by openly journeying from Moscow to Khiva (now in modern Uzbekistan).

Observations on food are woven throughout the book. What is interesting is how these are all connected to his persona as a brave traveller in a very hostile physical environment. It would have been very easy for Burnaby to complain of the food, but this would mark him as delicate and boorish rather than hardy and stoic. Furthermore, he presented his guides and the local people as good fellows, worthy of British sympathy and support against oppression. Accordingly, their culture and cuisine was constructed as novel, but not nightmarish.

In the depths of winter, he suffered from the cold and exposure and was grateful for the food he received. At day's end, he was served 'a strange culinary composition of Nazar's [his guide], made of rice, eggs, and chocolate, boiled in milk, over a spirit lamp – this strange mixture proving in our ravenous state the most savoury of dishes' (Burnaby, 1877: 119). On another day, dinner was a pot of fatty mutton and rice:

> It was not a very appetising spectacle, nor a dish that Baron Brisse [a noted French food writer of the time] would have been likely to add to any of his *menus*, but after a ride across the steppes in midwinter the

traveller soon loses every other feeling in the absorbing one of hunger, and at that time I think I could have eaten my great grandfather if he had been properly roasted for the occasion. (Burnaby, 1877: 205)

Even when honoured with a feast of horsemeat, Burnaby made no direct criticism. Instead he described the guests' ravenous consumption, sure that most of his readers shared similar feelings to him. Only once did he strategically allow the facade to fall. As a true explorer and adventurer, he could stomach almost anything. However, there was one exception that he shared with the readers, demonstrating his gentlemanly tastes and manners in the face of adversity. That was a cup of tea. Here he revealed the full horror:

It was not tea in our sense of the word, but a mixture which had the peculiar flavour of grease, salt and tea-leaves. Swallowing my nausea as best I could in order to avoid offending my host, I drank off the nasty draught, and exclaimed in the best Tartar I could master for the occasion, 'Excellent!'. (Burnaby, 1877: 209)

Changing Views

Despite the long-held view that food was one of the travails of travel, food often functioned as more than fuel or danger, even if that was often barely recognised. In prehistoric times, surplus food harvests were the catalyst for travel to cross-tribal gatherings. These early festivals were characterised by feasting and had an important social role of providing a temporary peace for settling disputes and arranging marriages. An example of this occurred in south-eastern Queensland, where Aboriginal groups would travel hundreds of kilometres to partake in the consumption of Bunya nuts. Highly rich in fat (making them deliciously attractive), these trees fruited prolifically, but only every two to three years (Frost & Laing, 2015a).

As modern societies developed, harvest festivals and other food traditions sometimes remained and these would attract recent emigrants to return temporarily to their home regions. The extraordinary flows of travel within China for the feasting and celebration of New Year remain a striking example of this today. Some regional specialities drew in visitors eager to try for themselves. In the 19th century, for example, Devon became famous for its dairy produce and afternoon teas featuring scones, jam and clotted cream. This meal became the major feature of the region's destination image and generated strong repeat visitation. Mass tourism to the seaside, also a product of the 19th century, generated its own foods and traditions, such as the consumption of fish and chips wrapped in newspaper. Similarly, carnivals, amusement parks and international expositions created fast food offerings for time-poor visitors who preferred to queue for rides and attractions rather than sit-down meals. Accordingly, hot dogs, hamburgers and ice cream cones were all invented for these markets.

However, it was late in the 20th century that there was a revolution in the relationship between food and tourism. In a relatively short period of time, food and cuisines shifted to being one of the key motivations for travel. To better understand this shift, the following seven qualifications need to be made:

(1) The enjoyment of food while on holiday becomes a mass phenomenon. Trends, fashion, media and marketing combine to link food to culture and to provide it with status as an integral part of the tourist experience.
(2) Travelling for food shifts from the domestic (as in the examples above) to the international. The status now arises from consuming the exotic.
(3) The changes are demand centred. Tourists want to indulge in food and associated cultures. Adventure replaces risk in influencing food experiences. This could include interactions with exotic sellers of food and beverages (Figure 1.1) and the consumption of unusual – even normally repulsive – foods and meals (Figure 1.2).
(4) Interest in food and cuisine becomes an example of *serious leisure* (Stebbins, 1992). People are interested in learning about food, having

Figure 1.1 Adventurous interaction with a street food vendor in Istanbul, Turkey (photo S. Harvey)

Figure 1.2 Adventurous menus – rattlesnake bratwurst, Cowgirl Restaurant, Santa Fe, USA (photo W. Frost)

new experiences and seeking out new tastes, and they link this to their own personal development and identity.

(5) The *demonstration effect* is critical. To gain status, people copy others. A food-savvy elite leads the way, but is quickly followed by the mass market. There are leaps across cultures. The rapidly expanding Asian middle class, for example, follows Western trends, although in recent years there has been a refocus on their own traditions and cultures.

(6) These interests in gastronomy and tourism are often constructed in opposition to modernity, both as a reaction and as an antidote. *Globalisation*, for instance, generates a movement towards *localism*. The growth and ubiquity of *fast food* leads to *slow food*.

(7) Supply is altered to cater for demand. Tour operators develop food-themed tours. Certain destinations reinvent themselves as attractive *food destinations*, through marketing campaigns and the development of culinary attractions, trails and routes.

Causes of change

The reasons for these changes are a combination of economic, social, technical and cultural. It is valuable here to briefly consider some of the reasons for these changes that have been advanced in the recent literature. These fall into two camps. The first recognises changes in the scale and nature of global tourism. Richards (2002) highlights both increased tourism mobility and growing competition between destinations as forces for new gastronomic products. Others see destinations as actively entrepreneurial, developing gastronomic products to attract more tourists (Du Rand & Heath, 2006; Gössling & Hall, 2013).

A second grouping identifies dissatisfaction with modernity as stimulating interest in food and tourism. Boniface (2003: 16) sees the catalyst as a 'world crisis of confidence in the way of life now come to be its routine'. Accordingly, anxious and insecure tourists are seeking out different foods and cultures – usually traditional and local – as a means of constructing a new self-identity that contrasts with the sameness of the everyday. As Richards (2002: 4) puts it, 'with the disintegration of established structures of meaning, people are searching for new sources of identity that provide some security in an increasingly turbulent world'. As such, food becomes a quest, perceived as having the power to effect personal transformation.

The Role of Media

In this book, our aim is to explore these forces in depth, with a particular focus on the media. In adopting this approach, we view media as important in two ways. The first is as instruments for disseminating and influencing attitudes, ideas and ultimately change. The second is as a lens for examining and understanding the processes and outcomes of these changes. These two approaches are built on two broad paradigms. The first links the media with marketing and may be viewed from a business or industry perspective as a way of increasing sales for destinations and operators. The second views the media from a sociological standpoint, utilising media as a means to better understand what is happening within societies. For this book, we are attempting a delicate balancing act of examining and analysing these phenomena from both business and sociological perspectives. Our view, which we try to communicate to our students, is that to understand disciplines such as tourism, media studies, hospitality, gastronomy and events, both approaches are equally important and need to be fully considered.

What part, then, does the media play in these changes towards food and travel? While tourism researchers have long been interested in media, the tendency has been to consider it in terms of destination imaging and marketing. How can we extend this consideration more broadly, particularly to the phenomena of increased interest in food? In this introductory chapter, it is instructive to examine some of the main themes and theories in tourism and the media and begin to explore how these might be applied to gastronomy and tourism.

Induced and organic messages and images

The early work on tourism and the media made a simple division between induced and organic sources. Where the industry created the media, as in advertisements, this was designated as *induced*. Where the media was created by forces other than the tourist industry, such as filmmakers or novelists, this was seen as *organic*. Induced media marketing was a conventional approach, which allowed operators and destinations to have control over the messages and images that were disseminated to the public. However, it had a drawback in that consumers could see that it was advertising and accordingly might not be convinced of its veracity or liability. Organic sources, in contrast, were outside the control of the industry, but had higher levels of trust and engagement.

This opposition of control and trust may be seen in media commentary and restaurant and travel reviewing. Independent travel writers are more likely to be critical. Indeed, their readers expect this. These writers may even go so far as to ridicule the pomposity and pretensions of some operators and their practices. For example, American travel writer Bill Bryson stays at a hotel in Dorset, England:

> Given the nature of the hotel, I'd expected the menu to feature items like brown Windsor soup and roast beef and Yorkshire pudding, but of course things have moved on in the hotel trade. The menu was now richly endowed with ... words that you wouldn't have seen on an English menu ten years ago – 'noisettes,' 'tartare,' 'duxelle,' 'coulis,' 'timbale' – and written in a curious inflated language with eccentric capitalizations. I had, and I quote, 'Fanned Galia Melon and Cumbrian Air Dried Ham served with a Mixed leaf Salad,' followed by 'Fillet Steak served with a crushed Black Peppercorn Sauce flamed in Brandy and finished with Cream'. (Bryson, 1995: 98)

Bryson's literary persona is of a humorous curmudgeon, so he sends up this menu *newspeak*:

> I was greatly taken with this new way of talking and derived considerable pleasure from speaking it to the waiter ... when he came around with the bread rolls I entreated him to present me a tonged rondelle of blanched wheat, oven baked and masked in a poppy-seed coating ... [and when finished] I dressed the tabletop with a small circlet of copper specie crafted at the Royal Mint. (Bryson, 1995: 98–99)

As a travel writer, Bryson is not dependent on funding from the destinations and operations he is visiting. He is an independent journalist, with no obligations as he is paying his own way (indeed, he both complains about high prices and values the bargains he stumbles upon). He praises certain restaurants and slams other. For his readers, his independence and objectivity translate into strong trust.

In contrast, some media personalities risk losing such trust through their commercial connections. Television chefs may promote cookbooks and pots and pans without diminishing their appeal, but some have perhaps gone too far. That some chefs advertise packaged stocks, for example, seems contrary and confusing.

Media tourism and mediatisation

Initially, much of the research into media and tourism has focused on organic image formation through films. Generally identified as film-induced tourism, case studies of films triggering bursts of tourist visitation included *Field of Dreams, The Quiet Man, Braveheart* and *Lord of the Rings* (Beeton, 2005; Connell, 2012). In more recent years, there has been a shift to recognising that organic image formation is due to the consumption of narratives through a range of different media. Examples of this include the reading of books and the watching of films based on those books, as in the cases of *The Da Vinci Code, Lord of the Rings, Twilight* and *Harry Potter*. Such productions encompass multiple media which people may consume in any order or even only partly. The rise of social media encourages tourists to go beyond what they have read or watched, posting their own commentaries, experiences, critiques and inventions. Accordingly, we can no no longer just see media as produced and consumed by separate entities, but rather see it as *co-created*, with producers and consumers both engaged in the process (Månsson, 2011; Mercille, 2005).

A good example of both co-creation and multiple media sources concerns blogger Julie Powell. In 2002, she launched her blog in which she attempted all the dishes in the cookbook *Mastering the Art of French Cooking* by Julia Child (Vol. 1, 1961 and Vol. 2, 1970). Such was the popularity of her blog that she landed a publishing contract resulting in her book *Julie and Julia: 365 Days, 524 Recipes, 1 Tiny Apartment Kitchen* (2005) (later retitled as *Julie and Julia: My Year of Cooking Dangerously*). The success of that book led to the film version *Julie and Julia* (2009), with Amy Adams playing Julie and Meryl Streep as Julia.

Two further spinoffs are worth noting. As people engaged with the blog, book and/or film, their interest was stimulated in going back to the original Julia Child recipes, resulting in increased sales of her cookbooks. The other outcome – illustrating the processes of co-creation – was that other aspiring bloggers aimed for success through variations on the theme, either through recreating the feats of great chefs or through emphasising their personal transformation through setting themselves an arduous cooking test.

Media framing, signing, archetypes and tropes

In analysing the impact of media on tourism, some researchers have utilised theories from communications and literature studies relating to structures and underlying meanings. Santos (2004) highlighted the concept of *media framing* in her study of Portugal. This is where the media organises stories – both structurally and in terms of narrative and plot – along common lines that then tend to reappear time and time again. In addition, signs (or signifiers) provided audiences with direction towards certain cultural messages, not only providing a guide as to how to *read* the film, but also reinforcing attitudes. Laing and Frost (2012, 2014) drew on research into classical literature and mythology to apply *archetypes* and *tropes* to their studies of travel and explorer narratives.

These are complex concepts, but their application to gastronomy, tourism and the media may be illustrated by two simple examples. The first comes from the cooking/travel television show *Shane Delia's Spice Journey* (2013). Travelling to Istanbul in Turkey, he makes the promise that he is going to take his audience to a secret place and experience that tourists don't know about. Walking along with a guide, he speaks directly to the camera and repeats this idea that they are heading towards a secret that only the locals know about. Eventually he arrives at the Golden Horn and purchases a fried fish sandwich. Of course, this is hardly a secret, as these sandwiches have long been publicised in tourism guidebooks. However, by framing this segment in terms of revealing a secret, tensions and expectations have been heightened and the audience more strongly engaged.

A second example is that of the personal journey of a traveller, resulting in some inner transformation or better insight into their own lives. Julie Powell (mentioned above), seeks not only to duplicate Julia Child's recipes, but also to test herself by giving some meaning and direction to her mundane life. Elizabeth Gilbert, in *Eat Pray Love* (2006), journeys through Italy after the break-up of her marriage. Enjoying the lifestyle, particularly the food, helps her to battle depression and begin to reshape her life.

Places of imagination

Researchers into media and tourism are split into two camps in regards to what media consumers are looking for when they travel. The obvious motivation seems to be to *see* what they have seen or read about. In a quantitative study, Macionis and Sparks (2009: 97) identified that the main motivation for film tourists was 'to see the scenery and landscape in real life'. Similarly, Carl *et al.* (2007) emphasised the need to visit the actual places where their favourite films were shot. In contrast, others have targeted plot and character as critically important. Drawing on ideas of co-creation, Beeton proposed that 'we view movies through ourselves in such a way to gain some personal meaning' and 'we put ourselves in the stories, sights, sounds and emotions of the movie' (Beeton, 2005: 229). Arguing that 'projecting striking visual images is rarely sufficient to carry a successful production', Frost contended that the appeal, 'for the audience of potential tourists is these storylines present a "promise" of what might occur if they were to travel to the locations featured' (Frost, 2010: 723).

In analysing tourism arising from film and television productions, Reijnders (2011) has developed the concept of *places of the imagination*. He conceptualises this as a circular process. Artists are inspired by physical places, constructing imagined versions of real places in their media. These media productions attract fans, who then travel seeking physical versions of these imaginary places. These fans cum tourists are making 'concrete comparisons between imagination and reality ... driven by an emotional longing for the two worlds to converge'. Travelling to destinations featured or linked to their favourite media stories, they 'search for physical references to a phenomenon that actually takes place in their minds' (Reijnders, 2011: 233 and 234).

While usually seen as arising from fictional media, the concept of places of the imagination is equally applicable to food-related media. Foodie destinations, particularly those promoted as the latest hotspot, are hybrids of reality and imagination. For example, rural places are often constructed as traditional and artisanal, idyllic escapes for jaded urbanites. Nostalgia and fantasy combine in their image-making, while potential negativities, such as economic and social issues, are excluded (Boniface, 2003; Frost & Laing, 2014).

Fandom and authenticity

The engagement between fans, places and the media is often very intense and profound. It may also be very inclusive, with those involved forming their own *social worlds* (Unruh, 1979). These are loose groups of people with strong common interests who come together around their passions. In the past these have been seen as quite informal, although the rise of social media is resulting in more organised structures and new forms of interaction. Such social worlds may be highly exclusive, with participants constructing their identity in terms of insiders versus outsiders.

In studies of media and tourism, social worlds and fandom have generally been examined in terms of highly focused tour groups venturing to destinations linked with their favourite media narratives. On such tours, the fans seek intense intimacy with others through shared experiences and camaraderie. *Authenticity* is vital to these tourist experiences, especially *existential authenticity* where the fans see themselves as central and the aim is to feel better about oneself (Buchmann et al., 2010; Reijnders, 2011; Roesch, 2009).

Recent research has focused on *parasocial interaction*, characterised by 'an imaginary sense of intimacy by an individual audience member with a media figure' (Kim, 2012: 389). While this research has tended to focus on television dramas, it can be extended to food-related media. In particular, parasocial interaction is a distinctive feature of cooking reality shows, such as *Masterchef* and *My Kitchen Rules*. In these the audience are encouraged to become not only fans of the show, but more importantly committed and obsessive supporters of individual contestants. This heightened connection is encouraged through the producers of such shows focusing more on the individual traits and personalities of the 'stars', rather than their culinary skills. Again, existential authenticity is in evidence, with these *reality* shows striving to convey emotions and transformations vicariously to the audience.

Aims and Scope of this Book

With the growth of interest in linking tourism and food, this book is timely in considering the interaction between tourism, gastronomy and the media. While previous works have considered gastronomic tourism (from both research and operations perspectives) and the relationship between tourism and the media, our work aims to go further in considering all three fields. In undertaking such a study, we are conscious that these are disparate fields and that the interconnections between them are multiple, complex and nuanced. None of them is simply a subset of the others. They could be considered separately, but our view is that what is needed is to understand their connections and influences upon each other.

This volume is divided into three parts. The first considers foundations and principles. Covering the three core topics, it also delves further into related areas such as festivals, gastronomic history and etiquette. Our aim here is twofold: covering the basic principles that underpin each area and identifying some of the contentious issues and research questions that we will return to in the later sections.

The second part focuses on current trends and emerging innovations. These include issues of nutrition and diet, Slow Food, food gardens, pop-up cafés and vans and farmers' markets. These issues are mainly centred within modern gastronomy, influencing changing directions and debates. However, they also affect tourism and are greatly influenced by the media.

The third part emphasises the media as a force for influencing change in tourism and gastronomy. Its coverage spans a range of media, including cinema, television cookery shows, cookbooks and social media. It also stresses the importance of personalities – cooks, writers, restaurateurs – who often function equally effectively across a range of media and may even become champions for change in certain markets and destinations. Our final chapter considers issues of globalisation, tying together the themes of the book and providing an agenda for further research.

2 A History of Gastronomy

The Supersizers (2008–2009) and *Heston's Feasts* (2009–2010)

In recent years, there have been a number of television programmes that attempt to show viewers what it might have been like to dine in the past and how this diet compares to its modern-day equivalent. In *The Supersizers Go …* (2008) and *The Supersizers Eat …* (2009), comedienne and actress Sue Perkins, who became a co-host of *The Great British Bake Off* (2010 onwards), and food critic Giles Coren spend a week eating food from a particular era. They then have their health assessed, along the lines of the documentary exposé about junk food, *Super Size Me* (2004). Perkins and Coren experience an eclectic range of diets, ranging from the basic staples required by Second World War food rationing to the rampant flamboyance of the banquets beloved of the Georgians and those living in Versailles in the time of Marie Antoinette. It is done in a tongue-in-cheek style, often in costume, but is educational for the viewers at the same time. We laugh or marvel at some of the things that people ate in the past, but are also forced to reflect on what we currently eat, and why.

Another example of the genre is *Heston's Feasts* (2009–2010), featuring Heston Blumenthal (Figure 2.1), flamboyant head chef and owner of the Michelin-starred Fat Duck restaurant in Berkshire, UK. Blumenthal is famous for his use of science to understand the properties of food and the processes of cooking, and his passion for awakening all of the senses of the diner, not just taste, smell and sight. While often described as being a pioneer of *molecular gastronomy*, he disdains this association:

> We do not pursue novelty for its own sake. We may use modern thickeners, sugar substitutes, enzymes, liquid nitrogen, sous-vide, dehydration, and other nontraditional means, but these do not define our cooking … The fashionable term 'molecular gastronomy' was introduced relatively recently, in 1992, to name a particular academic workshop for scientists and chefs on the basic food chemistry of traditional dishes. That workshop did not influence our approach, and the term 'molecular gastronomy' does not describe our cooking, or indeed any style of cooking. (The Fat Duck, 2015)

Figure 2.1 Heston Blumenthal (photo Alisa Connan)

In fact, this most modern of chefs is fascinated with the *heritage* of food. His menu at the Fat Duck includes 'reinterpretation of traditional British dishes, such as Powdered Anjou Pigeon, Mock Turtle Soup and the Beef Royal served at King James II's coronation in 1685' (The Fat Duck, 2015). Blumenthal sees an understanding of food traditions as the starting point for experimentation. As he observed in his Food Statement:

> As with everything in life, our craft evolves, and has done so from the moment when man first realized the powers of fire. We embrace this natural process of evolution and aspire to influence it. We respect our rich history and at the same time attempt to play a small part in the history of tomorrow. (The Fat Duck, 2015)

As well as his restaurant, Blumenthal uses the medium of television to get this point across. The mission behind *Heston's Feasts* 'is to surprise jaded 21st century palates by scientifically reconstructing an inventive back-to-the-future banquet consisting of forgotten flavours, textures and taste sensations' (SBS, 2015a). This summary doesn't come close to conjuring up Blumenthal's creativity and singular ability to amaze and stun his customers and viewers. The programme has an accompanying book, *Heston's Fantastical Feasts* (2010), which contains the recipes for a variety of feasts. His *Titanic Feast* incorporates food inspired by doomed historical figures of the Edwardian period such as Robert Falcon Scott and Lawrence of Arabia, including duck liver ballotine, camel and ice-cream 'bergs'. The *Fairytale Feast* is equally quirky, inspired by the Prince Regent and his love of excess, and 'the most influential and celebrated chef of the Regency era – Antonin Carême' (Blumenthal, 2010: 10). He devises an edible house and cooks Carême's signature dish – stuffed wild boar. Through these fantasy feasts, Blumenthal emphasises the importance of food as a sensory pleasure, a message that is often lost in an era of Paleo or 'low-carb' diets, publicity about eating disorders and guilt about food more generally.

Introduction

There is conjecture about when the term *gastronomy* was first used. Despite its apparent antiquity and link to the Ancient Greek words *gastros* (stomach) and *nomos* (the law), the term is argued to first appear as the title of a poem published in 1804, *La Gastronomie, ou L'homme des Champs à Table* (Mennell, 2003; Scarpato, 2002a). Yet its origins stretch back at least as far as the Ancient Greeks, who espoused a philosophy of pleasure that became synonymous with the sensual delights of good food. Indeed, Santich (2004) noted that *Gastronomia* was one of the titles imputed to Archestratus' *Hedypatheia*, discussed below. In her opinion, the word gastronomy simply 'disappeared from the European lexicons for around 15 centuries' (Santich, 2004: 16). Beyond arguments about terminology, it is more important that we understand the *origins* of gastronomy, given the importance that food plays in our lives, both physically and emotionally, and the fact that 'there is a lack of historical research on the formation of gastronomy as reflective eating and cooking' (Scarpato, 2002a: 52).

The television programmes mentioned above pick and choose from our gastronomic past, and we will follow their lead. It is not possible in one chapter to provide an exhaustive history of gastronomy. Instead, we aim to focus on the key moments over the centuries that have changed the way we eat and drink, as well as the way we *think about* eating and drinking. Like the rest of the book, it takes a largely Western perspective, but recognises that there are influences on Western gastronomy from around the globe and provides examples from Asia, Africa and the Middle East to internationalise the discussion. We consider the role played by individuals such as Epicurus, La Varenne, Brillat-Savarin, Larousse and Escoffier in previous centuries, as well as social trends and contemporary influences on the development of gastronomy, particularly those involving the intersection with tourism and the media.

Gastronomy in the Ancient World

Our starting point is to consider four individuals in the ancient world who, through their writings, helped to establish the philosophical underpinnings of gastronomy, as well as allied concepts such as wellbeing and *eudaimonia* (happiness). The first is Archestratus, a Sicilian poet in the 4th century BC, known for his poem *Hedypatheia* (Life of Luxury). His curiosity about the subject led him to travel throughout the Mediterranean, 'thus establishing an early link between gastronomy and tourism – in order to discover what was best to eat and drink and where to find it. By recording his findings he offered guidance to everyone who came after him' (Santich, 2004: 16). Archestratus thus wrote some of the world's first travelogues, helping the neophyte traveller to understand the type of food that they will encounter on their journey. While he is often called 'The Father of Gastronomy' (Santich, 2004; Yeoman & McMahon-Beattie, 2015), he could just as easily be labelled 'The Father of Gastronomic Tourism'. His other contribution was to emphasise the importance of seeking out the best quality ingredients, and his recognition of 'what we would call "terroir" is unparalled in ancient literature' (Albala, 2011: 17).

Two centuries later in ancient Greece, Athenaeus in *The Deipnosophists* (The Wise Men at Dinner) 'wrote about the relations that historians, poets and philosophers had with food and dealt with subjects collateral to food enjoyment, such as the shape of drinking-cups' (Scarpato, 2002a: 52). This history of food and the exposure it gave to the work of Archestratus meant that Ancient Greece has been revered through the ages 'as a culinary culture as well conceived as their political forms' (Albala, 2011: 17).

The third founder of the roots of gastronomic philosophy was Epicurus of Samos (342–270 BC). His teachings were centred on the notion that the seeking of pleasure was the most important purpose in life (Pearce *et al.*, 2010), but not to the point of hedonic excess. Pleasure, in the *Epicurean* sense, is instead a function of the attainment of *ataraxia* or tranquility, 'which sets bounds to our pleasure-seeking' (Annas, 1987: 5), as well as the absence of *aponia* or bodily pain. Yet there are choices to be made, and sometimes pain in the short term is to be preferred where it leads to pleasures in the future (Annas, 1987). It is thus a more sober philosophy than Aristippus' (435–356 BC) exhortation that one should aim for the maximum amount of pleasure in life (Ryan & Deci, 2001) and is more in keeping with Aristotle's (385–322 BC) view of *eudaimonia*, which 'is to be found in the expression of virtue – that is, in doing what is worth doing' (Ryan & Deci, 2001: 145).

Perhaps the antithesis of *Epicurean* balance was Marcus Gavius Apicius (1st century AD), who was attributed as the author of the Roman cookbook

De re Coquinaria. Unlike the stress placed in Ancient Greek texts such as *The Deipnosophists* on taste, moderation and the health-giving properties of dining, *De re Coquinaria* accords with the way that we view the typical lifestyle of the ruling elite of Ancient Rome – as one of excess and over-indulgence (Albala, 2011) – even though most of the population at the time largely had a frugal diet (Strong, 2002). Interestingly, the name Apicius, during the Age of Enlightenment, began to be associated with the very refinement of taste that he was said to have mocked, and 'by the nineteenth century to be called an Apicius was fairly positive' (Albala, 2011: 20). The same could be said for the term *epicurean* (after Epicurus), which shifted from denoting a glutton to a term of admiration given to a discerning person who enjoyed good food (Albala, 2011).

It is fair to say that the recipes provided by Apicius would make many modern diners shudder, including delicacies like dormice, a sow's womb, fla-mingos and larks' tongues (Albala, 2011; Strong, 2002). In Ancient Rome, food was often made to resemble something else, such as quinces studded with thorns that were made to look like sea-urchins (Strong, 2002), which is reminiscent of Heston Blumenthal's contemporary efforts at surprise and trickery, such as his famous meat fruit. Heston's Roman banquet on *Heston's Feasts* (2009), in homage to the likes of Apicius, included pig nipple scratch-ings, calf's brain custard, and a slow-cooked hog, followed by an 'ejaculating cake' for dessert (SBS, 2015b).

While the discussion above focuses on ancient Greece and Rome, it should not be taken as suggesting that food was not similarly a philosophic concern in other parts of the non-Western world. For example, the Chinese teacher and philosopher Confucius (551–479 BC) was known for his apho-risms against food that was undercooked or not served at the appropriate time and 'likened a well-planned meal to a well-governed state' (Pilcher, 2006: 9). Teachings by other philosophers such as Laozi (470–391 BC) and Mozi (470–391 BC) exhorted followers to seek simplicity and in their lives, including the preparation and partaking of food, in contrast to the grandeur of imperial banquets of the period (Pilcher, 2006). These debates are still ongoing today, with contemporary commentators extolling philosophies around slow food and organic produce (see Chapter 6).

Feasting in the Medieval World

In medieval times, only the very rich could enjoy culinary excellence, yet feasting was not merely an excuse for debauchery or the pursuit of pleasure. The medieval banquet, often held in a purpose-built hall where guests sat on benches rather than reclining in the Roman fashion (Strong, 2002), was a mechanism for demonstrating the power of the host through serving the best food that money could buy. It was also an acknowledgement of the fealty owed by many of the guests (Carroll *et al.*, 2005). This form of communal eating can be contrasted with Japanese ways of serving food in a similar time period (c. 1100), where people ate their meals as 'individual place settings, [which] were first arranged on low wooden trays' (Pilcher, 2006: 39). In the European medieval world, feasts were a regular feature of the medieval calendar (Albala, 2011), often connected to religious holidays or observances, such as the approach of Lent, but these were interspersed with periods of fasting. Chapter 5 on food rituals and etiquette will consider these aspects in more detail.

It is a common misconception that medieval cooking used spices to mask the smell of rotting meat. As Dickie (2008) observed, meat was generally plentiful and fresh for those who had the financial means to pay for it, being butchered close to where it was to be consumed. He thus argued that 'if people liked their food heavily spiced it was because they liked the taste. And they liked it for two reasons: first, because they had learned to enjoy what was good for them; and second, because spices were expensive' (Dickie, 2008: 53). The use of spices therefore was evidence of a person's wealth and status. The use of sugar was also prestigious, and used to counteract the level of salt needed for preservation (Dickie, 2008). This is ironic, given the depths to which sugar's reputation has slid in recent years, in part owing to bestselling books such as *I Quit Sugar* (Wilson, 2012) and *Sweet Poison* (Gillespie, 2008). Spices are also generally cheap to buy and widely available in the modern era (Figure 2.2).

The transfer of knowledge about 'an embryonic form of gastronomy' during the Middle Ages often occurred through 'medicine books, herbaria, treatises on agriculture' (Scarpato, 2002a: 53), which are dedicated to health and living well, and refer to the role of food in this process. Sharing ideas about food preparation and consumption can be seen as a global preoccupation. The Chinese food tome, *The Illustrated Basic Herbal*, dates from 1061, while in the Middle East, recorded recipes appear around 1226, collected by al-Baghdadi (Civitello, 2004). The Japanese produced a treatise on tea, *Kissa Yojoki* (c. 1215), which formed the basis of their ritualised tea ceremony (Civitello, 2004). Later Western works such as *Le Viandier* by Guillaume Tirel, known as Taillevent (c. 1310–1395), and Martino de Rossi's *Libro de Arte Coquinaria* (*The Art of Cooking*) (c. 1465) are considered to be significant achievements in terms of culinary-related literature. The flurry of cookbooks is linked to growing interest in food amongst the late medieval courts (Strong, 2002), while their diffusion throughout Europe was aided by developments in printing around the middle of the 15th century. Here, we see a shift away from treatises about food as a component of health and wellbeing to dedicated collections of recipes, albeit not precise in detail like their modern-day equivalents. For example, *Le Viandier* contains no quantities for ingredients and timings for cooking in the recipes (Hertzmann, 2010).

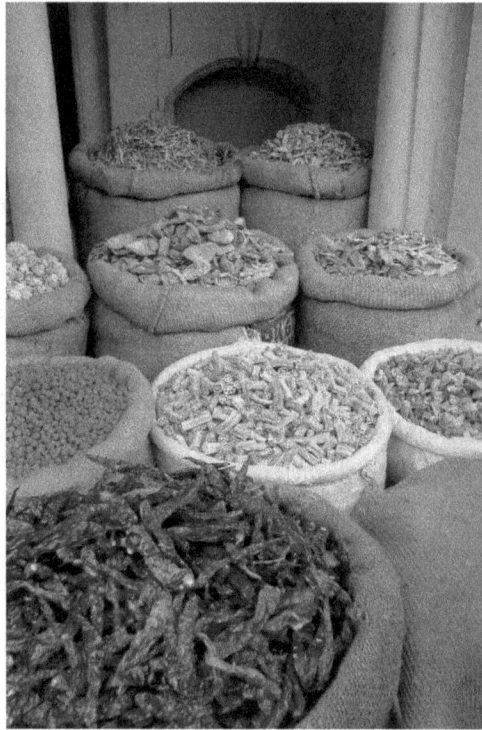

Figure 2.2 Spices sold on the streets of India (photo J. Laing)

The Renaissance and New Tastes from the New World

The Age of Discovery gave aristocratic patrons the opportunity to experience novel produce and ingredients, notably spices, coffee, tea and chocolate, from around the world. It also led to an exchange in food resources and thus improved the nutritional welfare of the poorer classes where 'long, intense, recurrent famines' were a constant threat 'making the subsistence of the poor especially precarious' (Mariani-Costantini & Ligabue, 1992: 316). Examples include the potato, the tomato and the kidney bean. While Mariani-Costantini and Ligabue (1992) argued that the Mediterranean diet, with its health benefits, is 'the outcome of Columbus's explorations', the popular view that Columbus discovered the tomato appears to be inaccurate, even though 'it is known that they were growing in Central America at the time of his visit' (Griffenhagen, 1992: 137). Nevertheless, the tomato is now so identified with Italian and Spanish cuisines in particular that it is difficult to imagine them without its presence.

These new ingredients were not however immediately popular in Europe, with the tomato taking nearly 150 years to be first included in an Italian cookbook – *The Modern Steward* (1692) – and the potato only becoming 'a regular part of the [Italian] peasant diet' in the mid 1800s (Dickie, 2008: 164). In contrast, 'peasants in China, Africa, and the Middle East began planting American staples as soon as they arrived in the sixteenth century' (Pilcher, 2006: 19), with, for example, the Chinese and Africans adopting chilli peppers to add heat to dishes and maize being ground into flour to create Chinese noodles (Pilcher, 2006).

French Haute Cuisine

The reputation enjoyed by France as a gastronomic leader and the height of culinary sophistication has had a remarkable longevity, continuing even to the present day. Menus at the royal banquets at Buckingham Palace are still written in French and the first professional chef to work in the White House was French-born, hired by the Francophile First Lady, Jacqueline Kennedy, in 1961. French tourism promotion strategies still largely rely on this association with outstanding cuisine (Du Rand & Heath, 2006; Frochot, 2003).

French training of young apprentice chefs is regarded as rigorous and a spring-board for a stellar gastronomic career, as the recent film *The Hundred-Foot Journey* (2014) illustrates. Chefs who acknowledge the debt they owe to their French culinary training include Thomas Keller (The French Laundry in the Napa Valley), Wolfgang Puck and Jamie Oliver. Others have benefited from the mentoring of expatriate French chefs and in turn have taught the next generation the classical French techniques of cooking. The Roux brothers in London trained chefs such as Marco Pierre White, Gordon Ramsay and Australia's Shannon Bennett (Vue de Monde in Melbourne). It must be said, however, that a young Heston Blumenthal only lasted a week with Raymond Blanc at Le Manoir aux Quat' Saisons and is one of the few chefs who is largely self-taught. As he explained:

> Going to the Manoir with Raymond Blanc spurred me on, but it spurred me on to go in a different direction ... Maybe if I'd gone to a smaller kitchen and I was a bigger cog in a smaller wheel, I wouldn't have felt the need to go down my own path, and maybe I wouldn't have ended up this way. (quoted in Dixon, 2008)

The other route to achieve French classical training is to attend the famous École du Cordon Bleu, a cooking school opened in Paris in 1895 by Marthe Distel, the publisher of *La Cuisinière Cordon Bleu* magazine. The term *cordon bleu* is a reference to a 16th century order – *L'Ordre du Saint-Esprit* – whose members wore a cross hung on a blue ribbon or *cordon bleu*. The name became identified with master chefs owing to the numerous magnificent feasts hosted by this order and the prestige with which they were held (Cordon Bleu, 2015).

Julia Child recalled that one of her teachers, Chef Bugnard, had worked for the renowned chef Escoffier (Child, 2006) and was effusive about his knowledge and technique. She received a diploma from the School in 1951, which paved the way for her famous cookbooks and subsequent television career. Even children's television referenced the institution, such as *Madeline at Cooking School* (1993), in which the French orphan is enrolled for lessons at the Cordon Bleu school after cooking a disastrous meal. *Quelle horreur!*

The origins of this French reputation for culinary excellence can be traced back to the 17th century, with the birth of *haute cuisine* and the notion of a *science* of food preparation and service. La Varenne's *Le Cuisinier François* (1651) was 'the first cookbook to represent a definitive break with the Middle Ages, opening with recipes for the bouillon, meat and fish stocks that served as bases or *fonds* for the repertory of dishes which followed and were the foundations of the new system' (Strong, 2002: 229). Then in 1691, *Le Cuisinier roial et bourgeois* by François Massialot was published, which listed recipes alphabetically and contained the kind of extravagant dish that was aimed at the cook working for the aristocracy (Strong, 2002). Despite its title, it was not until 1746 that a cookbook directed at the less exalted home was available – Menon's *La Cuisinière bourgeoise*. These texts formed the foundation of a distinctive French *haute cuisine*, a staple at the French court. They remained in favour even after the Revolution, thanks to the patronage and taste of men such as Charles de Tallyrand-Périgord, Napoleon's minister for foreign affairs. Ironically, Napoleon was no gourmand, but had a shrewd understanding of the value of diplomatic banquets to his fledgling reign as Emperor (Kelly, 2003).

It was the Bourbon dynasty, however, which was identified with French cuisine at its most decadent, contributing to their downfall. It is no surprise that one of the apocryphal sayings attributed to Queen Marie-Antoinette was 'Let them eat cake', a symbol of the callousness of the court in the face of mass starvation. The film *Marie Antoinette* (2006) satirised this image in the scene of the Queen frolicking amidst pastel-coloured *macarons* and sweets, to the strains of the pop classic 'I Want Candy'. Her predecessor, Louis XIV the Sun King (1643–1715), was notorious for wanting the very best of everything, including food and entertainment, which were seen as cementing the King's place as the centre of the court, France and the world, in that order. Louis stole the services of François Vatel, the head steward of his Superintendent of Finances, Nicolas Fouquet, to ensure the magnificence of his fêtes and banquets, a story brought to life in the film *Vatel* (2000) starring Gérard Depardieu. In the end, the talented but tragic Vatel could not cope with the pressure, killing himself with his own sword when the supplies of seafood for the royal banquet were inadequate (Clark, 1975; Kelly, 2003).

The events at the Palace of Versailles were an outré fantasy, including pyramids of preserved fruit and iced sweets, attendants dressed in allegorical costume such as signs of the zodiac and the four seasons, and the theatre

Figure 2.3 Antechamber of the *grand couvert*, Palace of Versailles, France (photo J. Laing)

created by myriad glowing candles, wreaths of flowers and greenery and fireworks (Strong, 2002). Even everyday meals at the Palace were subject to a complex and detailed etiquette, depending on whether the King was dining *au grand couvert* (in public) (Figure 2.3) or *au petit couvert* (in his own room), governing who was present and how those present were served (Strong, 2002). Eating was an opportunity to be close to the King, to see and be seen, akin to the elaborate ceremonies accompanying the monarch as he was getting dressed in the morning (the *grand* and *petit lever*) and going to bed in the evening (the *coucher*). The rituals and traditions surrounding royal meals influenced broader society, such as the popularity of *service à la française* (see Chapter 5) and the necessity of an array of tableware, both silver and china, in which to display and serve various dishes (Strong, 2002).

Birth of the restaurant

The end of the monarchy in France has been linked to the growth of the restaurant as we know it today. Before this time, most restaurants only served soup or *bouillon* as a restorative (*restauratif*) (Spang, 2000), and hence we see the origins of its name – *restaurant* (Kelly, 2003). Food could be served to patrons of taverns or chophouses (*gargotier*) or by caterers known as *traiteurs*, but this was small-scale compared with the industry that emerged after the French Revolution. The ingredients for the birth of the modern restaurant included the freeing up of the guild restrictions around catering, the growth of a new market for meals to be provided to regional deputies based in Paris and a host of unemployed chefs who had previously worked for the aristocracy and now needed to earn an independent living (Kelly, 2003; Mennell, 2003). Also important was the presence of a 'well-informed and knowledgeable eating public' (Mennell, 2003: 250), which increased competition between different restaurants.

Whatever the cause, the effects were momentous, with the number of Parisian restaurants growing from under 50 in pre-revolutionary times to more than 3000 in 1814, based on listings in the *Almanach des Gourmands* (Kelly, 2003). These new establishments, unlike chop-houses or taverns, were acceptable places for women as well as men to dine (Humble, 2002), which added to their appeal. It is hard to imagine modern life without the restaurant, a trend that has spread right around the world. As the sage Brillat-Savarin (1825) observed: 'Few among the crowds which patronise our restaurants every day pause to think that the man who founded the first restaurant must have been a genius endowed with profound insight into human nature' (p. 238).

Carême: The first celebrity chef

Like the restaurant, Antonin Carême's career was inextricably linked to the French Revolution. Abandoned by his poverty-stricken family on the streets in 1792, the 10-year-old was rescued by a cook who wanted his services as a kitchen boy (Kelly, 2003). He started as an apprentice to a pâtissier, and while he was eventually to become a master of the complete meal, it was his prowess with sweets and desserts that was his signature and led to him being noticed by the rich and famous. The towering *extraordinaires* or centrepieces that he made to grace banquet tables have fallen out of favour, with perhaps the only modern equivalent being the wedding cake, which takes pride of place at the wedding reception (Kelly, 2003). Carême himself made the wedding cake of Napoleon when he married Marie Louise of Austria in 1810, as well as a christening *extraordinaire* for their first child, the King of Rome, in the shape of a Venetian gondola. He also invented more humble fare such as the *vol-au-vent* and piped meringues (Kelly, 2003).

Other famous employers of Carême included the Tsar of Russia and the Prince Regent, both men who enjoyed their food and spent money on equipping their royal kitchens with the latest innovations. The kitchens at the Royal Pavilion in Brighton (Figure 2.4) were particularly fine and spacious, with a steam-powered table to keep the food warm, and the perfect exotic setting for his creations. It was his time in Russia rather than England, however, which was more influential on Carême and his culinary writing. He acknowledged service *à la russe* or Russian style in his book *Maître d'hotel français, ou parallel de la cuisine ancienne et modern* (1822), which he ultimately saw as more practical than service *à la française* for serving large numbers of people and ensuring people had enough to eat. It also allowed the chef to

Figure 2.4 The Royal Pavilion, Brighton, UK (photo J. Laing)

plate an individual dish in the kitchen and thus control its presentation. As Kelly (2003: 201) noted, by doing this, Carême 'cannily [pitched] his book at the growing restaurant market, which invariably favoured plated courses kept warm with bell-like covers or *cloches*'.

While many of his contemporaries slaved unnoticed in the kitchens of the rich, Carême worked as a freelance chef for most of his career. Unlike Escoffier, he never ran a restaurant (Kelly, 2003). Carême's profile was boosted by his association with royalty, but also because of the books he wrote, which were widely read, earned him a tidy sum in his lifetime and 'provided the methodological basis for the subsequent expansion of the profession later in the [19th] century' (Parkhurst Ferguson, 1998: 613). He was both a leader and a reflection of culinary taste and set the fashion even in small things, such as the stiffened white chef's hat (Kelly, 2003). His deep understanding of gastronomic traditions formed a launching pad for his new modern cuisine, much like Heston Blumenthal today. Carême's first book *Le Pâtissier royal parisien, ou Traité élémentaire et pratique de la patisserie ancienne et moderne, suivi d'observations utiles au progress de cet art, et d'une revue critique des grand bals de 1810 et 1811* (1815) was based on his detailed journal entries and contained recipes for such classic cakes and pastries as *madeleines*, *pithiviers* and *babas*, as well as descriptions of the banquets on which he worked and recommendations for dinner parties (Kelly, 2003). In 1828, *Le Cuisinier parisien* was published, complete with recipes and his illustrations, but his masterpiece was a five-volume encyclopaedia, *L'Art de la cuisine française au dix-neuvième siècle. Traité élémentaire et pratique* (1833–1847), the last two volumes of which were written by his pupil, Plumerey. Strong (2002: 283) observed that 'these volumes were to be the gospel of *cuisine classique* until replaced by the work of Escoffier at the opening of the twentieth century'.

Parkhurst Ferguson (1998: 619) argued that Carême's books, together with the gastronomic journalism of Grimod de la Reynière, the philosophical work of Brillat-Savarin and Charles Fourier, and the novels of Honoré de Balzac, have been instrumental in the creation of a strong French culinary identity: 'If French and foreigner alike have long considered cuisine quintessentially French, the explanation lies importantly in an expansionist culinary discourse that relentlessly associates (good) food and France, and has done so for some three or four centuries'.

Following in Carême's footsteps was Auguste Escoffier, who 'boasted that he had sent some 2000 French chefs from his kitchens all over the world' (Parkhurst Ferguson, 1998: 631). An apprentice at his uncle's restaurant in Nice and later an army chef during the Franco-Prussian war, he subsequently started up his own restaurant in Cannes. Escoffier's life changed in 1884 when César Ritz employed him to run the kitchens of the Grand Hotel in Monte Carlo and its equivalent in Lucerne during the off-season. In 1890, he accepted an invitation to preside over the menus at the new Savoy Hotel in London. During this time, Escoffier created dishes such as *pêche melba* and Melba toast after the Australian opera singer Dame Nellie Melba. After leaving the Savoy under a cloud, Escoffier and Ritz joined forces, and Escoffier supervised the kitchens at the Ritz Hotel in Paris and later the Carlton Hotel in London. Escoffier left many legacies apart from the culinary distinction of the hotels where he worked. His *Le Guide Culinaire* (1903) showed the influence of women diners (who could dine in public at his hotels) on 'the switch to lighter, more showy food' (Humble, 2002: 326) and was used to train chefs for years to come (Strong, 2002).

Brillat-Savarin: A philosophy of eating

It is impossible to talk about the evolution of gastronomy without turning to the subject of Jean Anthelme Brillat-Savarin, a man of the law who became one of the most famous gastronomic writers in history. His *La Physiologie du Goût* (The Physiology of Taste), has not been out of print since it was first published privately in 1825 and there are numerous translations available (Jaine, 2008). Unlike gastronomic writing by contemporaries such as de la Reynière, which focused on practical matters of sourcing and cooking food, *La Physiologie du Goût* focuses on 'the place of food in human existence, underpinned by medical and anecdotal evidence' (Jaine, 2008: x). Brillat-Savarin was satisfied by the simplest of meals but only those informed by the utility of gastronomical knowledge: 'Gastronomical knowledge is necessary to all men, for it tends to augment the sum of happiness'. He was no amateur dabbling in food. Instead, he anticipated the formal study of gastronomy with 'its own academicians, universities, professors and prizes' (Brillat-Savarin, 1825: 43).

The 20 aphorisms at the start of the book, which Brillat-Savarin intended to be 'a prologue to his work and an eternal foundation for his science' (p. 3), are often pithy and as fresh as the day he wrote them. They include:

- Animals feed: man eats: only the man of intellect knows how to eat.
- Tell me what you eat: I will tell you what you are.
- Gourmandism is an act of judgement, by which we give preference to things which are agreeable to our taste over those which are not.
- The pleasures of the table belong to all times and all ages, to every country and every day; they go hand in hand with all our other pleasures, outlast them, and remain to console us for their loss.
- The discovery of a new dish does more for the happiness of mankind than the discovery of a star.
- The right order of eating is from the most substantial dishes to the lightest.
- The right order of drinking is from the mildest wines to the headiest and most perfumed.
- Dessert without cheese is like a pretty woman with only one eye.

It would be wrong, however, to focus on these aphorisms to the exclusion of the rest of the book (Jaine, 2008). They are followed by 30 insightful meditations, which constituted the first rigorous – and exhaustive – interrogation of gastronomy, and continue to resonate today, in a manner that belies their early 19th century origins. They include discourses on appetite, gourmandism, the pleasures of the table, digestion, obesity, fasting and restaurateurs. Brillat-Savarin connects cooking with the advancement of *civilisation*, given that 'it was the need to cook which taught man to use fire, and it was by using fire that man conquered Nature' (p. 214). The birth of gastronomy was thus seen as a turning point in history.

Evolution of the Food Media

The genesis of food journalism started with Grimod de la Reynière, who published his first *Almanachs des Gourmands* in 1804, 'advising Parisians what was best to eat when, and how it should be prepared' (Santich, 2004: 16). His work covered food suppliers as well as restaurants and cafés (Mennell, 2003), and thus served a practical role for its readers (Jaine, 2008), rather like the modern equivalent of food supplements in newspapers and the ubiquitous Michelin Guide. This role was particularly important in post-Revolutionary France, 'translating the aristocratic culinary culture of the ancien regime for the use of a new public' (Parkhurst Ferguson, 1998: 606).

It is debatable whether the *Almanach* was the catalyst for the burgeoning growth in restaurants, or whether the development of the restaurant created demand for the *Almanach* (Mennell, 2003). Certainly, the two enjoyed a symbiotic relationship in Paris, unlike the USA during the 19th century, where hotel dining rooms rather than stand-alone restaurants were the norm (Freedman, 2011). The *Almanachs des Gourmands* has become an invaluable source for historians, providing evidence of the number and types of restaurants in Paris and their growth during the 19th century. Its readership extended to people living in London, which 'helped to foment the myth of gourmet Paris' (Kelly, 2003: 58).

In the modern era, food journalism takes three main forms (Jones & Taylor, 2013). The first involves trade publications aimed at the industry. The second is cooking magazines aimed at consumers, sometimes provided free at supermarkets as a branding exercise (Jones & Taylor, 2013), as well as commercial titles such as *Gourmet Traveller*, *Bon appétit* magazine and *Delicious*. The third form is journalism in newspapers, often in lift-out supplements at weekends, aimed at the foodie. We argue that the food blog is the emerging new form of food journalism, sometimes written by chefs, but often by amateurs, and allows for interactivity between reader and blogger, exemplified by Julie Powell's *Julie and Julia* blog (see Chapter 11), as well as providing a new source of 'taste preferences ... addressed to a potential community of taste' (Lane, 2013: 362).

Typical vehicles for writing about food are the cookery column, the restaurant review and the feature article (Jones & Taylor, 2013). Columns have a long history, such as Léon Brisé writing columns on gastronomy in several newspapers during the Second Empire as 'Baron Brisse' and Elizabeth David developing her reputation alongside her books in her columns in *Harper's Bazaar*, *Vogue*, *The Sunday Times* and *The Spectator*. More recent examples are often written by high-profile chefs, such as Hugh Fearnley-Whittingstall in the *Guardian's* Weekend magazine. This is another domain 'where the identities of celebrity cooks are established and sustained' (Jones & Taylor, 2013: 101).

Restaurant reviews are also omnipresent in the modern media and have led to well-publicised feuds between critics and chefs, notably that between A.A. Gill and Gordon Ramsay. The role of the modern food and wine critic in shaping and dictating culinary taste might, however, be under threat from a new form of *cultural intermediary* – bloggers and members of the public writing reviews of restaurants on social media sites such as TripAdvisor. These reviews can be characterised as 'citizen journalism' (Jones & Taylor, 2013: 103). Part of a restaurant review may involve a rating, sometimes in the form of a mark for a meal, but more famously as a star rating for the restaurant itself. The *Michelin Guide* awards one, two or three stars to the most exalted restaurants, but making 'their judgements without publicly discussing the grounds for reaching them in particular cases' (Mennell, 2003: 255). There are other guides that critique restaurants and cafés, including the *Gault-Millau* guide in France, the *Good Food Guides* in England and Australia and the *Zagat* ratings in the USA. The *Good Food Guide* in England is somewhat different, in that, rather than having professional judges, they rely on the feedback of the British public about their dining experiences (Mennell, 2003). According to Lane (2013: 360), these guides are taste makers, with the Michelin Guide occupying 'a particularly powerful position', given the financial consequences that may flow from these decisions (Clark, 1975). The tyranny of being a slave to the vagaries of the Michelin Guide and its stars is satirised in *The Hundred Foot Journey* (2014).

Gastronomy in the Modern Era

To conclude this chapter, we focus on a few of the issues and trends that are relevant to gastronomy in the modern era. The first is the burgeoning interest in experiencing international cuisine, notably from a non-Western background, as well as greater familiarity with it when returning home. This can be traced to the development of the airline industry and the growth in mass tourism that followed, as well as patterns and levels of migration, particularly after the Second World War. Diasporas took their food culture and traditions with them and ethnic restaurants became ubiquitous in many towns and cities around the world. The Italian cuisine in particular 'has become a world food, and comprehensive study of its history would encompass Britain, the USA, South America, and Australia as well as Italy' (Dickie, 2008: 9). The Italian diaspora thus invigorated the culinary life of the countries in which these people settled (Frost *et al.*, 2010; Frost & Laing, 2016). Similarly, the Chinese and Indian diasporas have introduced their food and restaurants to the places where they settled, often beginning within the enclave of a Chinatown or Little India (Frost & Laing, 2016; Pilcher, 2006), but then branching out to become a fixture of urban life. Fusion cuisine has taken these traditions and turned them into something new, a 'blend of past and present in cuisine preparation', which Ramshaw (2016: 59) argues 'is now, perhaps, an expectation of many consumers'.

Despite this, academic discussion appears to be divided with respect to the importance placed on seeking out new culinary experiences and maintaining culinary diversity in contemporary society. Symons (1999) referred to the *New Global Cuisine* and argued that there is an 'increased sameness' of menus around the world. Others such as Scarpato (2002a) and Santich (2004) pointed to the existence of a growing group of travellers who enjoy discovering new cuisines and cultures. Laing and Frost (2015b) labelled these individuals *food explorers*, while García (2013: 511) called them *culinary adventurers*, who are 'looking for the exotic and beautiful packaging of tradition and authenticity'.

Another trend has been the application of technological developments to the home. This has led to labour-saving equipment in the kitchen such as the refrigerator, the pressure cooker, the microwave oven and the food processor.

They have made it easier for those at home to recreate the dishes they see on television or read about in cookbooks, but have coincided with a time when home cooking is paradoxically on the wane. Current television series such as *Masterchef* (2005 onwards) have stimulated a demand for even more elaborate kitchen appliances such as *sous-vide* machines, ice-cream makers, blast chillers and pizza ovens. The question remains whether these gadgets are mostly aspirational, aimed in part at the time-poor or over-committed individual who embraces the fantasy of gastronomy but lacks the wherewithal or the impetus to make this a reality, as well as at the dedicated 'foodie'.

The kitchens presided over by Carême and Escoffier were mostly male dominated, although 19th century English aristocratic kitchens were generally headed by a female cook. While the film *Babette's Feast* (1987) tells the story of a former female chef at the Café Anglais in Paris, in reality, it was a male chef, Adolphe Dugléré, who made its name, including hosting the famous Three Emperors' Dinner during the 1867 Exposition Universelle for Emperor Wilhelm I of Prussia, Tsar Alexander II of Russia, the future Alexander III and Otto von Bismarck. The bill was 1200 francs, around US\$12,950 in today's currency, mostly owing to the calibre and the cost of the wines served (Lair, 2011). In the 20th century, small but growing numbers of women became top chefs in their own right. One of the earliest was Rosa Lewis, chef and owner of the Cavendish Hotel, which she bought in 1902. She claimed to have been trained by Escoffier and was nicknamed the Duchess of Jermyn Street. Her life has been serialised in the BBC television programme *The Duchess of Duke Street* (1976–1977). Others include the likes of Alice Waters at Chez Panisse, Elena Arzak of Arzak restaurant in Spain, Clare Smyth, Chef Patron at the three Michelin-starred Restaurant Gordon Ramsay in London and Kylie Kwong of Sydney's Billy Kwong. Despite this, it is probably fair to say that professional cooking at the highest levels is still a male-dominated industry.

Possibly one of the great changes in eating habits during the mid-20th century, post-Second World War, involved the availability of processed and packaged foods, as well as the so-called TV dinner. While this was promoted as lifting the burden from the (mostly) women running a household, in reality, they 'were expected to "be creative" with processed foods … [and employ] elaborate ruses to cover up the fact that they were using those convenience foods' (Neuhaus, 1999: 533). It was still important to give the impression that they *cared* about the food they served their families, even against the backdrop and distraction of watching television during meals (Neuhaus, 1999). Meals became more casual and the amount of cutlery used declined. This eventually contributed to the decline of fine dining restaurants.

Greater reliance on convenience food in the home occurred in tandem with the rise of fast food and snack food (Neuhaus, 1999), notably sold through franchised chain stores. However, fast food is undergoing a period of transition in the early part of the 21st century, tapping into concerns about health but also a growing sophistication about food and interest in its traditions. Burgers are being repositioned as a gourmet product (Yeoman & McMahon-Beattie, 2015), while food trucks and vans market fish tacos and fries as *dude food* and charge accordingly. While pizza, with its Neopolitan origins, formed part of 'a wide, ancient Mediterranean family of flatbreads' (Dickie, 2008: 186), it became associated with the proliferation of the pizza franchises with a quick family meal, often enjoyed around a television set. More recently, there has been a return to seeing pizza as an artisanal product, rather than mass produced, although chains still proliferate. The latter are forced to differentiate themselves with combinations such as the pizza with a cheese-stuffed crust or, more bizarrely, with tiny meat pies around the edge (Figure 2.5). Even McDonald's is offering patrons the opportunity to 'Create Your Taste' (Figure 2.6) through designing their own 'gourmet burger'. In Australia, this campaign is accompanied by the advertising tagline 'How Very Un McDonald's'.

We live in an age of industrial food production, which has seen 'small independent food producers, chefs and restaurateurs battling against the almost irresistible advance of industrial food' (Scarpato, 2002a: 56). However, there are clear trends towards *small is good*, with demand increasing for organic food and slow food. The growing prevalence of community and kitchen gardens and foraging are allied developments. This back to basics approach might be linked to scare campaigns about genetic modification of food, food adulteration, food fraud (where food is passed off as originating elsewhere or from another producer – see Cornish, 2015) and the

Figure 2.5 Pizza Hut Meat Pie Crust Pizza (source J. Laing)

Figure 2.6 Create Your Taste – McDonald's (source J. Laing)

level of preservatives in our diets. The growth in diagnoses of coeliac disease and allergies to foods such as peanuts has affected travel and food consumption experiences (Derham, 2013). There is a sense that 'food no longer feels safe ... We stalk the shelves of the supermarket, hackles raised, peering with paranoic intensity at the lists of ingredients' (Humble, 2002: 336).

Other food movements of note in the modern era include *nouvelle cuisine*, introduced in the 1980s. *Nouvelle cuisine* is a term that has a long heritage, dating back to works of the 18th and 19th centuries (Wood, 1991). In contemporary times, it was used by Henri Gault and Christian Millau in 1973 in an article titled 'Vive La Nouvelle Cuisine Francais' (Wood, 1991). Essentially it involved producing lighter fare, with less heavy sauces, and an emphasis on creativity. Mennell (1985) contrasts it to the 'Escoffier school' of cooking, which he argues was decaying until 'the *nouvelle cuisine* movement appeared' (p. 135). Wood (1991: 330) critiqued *nouvelle cuisine* as 'akin to a social purity movement ... in the emphasis on simplicity and freshness and also in the utilization by chefs of regional (country) cuisine for inspiration' and described it as a *middle-class* social rather than culinary construct. It has been lampooned for the emphasis on artistic presentation, with

Humble (2002: 335) referring to the fashion for magazine spreads with 'exotic foods air-brushed like models'. The size of the portions also attracted criticism (Cousins *et al.*, 2010), given the often high prices that accompanied them. Humble (2002: 336) poked fun at the pretentiousness surrounding *nouvelle cuisine*: 'Sales of kiwi-fruit went through the roof, plates were flooded with contrasting sauces swirled together, and every pudding had its coulis'.

Television has played a part in the trend towards so-called *molecular gastronomy* and has certainly piqued the public's interest in the creation of gels, foams, spheres and soils and use of liquid nitrogen to make ice-cream at the table. The term is often incorrectly applied to cutting edge techniques such as those employed by Heston Blumenthal or renowned Spanish chef Ferran Adrià from the three Michelin-starred elBulli restaurant in Barcelona, although both chefs have dismissed this association as a misconception (Cousins *et al.*, 2010). Adrià's innovation is probably more correctly described as *new Spanish cuisine*, which is challenging 'the centuries-long hegemony of France as the epicenter of international haute cuisine' (Svejenova *et al.*, 2007: 543). Other examples of Spanish gastronomic ingenuity include Juan Mari Arzak of the three Michelin-starred Arzak restaurant in San Sebastián and Joan Roca of the three Michelin-starred El Keller de Can Roca in Girona, named Number 1 restaurant in the world in 2015 by *Restaurant* magazine. It is Adrià, however, who is considered to be the culinary leader, whose 'artistry is in the contrasts (hot–cold, soft–crunchy, solid–liquid, sweet–savory), the concepts (e.g. foams), the techniques (e.g. spherification), and the creative methods (e.g. deconstruction)' (Svejenova *et al.*, 2007: 539).

The intersection between gastronomy and the media has changed from being largely text based (cookbooks, guidebooks, cooking columns) to being based on more visual media such as film and television. In this book, we focus in particular on the *mediatisation* of gastronomy, where 'increasingly, restaurants and chefs produce recipe/lifestyle books that may also serve as the basis for radio and television programmes or are simultaneously released as part of [a] total media package' (Hall & Mitchell, 2002a: 79). There is a growing number of reality television programmes such as *Masterchef* and *The Great British Bake-off*, where contestants vie for a cash prize to 'fulfil their food dream', often hosted by or with guest stars who are chefs of top restaurants or restaurant critics. Apart from their influence on demand for kitchen gadgetry, discussed above, these programmes have played a role in educating the public, particularly children, about culinary techniques such as smoking meat, tempering chocolate and understanding the difference between a *velouté* and a *jus*, as well as adopting professional kitchen jargon such as 'plating up' (Meryment, 2011). The evolution of social media is likely to represent another leap forward for gastronomic development, and further research is needed to consider the impact of food blogs and online restaurant reviews, as well as the relationship between platforms such as Twitter and Instagram and 'access to celebrity' (Stringfellow *et al.*, 2013), along with their effect on the evolution of gastronomy more broadly.

3   Food, Destinations and Tourists

Eat Pray Love (Elizabeth Gilbert, 2006)

Elizabeth Gilbert is a wealthy thirty-something New Yorker. After a messy divorce, her life lacks direction. She quits her job and decides to spend a year travelling. With an advance from her publisher for the book she will write about her journey, her first stop is Italy. Her justification is that she has always wanted to learn Italian, now she can spend a few months doing that. Arriving in Rome, her adventures start with dinner:

> The first meal I ate in Rome was nothing much. Just some home-made pasta (spaghetti carbonara) with a side order of sautéed spinach and garlic ... Also I had one artichoke, just to try it; the Romans are awfully proud of their artichokes. Then there was a pop-surprise bonus side order brought over by the waitress for free – a serving of fried zucchini blossoms with a soft dab of cheese in the middle ... After the spaghetti, I tried the veal. Oh, and also I drank a bottle of house red, just for me. And ate some warm bread, with olive oil and salt. Tiramisu for dessert. (Gilbert, 2006: 37)

This is a deliberately provocative passage. All the food taboos of a modern American woman are not only broken, but flagrantly flouted. There is garlic. There is pasta with a creamy sauce. Not beef, but veal. Bread. A rich dessert. A whole bottle of wine. Many courses, a large volume of food.

For four months, Gilbert enjoys Italian food. She still suffers depression and anxiety – her healing process has only begun. Revelling in Italian cuisine provides a release from the pressures of her old life. She eats pastries and gelati – even for breakfast. Pizza and pasta are her common meals, although on one occasion she tries a traditional speciality of lamb intestines.

Her food experiences are constructed as so much better than those she was used to in America. The man who makes her sandwiches calls her 'bella' (beautiful) whenever she places an order. When she and her Swedish girlfriend Sofie undertake a sidetrip to Naples, their friend Giovanni provides them with the address of the best pizza shop in that city, insisting they must go there. The effort is worthwhile, 'Sofie is practically in tears over hers, she's having a metaphysical crisis about it … [exclaiming] Why do they even *bother* trying to make pizza in Stockholm?' (Gilbert, 2006: 83).

With all this eating, Gibert puts on weight – 23 pounds, although she admits she was probably 15 pounds underweight when she arrived. The lifestyle, she notes, should be unhealthy. She is not exercising – by which she means she is not going to a gym, whereas she is doing far more walking than she would in New York. She is not taking any vitamin pills as she would in America. Yet when she glances in a mirror, 'I see a bright-eyed, clear-skinned, happy and healthy face. I haven't seen a face like that on me for a long time' (Gilbert, 2006: 85).

Preparing to leave Italy for India – the next stage of her journey – she reflects on how beneficial eating so much has been. She will easily lose the weight in India. She knows she has been self-indulgent, but muses:

> Is it such a bad thing to live like this for just a little while? Just for a few months of one's life, is it so awful to travel through time with no greater ambition than to find the next lovely meal? (Gilbert, 2006: 119)

No adventures, no romance, just food and personal transformation. A modern travel fairy tale. What is particularly important is that all of the food and wine that Gilbert enjoys is Italian. As a tourist in that country, her experience is all about consuming local food. When she travels to regional areas, such as Naples, Bologna and Sicily, she is delighted by the variations in regional cuisines. She is not at all interested in eating international cuisine in tourist hotels or restaurants. She wants to explore, to go where the locals go. That is her tourist experience and it is the one that increasingly the modern tourist desires. The appeal of her Italian travel narrative is not that it is extraordinary, but rather that it is accessible to most tourists if they travel there.

The Trip to Italy (2014)

Comedians/actors Steve Coogan and Rob Brydon play fictionalised versions of themselves. In *The Trip* (2010), they are commissioned by *The Observer* newspaper to write a series of humorous reviews of restaurants in the English Lakes District. In this sequel, they are asked to undertake a similar project in Italy, which will be not only a series of articles, but also a book.

As they drive from the north to the south of Italy, they dine at six top restaurants. At each they are presented with sumptuous feasts and beautiful views – very much the image of *La Dolce Vita* in Italy. Interestingly, when they make an unscheduled stop at a small town, they pronounce the food just as good as what they are eating in the upmarket establishments.

Eating together provides the venue for them to chat about a wide range of topics. There's an element of competition in their byplay, particularly apparent in their constant battle to upstage each other with impersonations of famous actors. Being a road trip through Italy, issues of reflection and transformation come to the fore. Initially, they are both a bit gloomy that they are approaching 50. However, as they proceed, this melancholy is shaken off. Steve (a notoriously wild man in Hollywood) resolves to quieten down, whereas the previously more stable Rob embraces his midlife crisis. In an interesting intertextual referencing, it is two female dining companions (their agent and photographer) who quote Julia Roberts in the film of *Eat Pray Love* (2010), highlighting that Italy is about immersing oneself in a glorious food culture.

Understanding Food Tourism

The examples of *Eat Pray Love* and *The Trip to Italy* illustrate how food has increasingly become a major component of tourism. For these tourists, the cuisine of Italy is not only exotic and satisfying, but it is also emotive and experiential. An important qualification to make is that food tourism is but one component of the whole tourist experience. Tourists travel for a range of reasons and in trying to separate them (and evaluate and measure them), often the bigger picture is lost. Food and cuisine cannot be separated from culture and heritage – and Italy as a tourist destination is an evocative example of this. Most tourists seek the whole package of experiences and their satisfaction is dependent on the right blend of these factors. In some circumstances, tourists will travel with food as the main objective – such as in a food tour or cooking school holiday. However, this is only a small section of the tourist market. Food may have become more important, but it is still firmly placed within the total tourist experience.

To better understand the broad phenomena that comprise food tourism, this chapter is divided into three sections, each examining a particular dimension of modern tourism. The first takes a demand-side approach, considering what tourists are expecting from food experiences while travelling. The second focuses on the supply side, particularly how destinations have changed what they offer in order to attract tourists. The third examines the role of media in these developments, emphasising the growth in television shows promoting food experiences and culinary destinations.

The Tourist

Understanding of the expectations and motivations of tourists can be approached by two pathways. The first is from a quantitative positivist paradigm. Generally the most widely used approach, it is particularly favoured in industry-based research. Utilising surveys of tourists and potential tourists, such research seeks to measure numbers of tourists with interests in food and evaluate their motivational factors and levels of satisfaction. Often utilising pre-existing national surveys and databases, a key aim of such studies is to identify market segments that have high interest or engagement with food and travel. Such studies are then put to practical use in underpinning the development of new tourism products and destination marketing campaigns.

An example of this research was conducted by Ignatov and Smith (2006), using a Canadian national tourist survey to understand the nature and various activities of food and wine tourists, resulting in the identification of a number of market segments. Another example is Mitchell and Hall (2003), drawing on data from the USA, Canada and Australia to identify key indicators and construct a typology of 'food tourist behaviour'.

The second approach tends to be conceptual and normative. It seeks to describe and interpret patterns and behaviours rather than measure them and its goal is to identify underlying causal factors. This is the approach that we will focus upon in this section.

Much of this research focuses on the personal benefit that tourists seek from consuming food as part of a wider cultural experience. In one of the earliest books focusing specifically on food and tourism, Boniface (2003) emphasised that tourists were seeking an escape from their everyday life. Part of this could be achieved by the food they chose. She especially identified that many tourists were nostalgic, looking backwards to an earlier time in history that they perceived as simpler and *better* and which could help them recover from the travails of modernity. While common in heritage studies, Boniface applied this concept to gastronomy and tourism. Taking an English perspective, she identified that many tourists indulged in meals and food rituals that were old-fashioned and no longer usually part of modern lifestyles. The full cooked English breakfast of bacon, eggs and fried bread was one example. Another was that of afternoon tea – particularly Devonshire Tea with scones, cream and jam. These nostalgic dishes, which involved greater preparation (and calories), had become part of people's holiday rituals, psychologically transporting them back to a romanticised past.

Richards (2002) similarly emphasised the importance of nostalgia. He also identified that tourists sought to acquire and display *cultural capital* through travel. Put simply, they hoped to show that they were better and more sophisticated people because they had travelled. For English tourists in Continental Europe, this cultural capital could be demonstrated through not only what meals they ordered, but also their expertise in pronunciation and knowledge of recipes and ingredients. Returning home, they in turn influenced domestic culture, demanding similar cuisines. Through these processes, accelerating at the beginning of the new century, forgotten foods – such as cider and polenta – were being rediscovered and adopted by a broader audience.

This interest in past and exotic cuisines raises questions of authenticity as a motivation for modern tourists. In an empirical study conducted in England's Lake District, Sims (2009) found that over 60% of respondents said that they deliberately chose to consume local foods on their holiday. Sims argued that 'tourists are seeking products that they feel will give them an insight into the nature of a place and its people'; or as one of her interviewees summed it up, 'get a taste of the place' (Sims, 2009: 329). Similarly, Timothy and Ron (2013a, 2013b) outline the rise of interest in heritage cuisines, driven by authenticity and nostalgia.

Authenticity, however, is a slippery concept. Arising in museum studies, it originally was used to signify that an artefact was certifiably true. In tourism studies it has increasingly been reinterpreted to focus on the tourist's experiences, particularly that the tourist feels fulfilled and psychologically better for their travel (Cohen, 2004; Wang, 1999). Such satisfaction may occur even if the tourism experiences consumed were not arguably true. In her study of Lake District tourists, Sims found that authenticity was highly important, with respondents seeking to 'experience a more authentic sense of self' (Sims, 2009: 325). For these tourists, authenticity was couched in terms of a romanticised view of English traditions and history. Furthermore, the tourists' definitions of authenticity were often expressed in negative terms – they did not want plastic, they did not want microwaved food. A telling disconnection emerged from discussions of local food and produce. Producers wanted a geographical definition. In contrast, the tourists identified local as iconic products associated with the region, such as particular cheeses and biscuits, and their origin was relatively unimportant (Sims, 2009).

A fascination with the past leads some tourists to seek out historic dishes, valued as a means to experience – even immerse oneself in – the past. Examples include taking part in a medieval banquet (Robinson & Clifford, 2012) and the eating of an arcane dish that had previously fallen out of fashion, such as the traditional sheeps-head meal in Voss, Norway (Mykletun & Gyimóthy, 2010). Ethnic heritage cuisines are increasingly subject to a cultural cross-over, as their popularity leads to consumption by groups that do not share the source cultural heritage. Accordingly, Italian, Indian, Mexican and Chinese meals are consumed all around the world, including in major tourism precincts. The catalyst for this spread has often been mobility, with diaspora societies retaining food cultures which gradually spread, albeit in a hybridised form (Frost & Laing, 2016; Gabaccia, 1998; Pilcher, 2006; Timothy & Ron, 2013a, 2013b). Nonetheless, such cultural sampling may be limited. Haverluk (2003), for instance, argues that while Mexican food has become mainstream throughout the USA, the broader Hispanic culture remains marginal.

The modern interest in food as a marker of a sophisticated lifestyle is now reflected in tourist behaviours. Getz *et al.* (2014) have identified the *foodie* as a key tourist segment. Defined as 'one who incorporates food, its preparation and enjoyment into their lifestyle' (Getz *et al.*, 2014: 51), the term 'foodie' was originally coined in the 1980s and became well known through the humorous bestseller *The Official Foodie Handbook* (Levy & Barr, 1984). Unlike many tourist descriptions, it is a term that many people will happily and proudly apply to themselves and, despite its comic origins, it carries no negative connotations.

Based on an empirical factor analysis, Getz *et al.* argued that there are four dimensions that are critical for people self-identifying as foodies. These four dimensions are (Getz *et al.*, 2014: 61–62):

(1) food-related identity, 'the importance of cooking to self and social identity';
(2) social bonding, 'foodies like to please and entertain others, to join others in a great food experience';
(3) quality;
(4) conscientiousness, being 'fastidious about how they buy, use and dispose of food'.

Getz *et al.* link foodies to two concepts from leisure studies – *serious leisure* and *social worlds*. The first was developed by Stebbins, who defined serious leisure as the 'systematic pursuit of an amateur, hobbyist or volunteers activity that is sufficiently substantial and interesting for the participant to find a career there in the acquisition and expression of its special skills and knowledge' (Stebbins, 1992: 3). In this sense, the career that is sought is unpaid, but is approached with just as much passion and intent as a work career. Social worlds are flexible units of social organisation. Although without formal boundaries and entry criteria, they are groups of like-minded people pursuing shared experiences and objectives (Unruh, 1979).

Similarly, Laing and Frost have identified the *food explorer* as 'independent travellers who are keen to experience food and wine that is distinctive of a place and they enjoy discovering and learning about different food styles, traditions and heritage' (Laing & Frost, 2014: 236). These food explorers have three distinctive characteristics (Laing & Frost, 2014: 236–237):

(1) They avoid commodified tourist experiences, guided tours and tourist menus. Instead they want to eat like locals and are happy to be surprised and challenged.
(2) They value food and drink that is authentic to the destination.
(3) They are concerned about cultural and environmental sustainability. The parallel may be drawn with ecotourism and, indeed, the same people may be involved in both forms of tourism, even on the same trip. This concern attracts them to movements like Slow Food (see Chapter 6).

The Industry

Culinary destinations

In the past, a small number of destinations were noted for their culinary attributes. France was the home of *Haute Cuisine* and restaurants with Michelin Stars, Italy was noted for *La Dolce Vita* and India, Thailand and Japan promised exotic fare. Nowadays, increased competition has led to a far wider range of destinations, all marketing their culinary expertise as one of their main attributes to encourage tourism (Richards, 2002).

Gastronomic tourism used to be based on place advantage – there was an existing well-known cuisine. The shift of recent decades has occurred through the widespread adoption of an entrepreneurial approach (Gössling & Hall, 2013). In order to capture greater market share, destination marketing organisations have repackaged their food offerings, sometimes trading on certain key strengths, at other times simply copying others.

In Europe, France and Italy retain the highest spots, but they have now been joined by other countries. Spain has marketed a distinctive cuisine and lifestyle built around *tapas*. Belgium has utilised its enormous variety of beers as a foundation, linking that with *moules and frites* (Figure 3.1). Denmark, Czech, Slovenia, Greece and others now enjoy an enhanced reputation for food and other European destinations are attempting to close the gap.

Over the last 40 years or so, there have been greatly increased tourism flows to Asia and a number of destinations have capitalised on their distinctive cuisines as key tourism attributes. India, Vietnam, Thailand and Bali have been particularly successful with cuisines that are viewed as perfect holiday fare in being spicy and cheap. For many tourists, this has been an enlightening experience of tasting highly exotic cultures and, in turn, this has influenced the growth of restaurants serving these cuisines in Western countries (Hall & Mitchell, 2002b). Similarly, Japanese food – although sometimes far more expensive – has shifted from a style consumed on holidays to high popularity around the world. A recent study of tourism associated with udon noodles has demonstrated that both domestic and international tourists have been drawn by the heritage and stories linked to this food (Kim & Ellis, 2015). Contrasting with these emphases on local culture, entrepots like Hong Kong, Singapore and increasingly Shanghai have specialised in providing an eclectic mix of restaurants and fusion cuisines (Henderson, 2009).

Similarly, Australia and New Zealand offer tourists diversity rather than specific indigenous cuisines. While there have been attempts to develop the latter, their success has been patchy; kangaroo and kumara are sometimes on the menu, but are still not mainstream. Instead the emphasis has tended to be on diaspora cuisines and modern international. In these countries, Melbourne has been the most successful destination in marketing itself as a

Figure 3.1 The café lifestyle, beer in the city square, Antwerp, Belgium (photo W. Frost)

food city. Interestingly, its success is built on a wide variety of medium -range restaurants and cafés – sometimes described as casual dining – appealing to both locals and tourists (Frost *et al.*, 2010; Frost & Laing, in press).

In recent years, North America has been strongly influenced by the rise of *dude food*. Through the mediation of pay television shows produced for the Food Channel, dude food has now spread globally. It is categorised by burgers, ribs, bacon, fried chicken, tacos, high calories and strong popular culture theming (Figure 3.2). At its extreme, it includes candied bacon and *turducken* (a chicken inside a duck inside a turkey and deep-fried, see Figure 3.3). As a trend it draws on notions of *comfort food* and a return to dishes from one's childhood and may be a reaction to increasing formalisation. Its roots – as with much of American cuisine – can be traced back to European migration, particularly from Germany. It is noticeable that variations of this style occur in Germany, such as the *Schweinshaxe* (roasted pig's knuckle or kneecap, see Figure 3.4). This dish is very popular in cities like Munich and Prague, where its consumption is marketed as a rite of passage for macho male tourists.

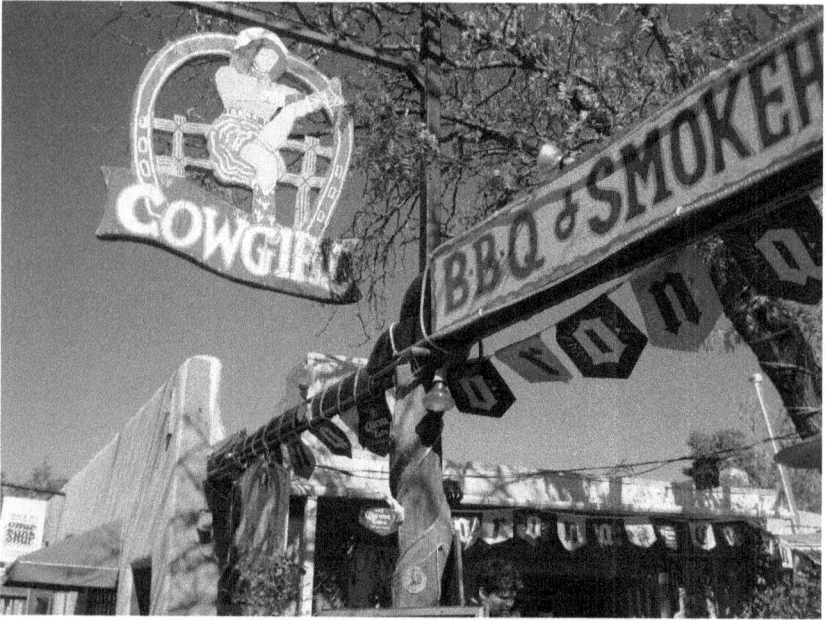

Figure 3.2 Dude food theming, the Cowgirl Restaurant, Santa Fe, USA (photo W. Frost)

Figure 3.3 Dude food – turducken, Alexandria, Virginia, USA (photo W. Frost)

Figure 3.4 The macho challenge of a 1.2 kilogram roasted pig's kneecap, Prague, Czech Republic (photo W. Frost)

While food tourism (and tourism in general) is often centered on major cities; there has also been interest in the development of rural-based food tourism. This may be viewed as having the following dimensions (based on Beer *et al.*, 2002; Connell, 2014; Frost & Laing, 2014; Sims, 2009):

(1) Food production and consumption are closely linked, with a strong emphasis on local ingredients and cuisine.
(2) Rural locations are imagined in nostalgic terms, as better and more authentic than modern urban cities. Food plays a strong role in this 'escape to the country'.
(3) This imagining is highly mediatised, particularly through magazines, novels, television and film.
(4) The economic impact of this tourism is seen as highly desirable, providing employment in agriculture and service industries and potentially arresting rural decline and a population drift to the cities.
(5) There are, nonetheless, possibilities for dissonance and tensions. The gentrification of the countryside might push up property prices and lead to pressure to restrict agricultural production that may be seen by newcomers as industrial and disturbing of their idyll.

Gastronomic public policy

Some destinations have successfully positioned themselves as highly attractive to tourists interested in gastronomy. Others have not. Is there some sort of recipe that allows places to strategically transform themselves? As with other forms of tourism, some places have initiated partnerships between governments and businesses – often through destination marketing organisations – with the aim of becoming a food destination.

Such public policy strategies may operate at the country, city, region or local level. Du Rand and Heath (2006) have developed a framework that includes food as an element of destination marketing. They argue that food may be either a key or a supportive attraction and that its inclusion in destination marketing is increasing. Similarly, Richards (2002) sees an increased emphasis on food in destination marketing, with this change driven by greater competition between destinations around the world.

An illustrative example of such a national strategy is the *Restaurant Australia* marketing campaign, launched by Tourism Australia in 2014 (Tourism Australia, 2014). Financed by $10 million of public expenditure, it targets 12 key international markets with the aim of raising Australia's profile as a gastronomic destination. This is justified by Tourism Australia as addressing a perception gap identified by empirical research. Their argument is that, of those surveyed who had never visited Australia, only 26% identified it as a destination they associated with food and wine. In contrast, of those surveyed who had visited Australia, 60% associated it with food and wine. Amongst the strategies implemented by the Restaurant Australia campaign was an international media familiarisation programme, involving hosted visits by 80 food writers and chefs.

At the more local level, public policy often takes the form of developing trails or marketing programmes. Examples include the Isle of Arran Taste Trail in Scotland (Boyne *et al.*, 2002), A Taste of Wales (Jones & Jenkins, 2002) and the Waterloo–Wellington Ale Trail in Canada (Plummer *et al.*, 2005). Associated with such marketing enterprises are schemes to regulate and certify the regional authenticity of local products and businesses (Beer *et al.*, 2002; Sims, 2009). The latter approach raises issues of commercial dissonance, with certification sometimes becoming self-serving, bureaucratic and distanced from commercial considerations.

Regional trails and programmes face problems of viability – a common issue for many tourism operations in rural and peripheral areas. The Taste of Wales was viewed as a failure owing to a lack of tangible benefits for participants, unfocused marketing and a confused identity (Jones & Jenkins, 2002). The Waterloo–Wellington Ale Trail only lasted for three years. While popular with tourists, it was the producers who decided to pull out (Plummer *et al.*, 2005). A study of the Isle of Arran Taste Trail proclaimed it a success, but this was only after two years of operation. Indeed, that study raised the concern of whether it would be viable in the long run, once the public seeding grant ran out and it had to shift to a tourism operator member-funded model (Boyne *et al.*, 2002). Unfortunately, a 2015 internet search for the Arran Trail shows no current website, suggesting that it is moribund.

The Experience Economy

In recent years, almost paralleling the rise of gastronomy and food tourism, the tourism industry has wholeheartedly embraced the concept of the *experience economy*. Getz *et al.* (2014), for example, apply it to the desires and motivations of their foodies. Initially developed by Pine and Gilmore (1999), this theory has evolved and adapted, often with the input of operators who are unaware of its origins, but just see it as an influential trend. The experience economy attractively promises increased profits whilst improving the quality of the tourism product offered to tourists. The key is to move away from an old-fashioned view of services – accommodation, meals, transport, tours – towards the planned creation of satisfying experiences. As this new paradigm has taken hold, there has been a clear shift in destination marketing. Rather than merely places and sights, the new approach focuses on the experiences that the tourist will encounter. Furthermore, the emphases are on the quality and intensity of these experiences. These are exclusive and tailored to the tourist's wants (the term bespoke is increasingly used) and are at their peak even profound and life-changing.

Pine and Gilmore's theory is built on five propositions:

(1) As the service economy replaced a manufacturing-based one, so now the experience economy represents the next step beyond services.
(2) More complex and satisfying than mere services, experiences can be sold at a higher price, thereby increasing yield.
(3) There are four *experience realms* – entertainment, education, escapism and aesthetics. Ideally, *memorable experiences* occur in the *sweet spot* where all four realms intersect.
(4) Experiences are produced and staged like a play. The consumers are the audience who are entranced by the performance and actors. Surprising elements and special effects are included, 'staging the unexpected' (Pine & Gilmore, 1999: 96), to create the impression that this is a bespoke production.
(5) Experiences are scripted to control quality. Like a play, the actors read their lines while maintaining an illusion of naturalism.

In gastronomy, the Experience Economy has been highly influential on high-end dining (even though Pine and Gilmore limited their initial analysis to franchise chains like the Rainforest Cafe). A significant manifestation of the approach has been the recent trend to *degustation* menus. Originally coming from French and generally meaning a tasting, it has come to signify a set menu including a range of the chef's best – or *signature* – dishes. As opposed to à la carte menus, there is no written description. Instead each arrives and is only then described by the waiter. In addition, it is common to have a series of matching wines; again these are only revealed upon being poured. Such an experience combines the idea that this is the chef's best and that there are spectacular surprises in store. It is notable that such a menu is staged for each group of diners, who may choose the number of courses and nominate foods they do not like. Reinforcing this impression of a bespoke experience, the waiter is the key actor, interacting with the diners and replacing the printed menu as the provider of information. This may or may not be done with a theatrical flourish, depending on the house style. In accordance with the principles of Pine and Gilmore, the waiter is but an actor reading from a set script, but skilfully providing an illusion of spontaneity and personal flexibility.

Another key manifestation of the Experience Economy is the provision of dining in a novel setting. One company, appropriately called 'Dining in the Sky', provides patrons with the experience of eating while suspended from a crane (Figure 3.5). While an extension of an older

Figure 3.5 Dinner in the Sky in Brussels, Belgium (photo J. Laing)

notion of locating restaurants in high structures with iconic views – such as the Jules Verne Restaurant in the Eiffel Tower – this new trend adds the experience of the thrill, perhaps owing something to the success of bungee jumping.

Another example is the concept of *imaginative dining* promoted by the Thailand based Minor Hotel Group. Arguing that 'bespoke culinary concepts are reaching a pinnacle of popularity and diners are eager to see who can pull out the stops for the most imaginative gastronomy', they offer 'gourmet international cuisines and local exotic flavours expertly prepared by a personal chef'. These are for couples or small groups and take place in 'idyllic settings that capitalise on the distinctive landscapes and views of each unique locale'. At the Antara Golden Triangle Elephant Camp and Resort in Thailand, the experience is marketed as Propose in the Jungle:

> Dine beside a scenic rice paddy, on a hilltop overlooking three countries and the Mekong River, or at the jungle elephant camp, and at the time of your choosing a baby elephant will present a bouquet of flowers with the ring safely hidden inside. (Minor Hotel Group, 2014: 11).

Despite its widespread adoption, the experience economy is subject to criticism (see Laing & Frost, 2014, 2015b; O'Dell, 2005; Ooi, 2005). It is essentially a supply-side view of tourism, with a focus on how operators can increase yields through careful planning and staging. The emphasis on scripting seems at odds with what modern tourists want. Research into existential authenticity indicates that many tourists are searching for meaningful encounters and experiences that will make them feel more complete, more real (Cohen, 2004; Wang, 1999). Will a meticulously scripted and staged performance satisfy such consumers? Or is this the sort of production they will associate with Disneyland and Las Vegas?

We propose that many modern tourists want to go well beyond the experience economy. Yes, they want personally engaging experiences, but they do not want them constructed and scripted. Savvy modern tourists want engagements that they seek out, that they choose and even construct themselves. Nothing is a bigger turn off for them than the idea that they are consuming a staged product. What they see as personally fulfilling is to *explore* and create their own experience.

Utilising the Media

Destinations and operators seek to use the media to help market their offerings. Through the media, images of places and experiences are created that will stimulate potential tourists to travel, possibly even with the aim of recreating these for themselves. Such imaging may be organic or induced.

Eat Pray Love provides an example of organic image formation. Elizabeth Gilbert – the writer – worked completely independently of any destination marketing organisation. While it might encourage tourism to Italy, it is not an advertisement for that destination. In contrast, *The Trip to Italy* tells a tale of induced image formation. Steve Coogan and Rob Brydon have been hired by a newspaper to write a series of restaurant reviews/travel stories. Organised by the newspaper in conjunction with the destination marketing organisation, their meals, transport and luxurious accommodation are provided for free by the various operators. This is a media familiarisation trip, commonly known in the industry as a *famil*. For the operators, it is part of their marketing budget and they are hoping for a strong return from the flattering newspaper stories.

The key to effective induced image formation is trust and yet – paradoxically – it relies on a certain amount of deceit. To work, the media presenter (whether writer or television host) has to project a strong and intimate connection with the audience. They have to be friendly, likeable, authoritative, authentic; they must connect and engender a sense of trust. This trust directly affects the ability of the media production to influence consumers and translate into future travel. Projecting that trustworthiness requires the downplaying, even the omission, of the financial support of operators and destination marketing organisations. The production cannot look like an advertisement, but rather the naturalistic wanderings of the host or writer.

Such an approach has been apparent in travel writing from at least the 19th century. In terms of gastronomic tourism, an early example was the 1991 television series *Floyd on Oz*, made with strong support from Tourism Australia (Hall & Mitchell, 2002a). Keith Floyd was a popular English chef and television personality, noted for his engaging eccentricity and down to earth persona. He had previously made six television series before being approached by Tourism Australia. The resultant 10 episode series took in all six states and two territories, covering a vast distance that would have made the production uneconomic without the financial support from the destination marketing organisation. Rick Stein reinforces this view of Keith Floyd as a pioneer, commenting that 'the fact Keith didn't cook in a studio was radically new' (Stein, 2013: 227).

A generation on, it is intriguing to see how Tourism Australia continues to use the media. At the 2014 Restaurant Australia campaign launch, international culinary guests of honour were Heston Blumenthal, Alice Waters and A.A. Gill (Tourism Australia, 2014). Paying for such international celebrities to attend makes the launch newsworthy, gaining valuable publicity across a wide range of media. Most importantly, it is part of an integrated marketing strategy to position Australia as a gastronomic destination.

4   Festivals and Gastronomy

La Dolce Vita Festival

The festival is staged at multiple locations – a dozen wineries throughout the valley. La Dolce Vita means 'The Sweet Life' in Italian and this festival celebrates Italian food, music and culture. What is on offer differs from winery to winery, but there is plenty of pasta, pizza, salami, wine and gelato. As travel and food writer A.A. Gill has put it, 'no nation, no culture on Earth has been as successfully rolled out as a global brand as Italy has' (Gill, 2010: 115). As we argued in Chapter 3, food and cuisine are central to that attractive brand image and it has been heavily reinforced by the media. Through its name, the La Dolce Vita Festival calls to mind the iconic film *La Dolce Vita* (1960). For festival goers, the imagery of the Italian lifestyle could equally come from films such as *Roman Holiday* (1953), *Moonstruck* (1987), *Under the Tuscan Sun* (2003) or *Eat Pray Love* (2010).

Yet, this festival is not in Italy. Despite its Italian food and theming, it is over half a world away. The setting for La Dolce Vita is in Australia's King Valley (Figure 4.1). Staged annually since 2001, it is operated by a group of winemakers. Most, but not all, of these winemakers have Italian heritage. Migrating after the Second World War, they originally focused on tobacco, with wine only really developing on a commercial scale right at the end of the 20th century. In the southern end of the King Valley, 19% of the population claim Italian heritage. In comparison, about 5% of all Australians are of Italian descent (Laing & Frost, 2013). The great majority of people who attend the festival have no ethnic connection to Italy. What draws them is their love of Italian food and culture. This interest in diaspora cuisine – its adoption and consumption by broad populations outside the diaspora communities – occurs around the world. It is not just a phenomenon linked with Italian food; it is also notably connected with a wide range of cuisines and foodways, including Chinese, Indian and Mexican (Frost & Laing, 2016; Gabbacia, 1998; Timothy & Ron, 2013a, 2013b).

Regional communities rely heavily on festivals to attract visitors, sell produce and maintain their identity (Frost & Laing, 2015b). However, faced with limited resources, they often struggle to find their niche, the distinctive

Figure 4.1 La Dolce Vita Festival at Pizzini Winery, King Valley, Australia (photo J. Laing)

theme that will distinguish them from other rural areas (Higham & Ritchie, 2001; Lade & Jackson, 2004). Food that is 'expressive of a region and its culture' may be a way of differentiating a destination from its competitors (Lee & Arcodia, 2011: 356). We interviewed organisers of the La Dolce Vita Festival, and they emphasised the effectiveness and power of theming their food and wine festival as *Italian*.

As one of these organisers said, 'there was a need for promotion of the area and what better way to hang your hat on than being an Italian family with heritage and tradition'. Another noted the appeal of a family party atmosphere, as it is 'part of that Italian heritage ... [that] you go to someone's house and you're treated as part of the family'. Yet another emphasised the distinctiveness of the landscape: 'you don't feel like you're in Australia ... you just feel like you're in another country, it's just so different'.

For these winemakers, the festival has become an essential part of their marketing mix. Whilst they value their Italian diaspora heritage, they also recognise that their family businesses are commercial and they need to be viable. As one explained the aim of the La Dolce Vita Festival:

It's a big promotional role, very big. Because people will come to these events and go, God, we had a good time. Then they will come outside of those events. That's what we hope, not just to attract them to the events.

It's about getting people in the door, so they get to know us and then want to come back.

Introduction

While the Dolce Vita Festival is themed around diaspora heritage, food and wine play a major role in its success, with the connection to ethnic cuisine helping to reinforce cultural identities, as well as providing the opportunity to increase sales, promote persuasive messages and expand markets and construct a satisfying experience for participants. The festival offers an alternative distribution outlet for local wine, while educating consumers and generating awareness in an informal environment (Bruwer, 2002). It also becomes a powerful tool for disseminating the culture of a place (Cavicchi & Santini, 2014), in this case, the Italian heritage of many inhabitants of the King Valley.

In this chapter, we explore some of the common linkages that exist between festivals and gastronomy and why they are important to many destinations. To illustrate these connections, two case studies are considered: the Melbourne Food and Wine Festival in Australia and Galway International Oyster and Seafood Festival in Ireland. While both festivals are a celebration of regional produce, the Galway International Oyster and Seafood Festival focuses specifically on the harvest of the native oyster, over an extended weekend, while the Melbourne Food and Wine Festival celebrates a cosmopolitan array of cultural cuisines over a two-week period with some events extending throughout the calendar year. Both are examples of *hallmark events*, which 'provide their host destinations with a competitive advantage, due to their significance and intimate association with the destination' (Frost & Laing, 2011: 6). The name of these events typically includes the destination name, connecting the two in people's minds.

Gastronomic Events

Many festivals utilise gastronomy as a theme. Their objectives include reinforcing cultural identities, increasing sales, expanding into new markets, promoting a brand, preserving artisanal production and delivering persuasive messages about health and the environment. A food-themed festival provides a great opportunity to increase awareness, visitation and the profitability of a destination and its surrounding region (Hall, 1992).

The history of festivals is intertwined with gastronomy, mainly because it is almost impossible to imagine a festival that does not have some element of food provided or sold to attendees. Falassi (1987), in his analysis of the ritual structure of events, has identified a number of rites that are common to many festivals and provide them with meaning and significance. One of these is the rite of *conspicuous consumption*, where an abundance of food and drink is available, beyond the everyday norm. This may take the form of special festival food (see Chapter 5), such as fairy floss/cotton candy, hot dogs or ice-cream cones or feasts or banquets. In Sardinia, festivalgoers at the Sant'Antonio's Day festivities consume a traditional sweet called *pobassinos* as the masked procession moves from bonfire to bonfire (Iorio & Wall, 2015). Chinese New Year celebrations involve families eating eight or nine specially prepared dishes that have a ritual significance:

> For example, in northern China, steamed dumplings (jiao zi) symbolise wealth and prosperity as their shape resembles a Chinese tael (a weight measure) and a money bag, while in southern China, a sticky cake or rice pudding (nian gao) is popular as it represents progress and continual improvement. (White & Leung, 2015)

The origins of this over-consumption of food at festivals can be traced to prehistoric times, where 'ceremonial feasting developed as a reaction to inconsistent food supplies. Periodically there would be massive surpluses of food, far more than small groups could consume and with little prospect of preserving for future years' (Frost & Laing, 2015a: 7). It also reflects the role of festivals as *ludic spaces* (Ravenscroft & Matteucci, 2003), where people can let off steam and indulge in practices that would be otherwise frowned upon or unavailable to the average person. It is still the case today that festivals provide a means of *escape* for attendees. They add colour to a destination and to people's lives. They may also be a focus for deviant behaviour (Sharpe, 2008).

An example of the latter is La Tomatina, the tomato throwing festival staged in Buñol, Spain. It may have originated from religious observances connected to San Luis Bertran, with the tomato throwing believed to have started at the end of the Second World War as a political statement and form of protest against the fascist dictator Franco. Throwing tomatoes was an anti-authoritarian gesture, but is now just an anarchic activity, enjoyed by many tourists. Unlike many food-themed festivals, La Tomatina was not created to leverage off the advantage of a product that is grown locally, although the town's identity is now bound up with the tomato.

Aside from the presence of food at festivals more generally, a wide range of festivals and events are *themed* on food and gastronomy. Some common types are discussed below (expanded from Frost & Laing, 2011: 50).

Food associated with a place

Particularly in rural areas, there are festivals celebrating the main agricultural produce of the region. Common examples include apple and strawberry festivals. The Fête du Citron (Lemon Festival) has been staged since 1929 in the French town of Menton on the Côte d'Azur, famous for its lemons, and features a parade with lemon-decorated floats. Sometimes festivals are themed around unusual products, utilised to provide a distinctive competitive advantage. Two examples from California are the Gilroy Garlic Festival and the Stockton Asparagus Festival (Lewis, 1997). Both evolved from a strategic decision to bring more visitors to their regions. Lee and Arcodia (2011) refer to the contribution made by these festivals to destination brands.

In some instances, the product may have strong connotations of appealing to the gourmet market, as in festivals themed on truffles or lobsters. There are a number of festivals themed around oysters, including the Bluff Oyster Festival (Panelli *et al.*, 2008; Rusher, 2003), the Galway International Oyster and Seafood Festival and Oysterfest in Ceduna, South Australia.

Generic food and wine festivals

Found around the globe, these are staged by cities that aim to project an image of sophistication. Their organisation brings together destination marketing organisations, local restaurants and food and wine producers. Examples include the South Beach Food and Wine Festival in Miami, Florida (Park *et al.*, 2008) and the Melbourne Food and Wine Festival. These events are often part of a calendar of hallmark events, which collectively form an *event portfolio* (Ziakas, 2013), discussed later in this chapter.

Regionally based wine festivals

Staged in wine regions through the cooperative efforts of wineries, these often have a food component, although the wine is paramount (Cavicchi & Santini, 2014; Strickland *et al.*, 2016). The La Dolce Vita Festival is an example of this type of event. They may offer 'a one-stop shopping opportunity for participants to sample all the wines from a particular region' (Yuan *et al.*, 2005: 43), or encourage visitors to travel to different wineries, which each offer a special attraction or activity, such as music, in addition to the wine tasting and food.

Harvest festivals

Found in agricultural areas, these build on traditions of the harvest and generally feature a wide range of produce (Janiskee, 1980). Historically, the harvest festival marked the passing of the seasons and celebrated and gave thanks to God or the gods for the abundance of produce able to be stored away for the winter (Barber, 2013). The distinction between harvest festivals and product-themed festivals may be at times blurred and there are indications that the term *harvest festival* is increasingly being generally applied for marketing purposes. Examples are the Sonoma County Harvest Fair in the Napa Valley (Figure 4.2) and the Williamsburg Harvest Festival in Ontario, Canada.

Figure 4.2 Visiting stalls at the Sonoma County Harvest Fair, Santa Rosa, USA (photo J. Laing)

Farmers' markets

These events (see also Chapter 8) are growing in popularity, in both rural and urban settings, as distribution points for fresh produce, but also as a way for people to connect with food growers. Alice Waters 'is credited with kick-starting farmers' markets across the US' and is a regular visitor at the Saturday morning farmers' market in Union Square in New York, which attracts around 250,000 customers a week (Bryant, 2014: 27). Dublin boasts the popular Temple Bar Farmers' Market, also held on a Saturday, in a precinct that becomes an entertainment area by night (The Age, 2015). Barbara Storey, Manager – Communications and Promotions for the Barossa Grape & Wine Association in South Australia, spoke at the Global Events Congress in Adelaide in 2014 on the appeal of farmers' markets in the region: 'We are starting to question our food now'. Like Alice Waters, she felt that these markets 'offer an experiential education ... kids learn about food, how to eat it, how to grow it'.

Agricultural shows and fairs

These often have a long tradition and date back into the 19th century. This type of fair 'allows visitors to experience a wide array of agricultural products within a themed setting' (Mitchell, 2006: 1298). In addition to displays and competitions for the best agricultural produce, they feature competitions for excellence in home produce, such as cakes, pies and preserves. The Bloomberg Fair in Pennsylvania, officially the Columbia County Agricultural, Horticultural, and Mechanical Association, started back in 1855 and attracts '500,000+ visitors in an 8-day period' (Mitchell, 2006: 1298). A derivative of the agricultural show is the dedicated cake show or cake decorating championship.

Diaspora-themed festivals

These have a strong emphasis on the diaspora's cuisine. While staged by people who identify with a particular diaspora, attendees will be drawn from the wider community, particularly if the cuisine is well known and popular (Frost & Laing, 2016; Timothy & Ron, 2013a, 2013b). An example is the Dolce Vita Festival, mentioned above. There has been a burgeoning of Mexican-themed festivals in the USA, such as the chilli festival, although the acceptance of this food does not mean that Hispanic culture itself has been totally embraced within mainstream society (Haverluk, 2003).

Special dinners and other themed events

Staged by restaurants or tourist attractions – or as part of non-food festivals – these events have a special theme linked to gastronomy. One example is the Medieval Banquet staged as part of the Abbey Medieval Festival in Brisbane, Australia (Robinson & Clifford, 2012). Another is the re-enactment of the dinner served in the film *Babette's Feast* at Thomas Keller's New York restaurant, Per Se, discussed in Chapter 15.

Food Festivals and Destination Marketing

Gastronomy is increasingly being seen by destinations as a means to add value to the tourist experience and is associated with high-quality and high-yield tourism. Festivals using gastronomy as a theme especially provide destinations with an opportunity to promote their local produce, often reflecting their cultural identity, and offer an alternative distribution outlet while educating consumers and generating awareness in an informal environment (Bruwer, 2002; Hall, 1992; Hall & Sharples, 2008; Kivela & Crotts, 2006). Food festivals are part of the intangible cultural heritage, for during festivals, product knowledge is spread among participants and local communities and local products become a powerful tool for disseminating the culture of a place (Santini et al., 2013). Accordingly, festivals are an important means of preserving heritage cuisines, foodways and artisanal production (Timothy & Pena, 2016).

Food experiences at festivals contribute to the development of a destination image. Marketing material will often depict food experiences using gastronomic cues through images and words and it is these cues that may raise emotions and attract culinary tourists (Silkes *et al.*, 2013). Destination marketing organisations are often involved in food festivals as an effective means of highlighting and communicating their food and other attractive attributes to potential tourists. An example of such a strategic process is the Stockton Asparagus Festival in California. Located in the rich Central Valley agricultural region, Stockton produces a wide range of irrigated crops. In developing the concept for a festival, the local tourism organisation and businesses chose asparagus as a theme, because they saw it as a distinctive and high-status gourmet food product. This, they reasoned, was the image to attract the right sort of tourist for a weekend festival (Lewis, 1997).

Whilst some areas have a tradition of food festivals, other destinations see them as a strategic tool to rejuvenate an image that may be tired and stale. Again, here there is a notion of tapping into food and gastronomy as being increasingly attractive to tourists and complementary to existing local foods, regional cuisines, wine and traditional practices (Kivela & Crotts, 2006; Lade & Jackson, 2004; Lee & Arcodia, 2011). Creating a positive destination image increases the overall attractiveness of these regional destinations, producers, brands and food experiences and encourages visitation. Strategically, destinations may utilise one of three approaches to project an attractive image to tourists via festivals. The first is *reinforcement*, whereby an existing image is strengthened through being utilised as a festival theme. The second is *repackaging*, where existing images are used that, while known to locals, are not particularly known to potential tourists. The third is *reimagining*, which involves an invention of a completely new image, often one that contrasts strikingly with a previous tired image (Frost & Laing, 2011).

Kangaroo Island off the coast of South Australia has used food festivals such as the Kangaroo Island Art Feast and Kangaroo Island FEASTival to help *reimagine* itself as a foodie destination, focusing on local honey, seafood, cheese and wine. Prior to this, it was promoted more for its nature-based tourism, particularly connected to wildlife. Its festivals combine natural outdoor settings with food experiences, and they aim for small-scale events, such as helping to catch and shuck local oysters. At a workshop at the Global Events Congress in Adelaide in 2014, industry speaker Justin Harman of Island Pure Sheep Dairy commented that this focus on getting close to the produce is part of the attraction for visitors, as 'we've never been so disconnected from our food'. These festivals are not just preaching to the converted. They also attract 'those who didn't come there to learn about food culture, but they get it'.

A contrasting urban example of reimagining is the Nottingham Food and Drink Festival in the UK. This was developed partly to combat an image of central Nottingham as being dominated by a strong heavy-drinking culture, with bars and discos dominating a night-time economy that was viewed as unattractive and dangerous. Through the Food and Drink Festival, a conscious strategy was followed of encouraging families to come into the city at night and highlighting that food and drink should be enjoyed together (Hollows *et al.*, 2014).

In recent years, some destinations have adopted the strategy of *the event portfolio*. This involves the construction of a series or calendar of events, spread across the year. The rationale for this is one of risk management. Rather than taking the risk of one high-profile event – which may be affected by bad weather or only appeal to a certain market – the strategy is to have a range of events that spread the risk (Ziakas, 2013). This strategy is particularly adopted by cities that wish to project an image of being *eventful cities*, which are attractive to tourists through the vibrancy that comes from a packed events schedule. Melbourne is the exemplar of this kind of strategy, which will be discussed in the case study later in this chapter. For destinations that take this approach, the development of a food and wine festival becomes almost mandatory, partly because of its broad appeal and partly because competing destinations are staging similar events.

A number of benefits associated with staging food festivals are identified in this chapter and the contribution of these food events and festivals to national, state and regional economies is important. Critical success factors include strong community involvement and support, strategically focused management and planning functions and effective marketing strategies (Mayfield & Crompton, 1995). However, some festivals are planned and staged in a manner that may not lead to the success originally anticipated by their organisers (Lade & Jackson, 2004). Often there is huge dependence on volunteers to stage the event who, despite their strong commitment and devotion of considerable time, may lack expertise and experience (Getz & Brown, 2004). Many events are not operated on a regular basis, or are held only on one or a few days or weeks annually, limiting benefits to local producers and communities. Additionally, the festival's development goals may vary between organisers, producers and community members, in relation to which fund raising and staffing may then become issues (Lade & Jackson, 2004).

Producers

Food and wine festivals are examples of industrial events, where the primary aim of organisers is to sell their products. Producer benefits of participating in a food and wine festival may include providing a more cost effective means of promoting their produce (food and wine), creating awareness of their produce in new customers and giving them the opportunity to engage with these new customers to gain immediate feedback (Bruwer, 2002; Getz & Brown, 2004). Along with initiating customer relationships, festivals may serve as an alternative distribution sales outlet and an opportunity to increase sales and expand target markets. Social media is now being increasingly used by wineries and food producers to complement festivals and strengthen ongoing relationships with customers (Hays *et al.*, 2013; Strickland *et al.*, 2016).

At the La Dolce Vita Festival, the organising committee comprises representatives of the local wineries. While competitors, they work co-operatively to market their wine region and they have developed the festival as a means to attract customers. Sales during the festival are important, but the ultimate goal is the long-term reinforcement of a brand that distinguishes this region as having an Italian flavour, inextricably linked to the food and wine. Research carried out by Lee and Arcodia (2011: 364) found that the use of a regional festival to enhance an existing destination brand is often dependent on a 'number of conditions: festivals' longevity, the number of visitors, government support and sponsors and media coverage'. The Dolce Vita Festival has been running for 14 years and attracts around 4000–5000 visitors to the King Valley. However, it is deliberately low key in terms of sponsorship, primarily because the organisers don't want the event to become too big, spoiling its authenticity and intimacy for visitors.

Festivals and the Tourist Experience

Food and wine festivals provide the opportunity for leisure, social and cultural experiences (Nicholson & Pearce, 2001). They often attract a large number of regional producers to a central location, making it convenient for the tourist to access them. Consumers seriously involved in gastronomy often seek experiences involving 'tasting, preparing, experimenting, researching, discovering, understanding and writing' about both food and wine (Kivela & Crotts, 2006: 354). Sampling local food and wine provides the tourist with an interactive experience and the opportunity to improve their knowledge of the wine and food product, while engaging in social interaction with producers and fellow festival attendees. Food and culinary experiences are drawcards for a destination, with tourists often seeking a local cultural experience with the expectation that the surrounding environment reflects an appropriate ambience and atmosphere. The existence of festivals and events is particularly important to the *creative class* identified by Florida (2002, 2005), who are looking for authentic, immersive and multifaceted experiences.

Authenticity is an important attribute of gastronomic festivals for many tourists. Generally, authenticity relates to offering products that originate from the area where the event takes place (Cavicchi & Santini, 2014; Clarke, 2014), but may also relate to the authenticity of the cultural cuisine that is showcased through the event (Laing & Frost, 2013; Timothy & Pena, 2016). It is a multidimensional concept, influenced by aspects of the production and delivery of the event in relation to its food and beverage products (Robinson

& Clifford, 2012). For urban dwellers, rural food and wine festivals may appeal, 'because they are local, celebrating a sense of place and community that are perceived as no longer available in crowded and alienated cities' (Frost & Laing, 2011: 51). Meeting and talking with food producers in a rural setting allows for intimate connections leading to greater satisfaction and well-being (Sidali et al., 2015).

Festivals and the Media

The nature of food and wine festivals means that they often attract media attention. This is often stimulated by the gaining of endorsements and appearances from celebrity personalities within the food and wine industries. Such occurrences not only add credibility but also serve as an additional attraction for the consumer. In regional locations, festivals are a means to promote both the region and celebrity personalities who may originate from these regions, own and/or operate a restaurant in this region and use regional produce from this region in their cooking/restaurant.

Social media is a platform more commonly being used in destination marketing as a tool to reach a global audience with limited resources (Hays et al., 2013). The majority of information from events may be contributed by individuals through social media channels, whether it be via photo and video sharing sites or social networking sites before, during or following the event (Becker et al., 2012). Social networking sites, such as Facebook, particularly serve as an important tool in enhancing marketing communications, by providing an opportunity for two-way communication between organisers and potential festival attendees to occur (Lee et al., 2012). Public relationships may be developed and potential festival attendees become more emotionally engaged, which may result in increased attendance of the festival. These public event pages developed by event organisers not only assist in creating awareness of local events but also enable potential attendees to encounter festival reviews and management to monitor and respond to any suggestions and criticisms concerning the event (Becker et al., 2009; Lee et al., 2012). The use of Twitter throughout an event can also be an effective means of promoting the event and raising interest in certain activities within the overall event itself. Research indicates that, in some instances, 60% of tweets are made during the event while the remaining 40% are split between before and following the event (Lee et al., 2012).

Potential issues associated with social media use in the development, promotion and extension of festivals and events do however exist. Owing to the nature of social media involving communication with potentially hundreds or thousands of consumers, managers cannot directly control the content and conversation. As examined in Chapter 1, there is a tension between induced and organic image formation. Induced is controlled by the organisers, but may have low levels of trust amongst consumers. Organic – which includes consumer posts on social media – may be seen as more trustworthy and authentic, but is far less controllable. Tourism industry concerns about the content and use of Trip Advisor are a good example of this issue. Festival managers may try to implement methods designed to shape and influence discussions that are consistent with the objectives of the organisation, although such attempts at control are recognised as difficult and may be counter-productive (Mangold & Faulds, 2009).

To conclude this chapter, we now shift to presenting two case studies that illustrate the different roles played by food festivals in the cities of Melbourne and Galway.

The Melbourne Food and Wine Festival

Melbourne has been voted the most liveable city for the fifth year running (2011–2015) and amongst the city's key attributes is its serious coffee and café culture, its mix of diverse cultures and an eclectic dining scene (Frost & Laing, in press; Frost et al., 2010; Holden & Scerri, 2012). Melbourne's restaurant and wine scene is well recognised internationally as a visitor attraction and the Melbourne Food and Wine Festival adds value to the tourist experience by both highlighting and reinforcing the city's cultural identity in connection to gastronomy. The Melbourne Food and Wine Festival, now in its 23rd year, has grown from a rather modest programme of 10 events to over 250 events in 2015, attracting over 200,000 participants (Melbourne Food and Wine Festival, 2015; Money, 2012).

The festival was founded in 1993 by Peter Clemenger, director of an Australian marketing agency Clemenger BBDO (Melbourne Food and Wine Festival, 2015). In 1990, Melbourne lost its bid for the 1996 Olympic Games (which went to Atlanta). Peter Clemenger was a committee member for the Olympic bid. Dejected, he went on holidays to Thailand. As he sat on the beach, he kept thinking about alternative event ideas that could stimulate the city. He came up with three possibilities where Melbourne excelled. These were fashion, gardens and food and wine. He evaluated each, but felt that food and wine was the strongest theme:

> In business I learned that you build on your strengths, but fashion was going to be too expensive and I didn't know much about gardens. So I chose food and wine because it is part of Victoria's way of life. It is very important to us. (Quoted in Money, 2012)

Interestingly, Melbourne now also stages successful fashion and garden-themed events as part of its event portfolio, such as the Melbourne International Garden Show, the Virgin Australia Melbourne Fashion Festival (previously the L'Oreal Melbourne Fashion Festival – see Webster, 2014) and Melbourne Spring Fashion Week.

Inspired by positive feedback on Melbourne's food, wine and restaurants provided by the visiting International Olympic Committee Officials, Clemenger championed the idea that the city could be promoted as a prime gastronomic tourist destination via the development of a food and wine festival (Scarpato, 2002b). The 'Visit Victoria' advertising campaign subsequently highlighted the festival in its destination marketing material, which contributed to the development of Melbourne's image as a *culinary capital.*

The festival is staged annually over 17 days from the end of February to the middle of March and relies on a core team of 18 staff members, along with hundreds of committed volunteers. Festival events are not just confined to Melbourne, with many events also being staged throughout regional Victoria, to involve the whole state in the festival. Regional Victoria is home to excellent quality food produce and the festival is a means of showcasing this to the public and potential tourists. It also contributes to an authentic consumption experience for participants.

The food and wine festival enables both locals and tourists alike to discover the city's various cultural traditions and lifestyles through gastronomic experiences. The festival initially targeted Melbournians but has grown to appeal to a broader audience of national and international visitors (Scarpato, 2002b), as well as attracting participation from both locally and internationally recognised chefs, restaurateurs and winemakers. Celebrity appearances and attendance over the years include Jamie Oliver (UK), Anthony Bourdain (USA), Nigella Lawson (UK) and Ferran Adrià (Spain).

Corporate professionals and food and wine industry members make up the Melbourne Food and Wine's honorary board, who work in conjunction with the festival's management team to stage the festival. The curatorial committees and creative consultants assist with developing a creative festival programme each year and include renowned Australian chefs/restaurateurs and food industry personalities such as George Calombaris (chef, restaurateur and a judge on *MasterChef Australia*), Gail Donovan (restaurateur and owner of one of Melbourne's most iconic restaurants, Donovans) and Matt Preston (award winning journalist, food writer and *MasterChef* judge). Having well-known local identities associated with the festival adds credibility to the festival as a whole.

The range of events staged is impressive, incorporating celebrity chef appearances, degustations, pop-up restaurants, cooking demonstrations and a range of family and children friendly events. The opening event, The 'Longest Lunch', attracted 1604 diners in 2015 (including over 200 international visitors) at a 530 metre table in Fitzroy Gardens. They experienced a three-course meal designed by renowned Australian chefs Shane Delia and Adriano Zumbo (Melbourne Food and Wine Festival, 2015). The 'Return to Terroir' event in 2015 attracted more than 50 of the world's leading biodynamic wineries

(Melbourne Food and Wine Festival, 2015). In addition to the festival in February/March, a programme of year-round events is staged under its brand.

The Melbourne Food and Wine Festival operates on a not-for-profit basis, relying on substantial financial funding from public institutions and support from private sponsors (Melbourne Food and Wine Festival, 2015; Scarpato, 2002b). Festival organisers credit the support and passion of their partners in making the festival internationally acclaimed. Community partners that are vital to the festival's success include the Stephanie Alexander Kitchen Garden Foundation (see Chapter 7), SecondBite, StreetSmart, Oxfam and HEAT (Hospitality, Employment and Training). Each of these organisations uses food in their programmes to assist the community. For example, SecondBite redistributes high-quality surplus fresh food to community food programmes around Australia using food generously donated by farmers, wholesalers, markets, supermarkets, caterers and events, while StreetSmart is a not-for-profit organisation that raises and distributes funds to reduce homelessness and assist families in need. HEAT is a practical youth re-engagement programme delivered in an informal learning environment, which assists young people who are disengaged from mainstream education. Involving these partners in the festival may have social inclusion outcomes, such as raising awareness of the need for equity and social justice and promoting accessibility to diverse community groups (Laing & Mair, 2015).

The staging of a generic food and wine festival as a hallmark event is not unique to Melbourne, but it has helped to put it on the map as a sophisticated destination, part of a destination marketing strategy that revolves around 'culture, cuisine, popular culture, fashion and lifestyle' (Frost et al., 2010: 99). Its longevity is testament to the way it has been able to adapt to the changing multicultural backdrop of Melbourne and the fact that it reflects and promotes the city's identity as a foodie destination, thus attracting local support as well as international tourists.

The Galway International Oyster and Seafood Festival

Galway is located on the West Coast of Ireland overlooking Galway Bay. Although not blessed with what may be considered a favourable climate (average temperatures range from 9° in winter to 20° Celsius in the summer months), it is renowned for its regional produce, particularly oysters and its cultural scene. Since 1978, the city has staged the Galway Arts Festival, a grass-roots initiative of local university students, which was designed to 'be as accessible as possible to as wide a number of people as possible' (Quinn, 2006: 292). In recent years, this festival has moved away from this focus on the region, now more strongly promoting itself to visitors and programming international content. This has met with some concern amongst locals, who see this shift as elitist (Quinn, 2006).

The other major city festival is the Galway International Oyster and Seafood Festival, staged on the last weekend in September to celebrate the city's rich annual oyster harvest (in season from September to April). It is a celebration of the Galway Native Oyster, harvested by the Kelly family for the last 61 years, and is the oldest oyster festival in the world, having been launched in September 1954. It was originally staged in conjunction with Paddy Burke's Bar in nearby Clarinbridge but moved into the city centre of Galway in the 1980s (Galway International Oyster and Seafood Festival, 2015). It was created by a local hotel manager to drive more visitation to Galway during the quieter months of the year, rather like the Parkes Elvis Festival, which was developed to give people a reason to visit and stay in the regional Australian town over the hot January period (Brennan-Horley et al., 2007).

The Galway International Oyster and Seafood Festival has managed to escape the criticism levied at the Arts Festival, by remaining true to its origins as an event that evokes community pride in Galway's oyster farming heritage, as well as reinforcing Galway's cultural identities through its association with the Kelly family, who claim 'a lineage that can be traced over 1000 years to the first kings of Connacht' (Kelly Oysters, 2015), and Irish music and culture. Approximately 60% of festival attendees live locally, with the majority of these locals being return visitors (Galway International Oyster and Seafood Festival, 2015).

The Festival has also been highly successful in attracting visitors to the region, with more than 22,000 visitors attending the event in 2012 (Galway International Oyster and Seafood Festival, 2015), thus adding value to the tourist experience in the city. The festival is the most internationally recognised Irish festival after St Patrick's Day and has been described by the *Sunday Times* as 'one of the 12 greatest shows on earth' and listed in the *AA Travel Guide* as one of Europe's Seven Best Festivals (Galway International Oyster and Seafood Festival, 2015). A number of celebrity guests have also attended the festival over the years, which adds to its credibility, including director John Huston, actor Bob Hope, golfer Christy O'Connor Jnr, Irish rugby hero Brian O'Driscoll and the Irish President Michael D. Higgins.

The four day programme includes the National Oyster Opening Championships followed by the Opening Night Party, the World Oyster Opening Championships, the Festival Parade, Masquerade Mardi Gras and Seafood Trail (Figures 4.3 and 4.4). The final day of festivities is a family day featuring musical performances, live cooking demonstrations as well as plenty of children's entertainment including face painting and circus skills workshops (Galway International Oyster and Seafood Festival, 2015). Although the main focus of the festival is the region's native oysters, the festival programme provides its attendees with many other interactive social

Figure 4.3 Traditional oyster-gathering boats on display at the Galway Festival (photo Boyd Challenger)

and cultural experiences, such as the Irish music night. The 'Seafood Trail' is a recent addition to the festival programme and involves a selection of Galway's best restaurants serving locally sourced ingredients and seafood throughout the duration of the festival (Galway International Oyster and Seafood Festival, 2015). Approximately 15 local restaurants participate in the Seafood Trail during the oyster festival and this provides these establishments with the opportunity to attract and create awareness to new customers. It also serves as a cost-effective means of promoting their produce and business, which may otherwise not occur without their involvement in the festival.

The festival brand is owned by the Galway Chamber of Commerce, with the festival staged by Milestone Inventive, an event management company based in Salthill, Galway. Milestone Inventive has a full-time staff of five people, which increases to between 10 and 15 during peak event times.

Figure 4.4 Oyster shucking at the Galway Festival (photo Boyd Challenger)

Guinness was the original sponsor of the festival in 1954 and remains one of its main sponsors. In 2015, other sponsors of the Galway International Oyster and Seafood Festival include Failte Ireland (the Irish National Tourism Development Agency) and local bars and restaurants (Galway International Oyster and Seafood Festival, 2015).

The success of the Galway International Oyster and Seafood Festival can be contrasted with the Bluff Oyster Festival in New Zealand. The Bluff festival has had a rocky history since its inception in 1996. In 2007, the then organisers, Venture Southland, a joint initiative of the Invercargill City, Southland District and Gore District Councils, planned to move it to Invercargill in 2007, to increase its patronage (NZPA, 2007). The local Bluff community were outraged at this attempt to take away their festival, and voted at a public meeting to take on the organisation of the 2008 festival. The new chairman, John Edminstin, 'set about taking the festival "back to basics" and putting the focus back on the people'. This had an immediate effect on attendance. As he observed: '[When] the committee scrapped the "corporate feel" introduced by Venture [we] immediately saw an increase of more than 1000 people through the gates in 2008' (Foden, 2015). In contrast, the Galway International Oyster and Seafood Festival continues to be able to attract large numbers of tourists, without losing sight of the importance of maintaining local support, ensuring its long-term survival (Rogers & Anastasiadou, 2011).

The Future for Food Festivals

Food festivals and the consumption of food at festivals have a long heritage and clearly fulfil a number of important needs, both social and economic. The case studies in this chapter, including the Dolce Vita Festival vignette at the start, illustrate how these events can play a part in the creation of regional identity and become a source of community pride. Sharing food and discovering new foods can bring people together and help to build *communitas*. At the same time, food festivals can contribute to their region's economic development through raising awareness of destination brands and increasing the numbers of visitors. Balancing these interests, so that the community maintains a sense of engagement and involvement in their local festival, is essential.

Another challenge for destination marketing organisations and festival organisers is to differentiate their festival theme from others. There are a multitude of festivals themed around fruit, vegetables and seafood, with the plethora of oyster festivals just one example. Choosing a food-related theme that is authentic to a destination and its culture makes it more difficult to be copied by others and may help to gain grass-roots support for the festival.

There are a number of trends affecting food festivals, notably the growing interest in slow and organic food, and the rise of the food van or truck, which makes serving food at festivals easier and more convenient. Both are discussed in Part 2 of this book. The growth in social media also affects festival organisation, and can be a useful tool for promoting a festival and delivering persuasive messages to different market segments (Frost & Laing, 2013). It might also help to build enthusiasm in attendees in the lead-up to the staging and gain feedback on different initiatives, thus increasing satisfaction with the event overall (Strickland *et al.*, 2016). More research is needed to explore the effect of social media on food festivals and its utility in marketing efforts.

5 Food Rituals and Etiquette

Downton Abbey (2010–2015)

> *'Marry a man who can barely hold his knife like a gentleman?'*
> Lady Mary Crawley, *Downton Abbey*

Lady Mary's contempt for the prospect of marriage to Matthew (the new heir to the Downton estate) is based not only on his middle-class upbringing as a suburban solicitor but her perception of his lack of social graces. Matthew's first formal dinner with the Crawleys involves service *à la française*, where each guest helps themselves from a serving plate or dish held by a footman. Even the servants aren't sure whether Matthew knows what he is doing. As the footman lowers the serving platter at Matthew's shoulder, he whispers 'I will hold it steady and you can help yourself, sir'. Matthew bristles at the slight: 'Yes, *I* know!'

Part of the fascination of the hit television show *Downton Abbey* (2010–2015) is the glimpse it gives of a world that has largely disappeared. Much of the plot is advanced through family conversations over a formal meal in the dining room. These scenes highlight the growing chasm between the elegant but stifling way of life that the Crawleys are accustomed to and broader social changes, exemplified by characters such as Matthew and his mother. The appeal is to *nostalgia*, in the sense of a 'longing for a culturally remembered past that may have occurred before one's birth and, hence, not have been experienced personally' (Caton & Santos, 2007: 372). Even if one had been born in this era, this lifestyle was essentially enjoyed by a rarefied few, rather than the masses. The television viewer gets to peep behind the curtain.

Dining in full evening regalia, with the men in white tie and the women in long gowns and fine jewellery, seated around a dining table laid with the finest linen, china, glass and silverware and being served multiple courses by a butler and footman is a world away from the casual TV dinners or simple family meals at home that most people (in Western society at least) are used to, let alone the growth of fast food eaten mostly with the fingers and on the run. The era of the dinner party is in decline, with more people eating out on a regular basis than ever before. Even in expensive restaurants, the trend

is towards simplicity and minimalism, with fewer numbers of establishments set up for or willing to offer a fine dining experience.

With the growing informality of dining, have the rituals and traditions
surrounding the preparation and service of food become passé or do they still
have a place in modern society? This is one of the central questions discussed
in this chapter. We are also interested in exploring changes to food etiquette
and rituals in a world dominated by the use of new technology, particularly
social media. Have these advances run ahead of etiquette, so that the latter
is struggling to catch up or adapt? Or have they also contributed to the death
knell for rules, rituals or social norms surrounding food?

While this chapter is largely based on a Western perspective, reflecting
the background of the authors, we have referred to other cultures and
attempted to analyse the issues presented as broadly as possible, through a
synthesis of the literature and our own experiences as researchers and travellers living within a multicultural society. We recognise, however, that more
research on food rituals and etiquette from a non-Western standpoint should
be carried out, in order to deepen our understanding of its changing nature
and imperative in a global context.

Historical Origins

Every society has its own rules governing the preparation and consumption of food. They acknowledge the fact that eating is more than just a necessity for maintaining health or survival, taking on a symbolic value, as a way
to build 'social relationships' and 'a means of creating community' (Visser,
1991: ix). Its rules, traditions and etiquette are like a language and a greater
understanding of them helps us to comprehend the history of human interaction and the way that society is organised (Beardsworth & Keil, 1997),
whether in the context of ancient Rome, Victorian London or our own new
millennium.

The first rules of etiquette for dining can be traced to ancient Egypt and
Mesopotamia, when feasts were used by various rulers to celebrate success
in military campaigns, shore up their political support with respect to both
their subjects and embassies from abroad, and demonstrate their wealth and
thus power. Their important symbolism was consolidated by the development of a number of rituals, which emphasised the shift of the guest from
the ordinary world into a special (*liminal*) space. Important rituals during a
Mesopotamian banquet included hand-washing, the anointment of oil, the
ceremony of wine being served by the cupbearer, and the seating of guests
on the basis of their status (Strong, 2002). Guests were given flowers at banquets in ancient Egypt. In both civilisations, guests wore their best clothes
to these dinners and were treated to a display of entertainment, aimed at
delighting the senses (Strong, 2002).

There is also evidence of elaborate dining rituals in ancient Greece and Rome, exemplified in the Roman *convivium* or dinner party. Guests reclined to dine and were attended to by a retinue of servants. Feet washing throughout the meal and even the cutting of toenails was a common ritual (Strong, 2002). The guest-list was dominated by men and these events were frequently the scene of debauchery, over-indulgence and tasteless excess. Live birds were placed in animals' bellies, flying out when the meat was carved, and every sort of exotica was served, from all parts of the empire, including peacocks and flamingos (Strong, 2002). Entertainment, often lascivious, was also a feature of these feasts (Carroll *et al.*, 2005; Strong, 2002). However, like their forerunners in Egypt, Greece and Mesopotamia, they served a serious purpose, one that has remained important to a degree across the centuries: 'The table and those bidden to gather around it and share its pleasures could be a vehicle for social aggregation and unity; but equally it could encourage social distinctions, separating people into categories by placement or, even worse, exclusion' (Strong, 2002: 7). Failure to receive an invitation was social death. The convivium contrasted with everyday dining, which often consisted of simple and frugal fare. The general public in imperial Rome would have been exposed to some of this ritual through their participation in free public banquets organised by and through their emperors, as well as politicians and aristocrats, which 'were designed to impress and win favour with one's fellow citizens and peers' (Carroll *et al.*, 2005: 15).

In medieval Europe, guests at banquets or court feasts were forced to adopt ways of dining that were more formal than the way they ate at home. As in the ancient world, they were a political tool to demonstrate status and acknowledge fealty: 'This was achieved through the quantity and quality of the food and drink on offer, and through associated festivities and rituals such as gift-giving' (Carroll *et al.*, 2005: 16). They also helped to cement social bonds (Strong, 2002). Seating arrangements, the order of serving diners and the table settings were decisions that were made according to rank (Hadley, 2005). Unlike their ancient forbears, medieval guests sat on long benches rather than reclining at the table (Strong, 2002). To modern eyes, however, these meals in the feast hall lacked refinement and were often plagued by violence owing to the overconsumption of alcohol (Carroll *et al.*, 2005: 16). They can be contrasted with the monastic meal, which was enjoyed mostly in silence and subject to a strict regime of table manners, based on courtesy towards fellow diners (Strong, 2002).

Guests who were not at the lord's or king's table in the medieval period bought along their own knives and spoons (forks were not in popular use then) and ate their meals off slabs of bread known as trenchers, rather than plates. All the food was laid out on the table and guests helped themselves. Honoured guests, however, were given their own implements and enjoyed individual dishes, rather than partaking from shared plates (Hadley, 2005). While Shuman (1981: 73) observes, 'The central matters of food etiquette were whether one ate directly from a serving dish or from the trencher and whether one sampled all of the foods or ate only one delicacy', there was guidance available on correct behaviour at the table. This came in the form of 'conduct books and manuals of household management' in which guests were counselled 'not to lean on the table, or dirty the cloth, nor to talk with a full mouth, break wind or look at what comes out of their nose when blown' (Hadley, 2005: 102). In the 13th century, the cult of chivalry resulted in the table becoming a place for civility and sociability, rather than drunken licence. Good order and good behaviour were seen as important: 'By adopting the code of courtliness at table, diners had another way of setting themselves apart – and above' (Strong, 2002: 69). One of the curious traditions that has disappeared since the medieval period is the rite of *assay*. This involved the testing of food and drink for traces of poison and was generally performed only for the ruler or monarch or high ranking nobility.

From the 14th century onwards, the range and number of dishes and implements found on the table expanded, with separate plates rather than trenchers, made from more varied materials, including ceramics and plate (precious metals) (Carroll *et al.*, 2005; Strong, 2002). This led to the development of rules on when and how to deal with these new table settings. Shared implements and vessels were phased out (Strong, 2002). The separate dining room came back into vogue during the Renaissance as a result of the rediscovery of Roman habits of dining, but this also reflected the fact that eating was increasingly seen as a private pursuit. Public dining became largely reserved for important occasions such as feast days or weddings, although there were exceptions, such as the daily spectacle of Louis XIV eating *au grand couvert* at Versailles, which acknowledged the link between power and dining (de Vooght & Scholliers, 2011; Lair, 2011). This ritual was shown in all its splendour in the film *Marie Antoinette* (2006), although it had become less frequent by this period. Even the Sun King increasingly dined in private in his chateau at Marly as his reign progressed. Conversation at the table took on a greater importance, again building upon the model of dining in the ancient world (Strong, 2002).

The intricate web of rituals surrounding dining led to these rules being written down in books of etiquette from the 14th century, although household regulations had made them clear to noble families and those serving them (Strong, 2002). This growth in books reflected greater levels of literacy beyond just the church and the association that was increasingly made between the possession of good manners and the possibility of social climbing (Strong, 2002). One of the most famous of these books was Erasmus' *De Civilitate Morum Puerilium* (1530), which argued that manners could set a human above animals, as well as his fellow human beings. The other highly influential etiquette guide of its time was de Courtin's *Nouveau*

Traité de la Civilité (1671), which documented the changes in dining ritual, including the use of forks. The latter had taken some time to be accepted, partly because it was less convenient than using the fingers, but eventually they gained popularity as a way to make eating neater, coinciding with the appearance of the dining room in middle class homes (Carter, 1998). The 17th century also saw the introduction of guides and manuals for banqueting and carving meat (Albala, 2011), individual served courses (Shuman, 1981) and the concept of a menu, which allowed guests to discern and anticipate what they were about to eat. The link between 'cuisine and class' was blurred after the birth of the restaurant in France. Preceding the French Revolution of 1796 (Spang, 2000), visiting a restaurant allowed those with the means to do so the right to dine handsomely without a formal invitation. It heralded the move of 'conspicuous eating and spending into the public arena' (Fox, 2014). However remnants of class distinctions lingered at the Victorian dinner party, when an invitation to dine was the highest possible tribute to the guest, as 'a demonstration that the person invited was accepted to be of the same social status as the host and hostess' (Strong, 2002: 273). The separate dining room was also a mark of good taste and remained so until the 1960s and 1970s, when the fashion for open plan living spaces took over.

The Victorian era spawned *Beeton's Book of Household Management* (1861), edited by the ubiquitous Mrs (Isabella) Beeton, which aimed to assist the neophyte mistress of the household on all aspects of her role in the home. It not only contained recipes but was also 'a detailed and fascinating directive for young wives on everything from how to manage a large household staff to how to judge, hire and address a second footman or upstairs chambermaid' (Fox, 2014). Despite the large numbers of servants that were needed to run a Victorian household, they paradoxically became less obtrusive – present in the background at meals or dinner parties to serve the food, but otherwise kept from view, a divide dramatised in the TV series *Upstairs Downstairs* (1971–1975) and more recently in *Downton Abbey*. These programmes provide a glimpse of what it might have been like to live and work in a great house. The only other writer who proved as influential with respect to etiquette was the American Emily Post, author of the classic *Etiquette in Society, in Business, in Politics and at Home* (1922) and a popular syndicated newspaper column.

Post-war, societal changes towards informality affected dining no less than other aspects of family life. There was a shift towards entertaining guests in a more relaxed style (Fox, 2014), with the need for servants obviated by technological innovations such as the microwave and the dishwasher (Strong, 2002). The TV dinner, a pre-packaged meal requiring heating up, was invented in the 1950s – convenience food for those (generally women) who wanted to watch their favourite shows without slaving over a hot stove. As we discuss at the end of the chapter, the way we eat dinner as a family has changed, as has the prevalence of the dinner party as a tool of socialisation, replaced in many cases by eating out. Despite these social trends, we argue that gastronomic rituals and etiquette are still needed and indeed desired, even if they come in different forms or have been adapted to meet modern lifestyles.

Influences on the Development of Food Rituals

Religious practices played a part in the development of some food rituals. For example, the Japanese tea ceremony, which can take up to four hours to perform, is based on Buddhist rites (Jolliffe, 2007). Other religions place restraints on the food that can be eaten or call for fasting at certain times of the year. Apart from the restriction of food before the hours of sunrise and sunset during the Muslim Ramadan celebrations, there were various periods of fasting throughout the Christian calendar during the medieval and Renaissance periods, notably the Lenten fast before Easter, with its 40 days being symbolic of Jesus' fast in the desert (Flandrin, 2007). Meat was forbidden during Lent, as were butter, lard, eggs and cream. The concept of meatless days meant that fish became a staple of Friday meals in some Christian countries. These days, this tradition is largely confined to Good Friday. Lent was then followed by *Carnival*, a period of feasting and revelry. The blessing of food and saying grace before eating is another acknowledgement of its importance in people's lives. This has developed into the secular toasts that express goodwill and honour to those with whom we are drinking (and eating). Various religions have also placed taboos on eating certain foods or require food to be prepared in accordance with strict rules, which will be discussed later in this chapter.

There are also distinct cultural foundations for some of these practices, which may have had a long evolution, accounting for different rituals being observed in different countries (Hegarty & O'Mahoney, 2001), and forming part of culinary identity (Danhi, 2003) and culinary heritage in some instances. For example, there are no universal laws with respect to the 'sequence in which dishes are served' (Flandrin, 2007: xix). Cheese is normally served in France before dessert, whereas in England it is the other way around. A salad is often served in the USA as a separate course before the main course. In France, drinking coffee with milk (*au lait*) is a *faux-pas* except at breakfast. Italians are often served a pasta course before the main course, which is not a staple of other national menus. In some countries, a series of appetisers is common at the start of the meal and served as finger food, sometimes to share, such as the Italian *antipasti*, the Spanish *tapas* and the French *hors-d'oeuvres*.

The third influence on food rituals and etiquette is the media. Historically, this has taken the form of books such as etiquette guides or cookbooks. The structure of a classical meal in the French style was often replicated in famous cookbooks in the 17th and 18th centuries, such as de la Varenne's *Cuisinier François* (1651) and Menon's *Cuisinière Bourgeoise* (1746), which organised dishes for readers by their function, e.g. soups, hors d'oeuvres, entrées (Flandrin, 2007). This structure is still followed by cookbooks today, with the order in which dishes appear in the cookbook reflecting the order in which they are normally served to diners. In more recent years, television programmes on food have taken greater prominence in shaping tastes and knowledge about food (Strong, 2006).

Rites of Consumption and Rites of Passage

There are rites of *conspicuous consumption* associated with food that are inherent within celebrations, special occasions and special events, particularly festivals (Falassi, 1987). There is often an abundance of food or the availability of food that has a certain status or is considered to be 'special'. Examples include a New Guinea feast marked by the serving of 3000 pigs (Fox, 2014); the rich food often served at Christmas time, such as plum pudding or roasted meats (Laing & Frost, 2015a; Visser, 1991); sweet food offered at the graves of loved ones during the Mexican Day of the Dead (Brandes, 1997); the suckling pig served whole at Chinese weddings (Fox, 2014); and *fair food*, which is generally easy to eat, portable and high in sugar and/or fat, such as hot dogs, hamburgers, fairy floss/cotton candy, ice-cream cones and soft-drink or pop (Prosterman, 1981). Generally speaking, fair food was not common in people's homes, and difficult to prepare without specialised equipment. It thus took on a festive character because it was a treat, associated with 'tinsel and transience' (Prosterman, 1981: 83). The taste or smell of these foods can bring back cherished memories of past celebrations (Visser, 1991), an example of the nostalgia referred to at the start of this chapter.

Formal meals or feasting can be linked to *rites of passage*, notably celebrations of births, deaths and marriages, which mark the transition from one stage of life to another (Falassi, 1987). The service of food is seemingly obligatory when 'life becomes dramatic', and these occasions often developed their own traditions, aimed at clarifying how people were supposed to behave at times that were otherwise unsettling (Visser, 1991: 22). While these rites were at their most flamboyant when associated with the ruling class, like the events created to commemorate the birthdays of royalty, some of these celebratory elements filtered down to the lower classes and became ubiquitous, such as the birthday cake. Meals served at a wedding are generally accompanied by speeches, and rituals such as cutting the cake with a ceremonial knife or sword (Charsley, 1992), or the pinning of bank notes to the bride's dress. Part of the wedding cake itself might be kept to celebrate the first wedding anniversary or the christening of the first child (Visser,

1991). Other examples are the giving of wedding or christening favours known as *bomboniere* as a token of the day – traditionally a small bag of sugared almonds, which symbolises that life is bitter-sweet.

Gastronomic Etiquette

There are several key reasons identified for why we have developed sophisticated food etiquette over the centuries. Gastronomic etiquette or 'manners' might be conceptualised as a marker of identity, helping us to fit in with others, particularly those within our own culture, ethnicity, class or religion, and to behave in predictable ways (Beardsworth & Keil, 1997; Visser, 1991). Fox (2014) argues that 'to set yourself apart from others by what you will and will not eat is a social barrier [and] the obverse of this is that you identify yourself with others by eating the same things the same way'. A lack of understanding of basic food rituals or etiquette thus marks a person as an outsider (Fox, 2014). Food is also a symbol of power, as discussed above, and rituals surrounding it help to show off that power, but also to keep it from waning. For this reason, the *potlatch* feast of the Native Americans was used as a means of cementing power relations through the giving of gifts.

These rituals might also be based on the desire to avoid being exposed to 'the unpleasant side of life' (Carter, 1998: 28). The medieval tolerance of belching or breaking wind at the table has changed to embarrassment at these manifestations of bodily functions (Beardsworth & Keil, 1997), although not all cultures share this response. In the film *Witness* (1985), the Amish boy Samuel (Lukas Haas) burps at a meal, to the approval of his mother (Kelly McGillis), who interprets it as an endorsement of the food, much to the surprise of the urban policeman John Book (Harrison Ford). For similar reasons, owing to squeamishness, animals are normally butchered and meat is generally carved out of sight of the consumer and mostly served without reminders of the animal that provided it. The trend for nose-to-tail dining, where all of the animal is used, runs counter to this, although it is still largely a niche experience, in contrast with 'a soft majority worldview promulgated by the supermarket experience of easy-to-swallow packaged meat that elides economic reality and anatomical fact' (Strong, 2006: 31).

While it is impossible to cover the various types of food rituals in this chapter, some key examples are highlighted below.

Styles of food service

Different styles of service of food have been in vogue and examples of each can still be found in restaurants across the world. They developed once 'more ceremony [was] accorded to the serving and eating of specific types of dishes' (Shuman, 1981: 74) and required servants (now waiting staff) to assist with food service to guests. For silver service, food is served by a waiter using a spoon and fork from a platter onto the plate of the guest, from their left. This is a theatrical practice that is still observed in formal restaurants, mostly in Europe, and requires large numbers of highly trained staff, adding to the cost. Service *à la française* or French style dates from the 17th century and involves the guest helping themselves from a platter or dish held by a servant or waiter. The rest of the dishes remain on the table, to be served in turn to guests. There was a set ratio of dishes per guest, reflecting a 'concern for order, balance, good taste and elegance' (Strong, 2002: 231), and each course encompassed multiple dishes. This was overtaken in the 19th century by service *à la russe* or Russian style, where the diner helps themselves to cold dishes from plates, bowls or dishes on the table, while hot dishes are passed around after being carved or plated in the kitchen.

Flandrin (2007: 94) observes that the differences between service *à la française* and service *à la russe* are often 'difficult to pinpoint' and that both had their critics as well as proponents. In the case of service *à la française*, food took some time to circulate around the table and guests could not go back for seconds or help themselves to as much or as little as they wanted. Any hot food remaining on the table until it could be served to guests also ran the risk of growing cold. It was, however, deemed more elegant and 'pleasing to the eye' (Flandrin, 2007: 94) than the alternative. Service *à la russe* became popular because it allowed food to be consumed when it was cooked perfectly and at the optimum temperature. It required a retinue of servants to carry it off, only possible where a host was financially secure enough to afford them, and overcame the need for the host to be involved with food service or handling (Beardsworth & Keil, 1997; Strong, 2002). The move towards service *à la russe* also significantly reduced the time taken to serve a meal. Despite the greater convenience, it was only at the end of the 19th century that the French relinquished the norm of service *à la française* (Strong, 2002).

Table settings and table manners

Rules of modern etiquette governing table settings and table manners have their origins in some of the historical practices outlined earlier. In formal Western table settings, the side plate is laid to the left of the diner, and glasses are laid to their right. Using the wrong implement is a social faux-pas. The rule with respect to cutlery laid in pairs on either side of a plate is to start from the outside and proceed inwards. Soup should be eaten with the spoon tipped away from the diner, rather than towards them. Where a knife and fork are provided, they should be used (although Americans tend to favour the fork only) and neither implement should be waved around, even to make a point while talking. There is a correct way to hold a knife, as Mary Crawley in the opening vignette makes clear! The knife should be held with the index finger pointing down the back of the blade, and the knife should point down towards the meal, not sideways. During the meal, the knife and fork should rest on the plate if not being used, in an inverted V shape. This signals to a waiter or the host that the diner is still eating their meal. At the end of the meal, the knife and fork are to be placed together, in parallel and in the centre of the plate, with the tines of the fork pointing up, to indicate that the diner is finished with their meal, although there are arguments as to whether this is still *de rigueur*.

The TV show *Agatha Christie's Poirot* (1989–2013) poked fun at this profusion of culinary rules about implements in the episode titled 'Four and Twenty Blackbirds'. Poirot, the famous Belgian private detective, serves some rabbit to his British offsider, Captain Hastings, and is aghast when Hastings takes up his knife and fork to eat it: 'No, no Hastings. Use your spoon. That is the Liège way. To use a knife is an insult to the cook. It implies the meat is tough'.

These rules have their counterparts in other cultures. For example, strict dictums of etiquette apply to eating Asian food, particularly the use of chopsticks. The latter have a practical purpose, as traditional Japanese etiquette requires eating small pieces of food, so as not to open one's mouth very wide (Ohnuki-Tierney, 1997) and the chopsticks help to lever the food into the mouth. Use of chopsticks also avoids contact between food and one's hands, which is taboo for the Japanese, except when eating prescribed foods such as rice balls. This makes eating fast food problematic in this culture, if not impossible, if one is to observe strict etiquette. The use of chopsticks to take food from a common bowl and move it to one's own bowl is seen as unhygienic by many Westerners, and there are calls within China to change this practice (Cooper, 1986). The use of a personal bowl for one's food is also subject to rules of etiquette. The bowl should be raised close to the mouth when eating, as if it is left on the table, it signifies that the guest or diner does not like the food (Cooper, 1986). It is considered rude to start eating before everyone has been served (which is also an edict in Western cultures) and all contents of the bowl should be eaten by the diner, including tiny grains of rice, as a mark of respect. Observing these rules represents more than just a display of good manners in Chinese society. It is tantamount to showing others the kind of person you are (Cooper, 1986), another example of how food rituals can be used to define membership of a group and a sense of identity.

Order of food service

Most of the sequencing of courses and later the order of menus across cultures has been shown to be a function of the rule that there should be a separation between sweet and salty dishes, and the latter should precede the former. We are therefore accustomed to the idea that a dessert or sweet course comes at the end of the meal, but this was not always the case. This innovation occurred in France from the 17th century and slowly made its way to other countries across Europe (Flandrin, 2007).

The recent popularity of salted caramel and the use of ingredients such as fruit and chocolate as an accompaniment to savoury dishes is, however, blurring the edges of this once obligatory rule and modern chefs are often extolled to mix these elements on the plate, along with different textures. It should also be noted that combining sourness and sweetness is a notable feature of Chinese cuisine, as well as being found in dishes such as the Italian *agrodolce* sauce, combining vinegar and sugar. Exposure to diverse combinations of tastes opens up opportunities to *fuse* cuisines across ethnic and cultural boundaries. Thus opinion of what is 'proper' or 'correct' may initially diverge but ultimately become homogenous.

Cutting-edge chefs such as Heston Blumenthal take great delight in ignoring or overturning received wisdom or historical custom about the compatibility of certain ingredients. In some cases, they are returning to the traditions of the past, such as Blumenthal's *Heston's Feasts* (2009–2010) TV series, where he discovers differences in the types of food and the order in which they were consumed in various eras. The medieval feast recreated by Heston Blumenthal includes meat fruit, where a meat dish is created to resemble raw fruit, while his Roman banquet showcases savoury custard as a delicacy.

Serving protocol

A variety of serving protocol has been developed based on the social background and/or gender of guests. In some countries, women are traditionally served before men. In others, it is the most senior person who is served first. In the Victorian era, those people sitting on the right of the host and hostess (generally the most important guests) were the first to be served (Strong, 2002). In these cases, the order in which people are served is based on their status as individuals. It is another example of how food rituals can be used to shape social identity, but also to entrench and symbolise power (de Vooght & Scholliers, 2011).

There is clear divergence between cultures and across eras regarding the type of food provided to guests. In most contemporary Western societies, it would be considered bad manners to serve one's guests with different food from the host, even in royal circles. However, in ancient Rome and medieval Europe, this was a common practice, with guests often given food that varied depending on their rank (Strong, 2002). Similarly, in some African societies, these privileges would be considered a demarcation of the elite status of the host as a king, noble or chief (Dietler, 2001). Thus in Uganda, the king could not eat certain foods regarded as low in status, e.g. sweet potatoes, while in Cameroon, the village chief had exclusive rights over certain 'noble' animals, e.g. leopards, but could share prescribed parts of these animals with senior dignitaries of the village. While Dietler (2001: 88) points out that these practices are not 'universal among African kingdoms and chiefdoms', they do however serve to emphasise the common link between feasting and the protection of self-interest throughout history (de Vooght & Scholliers, 2011; Dietler & Hayden, 2001).

Apportioning and accepting food

Even the simple activity of food apportionment might be important. According to Shuman (1981: 73), 'the accommodation of an unexpected guest, an offer to share food, or the delegation of the last piece of food on a serving dish are all social acts' and thus portions offered and accepted are forms of communication that can result in relationships being 'made, broken, reinforced, or strained'. Overfilling one's plate might be considered rude in some cultures, while to others, it is a sign that the guest is enjoying their meal. Offering a guest too little might similarly be symbolic of the importance of the guest in the eyes of their hosts. Refusing a helping several times might be a sign of good manners in some eyes, with women often tempted to play down an appetite, even in contemporary times, lest they be seen as less feminine or greedy. Taking the last piece of food on a plate is similarly understood as somewhat gauche. The latter is sometimes known as the 'old maid' (Shuman, 1981).

Refusing an offered delicacy could also be construed as rudeness. This is the dilemma facing the tourist who is offered something out of the norm or which perhaps offends food taboos from their own culture. An example might be the serving of whale-meat in Japan to Western tourists. A tourist was observed being offered some caviar in a hotel in St Petersburg by a waiter. She refused. The waiter was offended: 'This is [our] best Russian caviar!' He interpreted the tourist's response as an insult to his heritage. Sometimes the reluctance to try a new type of food is simply a fear of the unknown – known as *neophobia*. This may have a biological as well as cultural link, helping us to avoid eating unfamiliar foods that are potentially dangerous (Cohen & Avieli, 2004; Visser, 1991).

Social interactions while dining

There are rules with respect to social interactions while dining, which are shaped by seating arrangements (Prosterman, 1981), as well as cultural norms. Fast food is often eaten on the run, and thus may not constitute a social activity. Some fast food outlets encourage this lack of sociability by providing tables without chairs for customers (Ohnuki-Tierney, 1997). This has led to a partial relaxing of the Japanese rule against eating while standing up, which was previously considered to be highly ill-mannered. This was taken to the zenith in the traditional Japanese tea ceremony, where 'one must kneel even to open a door' (Ohnuki-Tierney, 1997: 178). Eating at a counter or bar generally makes it difficult to converse with the person sitting beside us, unless we know them already, as each person is facing ahead, rather than making direct eye-contact (Prosterman, 1981). In many of these establishments, there is an open kitchen in front of the diners, which becomes a type of theatre, to be observed in lieu of conversation with fellow diners.

It is also common these days to see a single diner sitting alone in a restaurant reading a book. This is generally acceptable behaviour in all but the most formal of restaurants, where it might be interpreted as disdain for the artistry of the chef. In some countries such as Italy, waiting staff will automatically sit single diners together, at adjoining tables or even the same table, to encourage socialisation. Sitting at a table with strangers is, however, a strain for some people, and runs against some cultural norms, whereas others enjoy making new acquaintances. It is normally good manners to exchange at least some pleasantries with the other diners at a shared table (Prosterman, 1981).

Food Taboos

There are a number of food taboos within certain societies, many of which are linked to religious practices (as discussed earlier). For example, Orthodox Jews eat kosher food, which corresponds to Jewish dietary laws, as laid down in the Bible. Various foods are outlawed, including pork, rabbit and shellfish, and those animals whose meat is not outlawed must be slaughtered in a prescribed manner. Meat and dairy foods cannot be prepared or eaten together, requiring a kosher kitchen that keeps these products separate. Other well-known food taboos include the Hindu prohibition on eating beef, owing to their belief in the sacred cow, and the Muslim refusal to eat pork (Beardsworth & Keil, 1997).

Other food taboos are subject to negotiation over time, as mores and habits change (Cooper, 1986). In some instances, these taboos are linked to the availability or inconsistency of a food supply to a particular society or community (Frost & Laing, 2015a). Thus the French eat horse-meat and some Asian cultures eat dog-meat, but this is generally not acceptable worldwide. The eating of whale-meat is a controversial subject, and is most notoriously associated with Japan, although it is also consumed in other societies with a fishing tradition, such as the Inuits, the Norwegians and the Icelanders. Objections to eating whale-meat are based on concerns about survival of various species of whale, and the availability of other sources of protein that are easier to obtain and less threatened as a species. Environmental organisations such as Greenpeace and many national governments have lobbied the Japanese to stop the consumption of whale-meat, but to date it has proved difficult to change this cultural norm.

In some cases, food taboos may be side-stepped. Tuchman and Levine (1993) examined the enthusiasm of New York Jews for Chinese restaurants.

They found that many of their interviewees happily ate Chinese dishes with pork or prawns – both taboo. This infringement was rationalised on the basis that these foods were minced and so were unrecognisable.

The ultimate food taboo is the eating of human flesh (Beardsworth & Keil, 1997), but even cannibalism is replete with etiquette. Narratives of cannibals who eat their fellow human beings often detail 'carefully prescribed ritual' (Visser, 1991: 8). This does not appear to be a mindless act, whether it be to placate the gods, satisfy hunger or deter acts of warfare or aggression from other tribes. How the body was eaten and by whom was socially sanctioned and thus regulated (Visser, 1991), however distasteful we might find such a suggestion. In popular culture, the closest equivalent we have is the serial killer Hannibal Lecter. In the film *The Silence of the Lambs* (1991), based on the novel of the same name, Hannibal (Anthony Hopkins) famously expounds how he ate a human liver 'with some fava beans and a nice Chianti'. The choice of fava beans is a macabre touch, given their taboo status in some cultures (Mintz & Du Bois, 2002).

The Future of Food Rituals and Etiquette

The opening vignette about *Downton Abbey* shows how important food was to sociality in that era, with food consumed at a communal table and conversation flowing during the meal. Even in more humble homes in the early years of the 20th century, people ate their main meal at night together. This is almost a rarity at the start of the 21st century, with family meals often either eaten off plates juggled on knees or trays beside the television or computer, or replaced by grazing on snacks grabbed from the refrigerator and eaten at the kitchen bench. Conversation is often absent, or exchanged during the breaks for advertisements. Others read or browse emails or social media during meals. These days, many families only eat at a common table when they eat out or when they entertain. Yet TV and films continue to show people, particularly families, eating at the table, perhaps because it is a clever way to advance plotlines and highlight conflict in a confined space. A generation of film families have followed this model, from *Leave It to Beaver* (1957–1963) through to *The Brady Bunch* (1969–1974) and the more recent *Modern Family* (2009 onwards). An exception is *The Big Bang Theory* (2007 onwards), where the four geeks regularly eat takeaway food on a couch around a coffee table, although a recent episode saw Leonard (Johnny Galecki) temporarily succumb to pressure for a dining room table, much to Sheldon's (Jim Parsons) disgust. This change was too much for Sheldon, and the group moved back to the couch.

The dinner party is another casualty of busy modern lives, despite the popularity of TV cooking programmes such as *Masterchef*, the strong global sales of cookbooks by celebrity chefs and the cornucopia of ingredients that is available to the home cook. Rather than entertain at home, many people prefer these days to join friends at a bar, café or restaurant and meeting for breakfast or coffee is increasingly popular, especially at weekends. Even when guests are invited to a home, this may be for a casual barbeque, rather than the traditional sit-down dinner around a dining table. Those who continue to throw dinner parties are perhaps concerned less with formal etiquette and more about the need to impress their guests with their culinary capital, 'where repute may be sought through the use of ingredients distinguished by their echt or recherché properties and through the casual display of tableware and culinary gadgets' (Strong, 2006: 36).

Although many modern restaurants are less formal and stuffy than their predecessors, we argue that they still constitute a move away from the everyday into a liminal space and thus are special occasions. Patrons at most establishments, except arguably the most basic of fast food chains, 'come to be cosseted, spoiled, smoothed down after the business of the day, made to feel like royalty, allowed to indulge themselves in a leisurely fashion, and generally to feel as far removed from eating at home as is possible' (Fox, 2014). Fast food patronage, on the other hand, alleviates the anxiety of not understanding basic rules of etiquette (Beardsworth & Keil, 1997). There are no confusing table settings or even implements, with the food mainly consumed with the fingers. Eating out may also expose diners to a multiplicity of ethnic cuisines, each of which have their own rituals that must be mastered, such as chopsticks. The importance of understanding this ritual is sharpened when the diner becomes an international tourist and is exposed to an unfamiliar culinary heritage (Cohen & Avieli, 2004).

The use of the mobile or cell phone in restaurants is now pervasive, with growing numbers of people unable to eat without obsessively checking their email messages and postings of Facebook friends or tweeting to followers. This may be viewed as an example of the growing incivility of society (Carter, 1998). Carter refers to the predilection for loud discussions on phones in restaurants as an intrusion 'into the most private moments of our lives' (p. 191). Technology has moved on since Carter wrote this, and these days people are more likely to be scrolling through screens, typing responses or photographing their food for social media, rather than talking out loud. The end result is the same, however – a disregard for the feelings of others and the end of the art of conversation, which has a further deleterious effect on the way people behave. As Visser (1991: 23) observes, 'The moment communication is lost, "manners" drop away'. Some restaurants have reacted by banning photography, arguing that the use of a flash is annoying for other diners, but it would be a brave establishment that outlawed the use of phones altogether.

Etiquette books are increasingly hard to find in bookshops, replaced in many cases by books on 'what to wear'. What we look like is seemingly more important to modern readers than how we behave. The vast shelves of how-to books are often self-centred, focused on our own personal lives, rather than how we might live more harmoniously alongside others. One of our authors received a book on etiquette when she was 10 years old from her mother, who wrote on the flyleaf 'May this book be a help and guide for you'. It has indeed been tremendously useful, giving her a sense of confidence and ease in social and work situations, but one wonders how many 10 year olds these days would receive such a present and how they might react to it.

Regardless of the more casual approach to dining, and the move away from formal dining etiquette in contemporary times, it appears that manners still matter, particularly in the business world, where formal meals are often used to close deals or to cement working relationships. In the TV series *Seinfeld* (1989–1998), the fear of not being up-to-date with the latest dining etiquette is the subject of satire. Upon being told that his friend Elaine's (Julia Louis-Dreyfus) employer eats a Snickers bar with a knife and fork, George Constanza (Jason Alexander) comments 'He probably doesn't want to get chocolate on his fingers. That's the way these society types eat their candy bars'. George follows this example at a work meeting, and his boss is impressed with his *savoir faire*. The trend spreads, and Elaine and George subsequently spy people eating a cookie and a doughnut with a knife and fork. The punchline is their friend Jerry's comment 'I saw someone on the street eating M&Ms with a spoon'. The humour emphasises the message that most of us in modern society want to avoid social ridicule for displaying our ignorance of accepted practice, even if we don't want our lives to be totally rule-bound.

Part 2
Trends and Innovations

6　The Quest for Good Food

The Art of Simple Food (Alice Waters, 2007)

In 1971, Alice Waters opened a restaurant in Berkeley, California. Close to the university, it specialised in fresh, local grown produce. Waters called her venture Chez Panisse, taking the name from the character of a kindly old gentleman in a series of 1930 films by Marcel Pagnol. Having finished her university studies, Waters had spent a few years in Europe, particularly France. The cuisine and culture of the French had become a major influence on her life and she wanted her restaurant to embody those French aspects that she felt were missing from American society.

As she later recounted:

> My delicious revolution began when, young and naïve, I started a res-
> taurant and went looking for good-tasting food to cook. I was trying to
> find ingredients like the ones I had loved when I was a student in France:
> simple things like lettuces, and green beans, and bread. I was searching
> for flavour, not philosophy, but what I found was that the people who
> were growing the tastiest foods were organic farmers in my own back-
> yard, small farmers and ranchers within a radius of a hundred miles or
> so of the restaurant who were planting heirloom varieties of fruits and
> vegetables and harvesting them at their peak. What was revolutionary
> about this was being able to buy directly from the source and not being
> limited to what I could find at the supermarket. (Waters, 2007: 3)

Waters was fortunate in the opportunities of the *terroir* of where she had chosen to set up her establishment. San Francisco – and Berkeley in particular – was a centre of the counterculture, providing a supportive market for such an experiment. Over time, Berkeley kept that radical edge while evolv-
ing a strong creative class. Furthermore, her notional 100 mile radius covered a wide range of farming environments. These included the Central Valley (regarded as one of the most fertile cropping regions in the world), Sonoma, Napa, the San Francisco Bay area and a range of coastal areas. Since the 19th century this had been imagined as America's food bowl and a place where unusual and distinctive crops – ranging from the Mediterranean to the

sub-tropical – could be viably produced by small family farmers (Frost, 2002; Tyrrell, 1999). Accordingly, Waters was able to source an extraordinarily rich variety of produce from within the surrounding hinterland (Figure 6.1).

Chez Panisse was a great success, gaining a Michelin Star and being awarded America's Best Restaurant by *Gourmet* magazine in 2001. Waters became a well-known media identity, often commenting on the need for good food. In her 2007 book *The Art of Simple Food*, she listed nine key principles. These, she argued, 'have less to do with recipes and techniques than they do with gathering good ingredients, which for me is the essence of cooking' (Waters, 2007: 5).

Her key principles are (Waters, 2007: 6–7):

(1)   eat locally and sustainably;
(2)   eat seasonally;
(3)   shop at farmers' markets;
(4)   plant a garden;
(5)   conserve, compost and recycle;
(6)   cook simply, engaging all your senses;
(7)   cook together;
(8)   eat together;
(9)   remember food is precious.

Figure 6.1 St Helena farmers' market, Napa Valley, California, USA. A place to buy local produce directly from the producer and within Waters' 100 mile radius (photo: W. Frost)

These key principles reflect and inform a strong movement within modern societies. Appearing in a wide range of forms and distinguished by various names, essentially this is a quest for better food. Paradoxically, parallelling this search is a growing unease that modern food is not very good; that despite our advances in technology and despite the ability of the media to disseminate effective messages like that of Waters, we are eating quite poorly. In this chapter we examine this debate in detail, considering two high-profile critics in writers Eric Schlosser and Michael Pollan and then analyse the rise of modern movements advocating change, with a focus on Slow Food. In the following chapters we continue with Waters's principles, examining the growth of farmers' markets and edible gardens.

Fast Food Nation (Eric Schlosser, 2001)

The starting point for Schlosser is the economic and cultural domination of fast food at the beginning of a new century:

> In 1970, Americans spent about $6 billion on fast food: in 2000, they spent more than $110 billion. Americans now spend more money on fast food than on higher education, personal computers, computer software, or new cars. They spend more on fast food than on movies, books, magazines, newspapers, videos, and recorded music – combined. (Schlosser, 2001: 3)

The evolution of the USA as a nation that identifies itself with fast food comes with costs. According to Schlosser, there is a hidden dark side to the ubiquitous burger and fries. Through a series of journalistic investigations, he uncovers three main areas of concern:

(1) The economics of mass production of cheap fast food lead to concentrated business ownership. Large agricultural corporations supply fast-food franchises which dominate sales. Economies of scale allow ultra-cheap production that has forced out traditional family businesses. Importantly, as Schlosser stresses, this is happening at every stage of the supply chain, from farming through to retailing. The American dream of operating a successful small business is rapidly dissipating.
(2) The quest for cheap production has seriously increased risks. Slaughterhouses used to be highly regulated, but this has all been swept away. Many slaughterhouse employees are now illegal immigrants – poorly paid and trained. Apart from the social justice issues of the exploitation of migrant workers, this change has resulted in a sharp increase in industrial accidents. Furthermore, declining standards have led to higher rates of meat tainted with animal faeces, causing outbreaks of food poisoning and other diseases amongst consumers.

(3) Greatly increased rates of fast food consumption are resulting in increased obesity with consequent public health implications.

Schlosser's book had a major impact, being released at a time when the issue of Mad Cow Disease was highly prominent. Although mainly confined to Europe, concern about Mad Cow Disease was worldwide. In particular, this crisis highlighted questionable practices in feedlot production of beef, such as feeding bone meal to cattle to increase their protein and growth rates. When Schlosser's book was made into a dramatised feature film (*Fast Food Nation*, 2006), the focus was primarily on the issues of slaughterhouse standards and posed the question: what exactly was in our favourite burger?

The Omnivore's Dilemma (Michael Pollan, 2006)

Journalist Michael Pollan poses the Omnivore's Dilemma. If we can eat everything – and modern technology allows us access to a wide range of cheap food – what should we be eating? Underpinning this dilemma is a 'national eating disorder' of contradictory fad diets and food trends, rising obesity and increasing diet-related disease across America. He terms this the American Paradox – 'a notably unhealthy people obsessed by the idea of eating healthily'. In contrast, 'there are other countries, such as Italy and France, that decide their dinner questions on the basis of such quaint and unscientific criteria as pleasure and tradition, eat all manner of "unhealthy" foods, and, lo and behold, wind up actually healthier and happier' (Pollan, 2006: 3).

To investigate what Americans should be aiming for, Pollan puts together four meals, each representing a different production and consumption paradigm. These are:

(1) takeaway from McDonald's, consumed while driving;
(2) a home-cooked meal made with ingredients bought from organics retailers;
(3) another home-cooked organic meal, but for which the food has been sourced directly from producers; and
(4) a third home-cooked meal, comprising ingredients that have been hunted or foraged.

Much of the book is a strong critique of modern gastronomy. Starting with supermarkets, Pollan notes that, while they seem to offer a wide variety of food, they are actually dominated by corn (i.e. maize):

Corn is what feeds the steer that becomes the steak. Corn feeds the chicken and pig, the turkey and the lamb ... even the salmon, a carnivore by nature that the fish farmers are reengineering to tolerate corn. The eggs are made of corn. The milk and cheese and yoghurt … Head over to the processed foods and you find even more intricate manifestations of corn. A chicken nugget, for example, piles corn upon corn: what chicken it contains consists of corn, of course, but so do most of the nugget's other constituents, including the modified corn starch that glues the thing together, the corn flour in the batter that coats it, and the corn oil in which it gets fried. (Pollan, 2006: 18)

As he visits farms and factories, he ponders whether such a corn monoculture is sustainable. Farmers complain of low prices and high debts. Massive government subsidies seem to be benefiting a few oligopolistic companies. Cattle and chicken in industrial feedlots are distanced from nature, in a system propped up by hormones and antibiotics.

This abundance of cheap food causes major problems for health. He finds that, in the last 20 years, the per person consumption of added sugar (primarily corn sweetener) in the USA has risen by 23%. Even though there is much media coverage of diet issues, it seems that this is being overpowered by evolutionary hard-wiring. As omnivores, humans react to surplus food by increasing consumption. When those extra calories are dished up in fat and sugar, the temptation is overwhelming. As consumption has increased – and work has become more sedentary – obesity and diseases like diabetes have increased. Furthermore, these health problems have disproportionately affected those at the lower end of the socio-economic scale. Here the problem is that cheap fast food is energy dense. Fried chips are five times cheaper than carrots. Similarly, soda is a fifth of the cost of fruit juice (Pollan, 2006).

Moving on to organics, Pollan considers the booming range of retailers in California where he lives. Their produce is what he calls *Big Organic* and it is still distributed in similar ways to mainstream agriculture. He is puzzled by a new range of frozen organic TV dinners. He talks to producers, who argue that they have to make compromises to gain a foothold and incrementally change attitudes and behaviours. He has mixed feelings about the meal he prepares, particularly when he finds that none of his family like the most expensive dish. This is organic asparagus, flown in from the Southern Hemisphere, so that consumers can eat it out of season.

Pollan then considers small organic producers who sell directly to consumers. He volunteers to work on a small farm in Virginia called Polyface Farm. His interest in this farm is piqued when he tries to mail order some produce. The farmer – Joe Salatin – not only refuses, but is scathing about mail order food. His farm is built on firm environmental principles, including minimising shipping. He only sells through local farmers markets or directly off the farm. Working on the highly productive farm, Pollan realises that it is grass-based, whereas all the other farms he has visited are corn-based. This has important implications for health:

A growing body of scientific research indicates that pasture substantially changes the nutritional profile of chicken and eggs, as well as of beef and milk. The question we asked about organic food – is it any better than the conventional kind? – turns out to be much easier to answer in the case of grass-farmed food ... the large quantities of beta-carotene, vitamin E, and folic acid present in green grass find their way into the flesh of animals that eat grass ... [and it will] have considerably less fat in it than the flesh of animals fed exclusively on grain ... [and] the [unsaturated] fats created in the flesh of grass eaters are the best kind for us to eat. This is no accident ... we evolved to eat the sort of foods available to hunter-gatherers ... [and] pastured meats [have] the nutritional profile ... which closely resembles that of wild game. (Pollan, 2006: 266–267)

Whereas the farms Pollan had previously visited were monocultural, Polyface grows a wide range of produce. This diversity, Salatin argues provides a healthier ecosystem. From an economic perspective, it allows the farmer and his family to take a portfolio approach, spreading risks across varied revenue-earners. Both his productivity and return on investment are much higher than if he farmed conventionally. For his consumers, the produce is valued as they know its provenance. Indeed consumers are encouraged to visit to observe the organic methods and can even engage in the slaughter of the chickens that they purchase. This last feature highlights Salatin's philosophy that humans need to return to the basics and if they are to eat flesh must recognise the need for humane killing practices.

In the final third of the book, Pollan produces a meal that he has hunted and gathered in California. Through a friend who is a chef (from Waters' Chez Panisse), he is introduced to the hunting of feral boar in the hills near the Napa Valley. Another enthusiast takes him collecting wild mushrooms in newly felled pine forests of the Sierra Nevada. He even makes a sourdough bread by leaving his mix outside in Berkeley, so that it attracts wild yeasts.

Pollan views the meals made through hunter-gathering and from Polyface Farm as highly satisfactory. He contrasts these to the disappointments of his corn-based McDonald's and his Big Organic meal. Nonetheless, he has some lingering doubts. Small, locally produced and grass-based is clearly best, but the question remains whether the modern world could really feed itself this way.

Slowing Down Our Food

Slow Food is the idea that, in our modern fast world, we need to slow down how we produce, cook and eat food. Simply defined, it promotes 'locally sourced ingredients, traditional recipes and taking time to source, prepare and enjoy food' (Dickinson & Lumsdon, 2010: 80). However, it is a broad concept, with multiple interpretations and perspectives. While there is a governing body in

Slow Food International (www.slowfood.com), it needs to be recognised that there is also a wider, grass-roots movement and advocacy. This varies across countries, affected by differing local conditions and environments.

Initially, Slow Food developed as a response to the globalisation and standardisation of fast food. Its genesis was in Italy, when in 1986 McDonald's announced plans to open a store near the famous Spanish Steps in Rome. Protesters, led by activist and journalist Carlo Petrini, focused on the need for an alternative based on tradition and good quality. Even today, Slow Food is often defined in the media in terms of being the *opposite* of Fast Food (Boyd, 2016; Hall, 2012). Certainly, amongst our students there seems to be little understanding of the concept until it is explained in this contrary way.

In essence, Slow Food celebrates traditional ways of preparing and consuming food. Rather than takeaway or heating in a microwave, meals should be cooked slowly, using traditional recipes that require hours of simmering. Within the European context that spawned the concept, this highlights dishes such as Bolognese sauce, osso bucco (veal shin and polenta) and cordero asado (roast lamb shoulder) – all dishes that cannot be thrown together quickly. This is because they use fattier cuts that are highly flavoursome if cooked for sufficient time for the fats to break down (or be rendered). Such a process takes a long time, perhaps 8–12 hours, and often requires that preparation begins the day before.

Nor should Slow Food be thought of purely in terms of Europe (see, e.g. Parsecoli and de Abreu e Lima, 2012). Many dishes from the Middle East, the Indian sub-continent, Africa and South America require long periods of simmering to achieve the required taste. In the USA, the concept has been applied to the increasingly popular method of brining meats in salted water for hours prior to cooking. Meats treated this way retain moisture and may be cooked slowly in pressure-cookers and barbecues (the latter referring to slow smoking in an enclosed device rather than an open grill). Dishes like pulled pork – where the meat is slow roasted or barbecued and then shredded – have now spread from Northern America and become popular around the world. A key part of that process has been the influence of American media, particularly the large number of television productions devoted to barbecuing and dude food. One example of this is *Man Versus Food* (2008–2012), in which host Adam Richman visits various restaurants and takes on competitive eating challenges.

Slow Food is not just about slow cooking. Dishes that take a short amount of time – such as the grilling of meat fillets, fish and vegetables – can be seen as part of the Slow Food approach. What includes them within the concept is an emphasis on fresh ingredients, choosing the most appropriate cooking method and the use of traditional recipes and ingredients.

Slow also extends to preparation. Examples including home curing and smoking of meats, fresh pasta making, the seasonal bottling of preserves and jams and a return to the baking of breads, cakes and pastries. All of these have experienced a strong resurgence in recent years, manifested in home production, artisanal operators and coverage in the media. The English television shows of Hugh Fearnley-Whittingstall, commencing with *Escape to River Cottage* in 1999, have been particularly influential. The emphasis on small-scale, seasonal and local production is critical to Slow Food. Originally conceived as a reaction to multinational food chains, it continues to advocate patronage of small, locally owned and operated businesses. In some cases, these changes in fashion have slowed or halted the spread of the franchise retailers. An intriguing example of this occurred in Melbourne, Australia; where consumer preference for independent baristas led to Starbucks closing most of their stores (Frost *et al.*, 2010).

Slow Food as heritage

In recent years there has been increasing interest in viewing food, foodways and cuisines as a form of heritage (Timothy & Ron, 2013a, 2013b). Considering Slow Food through a heritage framework provides a range of important perspectives and understandings (Boyd, 2016). Broad definitions of heritage include, 'anything that someone wishes to conserve or collect, and to pass on to future generations' (Howard, 2003: 6) and 'some sort of inheritance to be passed down to current and future generations' (Timothy & Boyd, 2003: 2). Whilst often associated with past history, heritage is better conceptualised as relating to three time periods (Harvey, 2001; Urde *et al.*, 2007). These are the *past* (when the heritage was created), the *present* (when it is now being evaluated and discussed) and the *future* (for which it will be preserved).

Such an approach is a good fit for understanding Slow Food. Within its promotional material, references to preservation for future generations abound. As is common with many heritage concerns, the call for preservation is couched in terms of the immediate threats from modernity. This concern for present action to protect the past for the future is strongly influenced by a nostalgia for the past. Filtered through modern travails, we tend to see the past in romanticised and sanitised terms – a period when life was simpler and better (Hewison, 1987). Such a qualification raises the issue of criticisms of Slow Food, a topic that deserves measured consideration.

Critiquing Slow Food

Most of the academic discussion of Slow Food and similar trends has been led by advocates of change. Such studies may be viewed as *action research*, where the researchers are direct activists within a change process, working with an objective of achieving changes, often associated with social justice, sustainability or community change. This approach is important in effecting the betterment of human conditions, but it may come at the cost of a limited critical enquiry. While keen fans of Slow Food, our aim in this section is to consider some of the criticisms and limitations of this trend in gastronomy. Four main areas of concern are examined.

An elitist practice?

In their study of websites for Slow Food festivals, Frost and Laing (2013) noted that the language and imagery were elitist – suggesting that Slow Food was only for those with discerning tastes and/or wealthy incomes. In this sense, Slow Food is no different to any other food trend, usually starting with a coterie of advocates drawn from the wealthier and better educated sections of society and then trickling down to a more general audience. What is distinctive about Slow Food is that *time* is particularly critical. If Slow Food takes many hours to prepare and cook, then this may put it outside of the reach of ordinary working people in our time-poor modern society. In addition to the costs of better quality ingredients, there is an *opportunity cost* of the time put into sourcing, preparing and cooking.

Advocates of Slow Food tend to tackle this issue head-on, arguing that there is a false perception that it involves so much time that the average person could not afford to cook this way. In slow-cooking meat dishes, for example, there is a short period of preparation, but the long cooking period requires little supervision as the pot simmers. Greater availability of modern electrical slow cookers makes the process even easier. Nonetheless, Slow Food – like many other gastronomic trends – suffers from two major constraints. First, it requires organisation and planning. Second, mass-produced fast food is temptingly very cheap. Accordingly, it takes conscious commitment for consumers to choose to take this alternative path.

An arcane and romanticised heritage

In the 1980s, two influential books challenged our notions of heritage. Hobsbawm and Ranger (1983) introduced the concept of *the invention of tradition*, arguing that, as a response to modernity, societies will invent new rituals and customs, which will often quickly become accepted as ancient and venerable. Hewison (1987) saw difficulties in the growing popularity of heritage. He warned that, 'commerce reinforces the longing for authenticity in order to exploit it ... nostalgia is also clearly linked with snobbery' (Hewison, 1987: 29) and 'when museums become one of Britain's new growth industries, they are not signs of vitality, but symbols of decline' (Hewison, 1987: 84). Such views are applicable to Slow Food, leading to criticisms of invention, arcaneness and romanticisation.

Given that Slow Food privileges tradition, it needs to counter arguments that all food traditions are worthy of preservation. Many peasant societies were beset by food shortages and nutritional deficiencies. For example, polenta – made from corn – has come back into fashion in recent years.

In the 18th and 19th century, it was the major staple of many agricultural communities in Spain and Italy. The result of a diet based strongly on corn was the hideous disease pellagra, resulting from niacin deficiency. Nor is this an isolated case; many peasant cuisines based on limited staples were characterised by chronic ill-health. Many of the dishes cherished today were not actually everyday fare, but rather those from feast days. As standards of living have risen, these dishes have tended to be modified, often becoming richer and meatier, so that they are no longer exactly what was consumed in the past (Gabaccia, 1998). Furthermore, it needs to be recognised that peasant cuisines were often based on mostly female labour devoting hours and hours of hard work to preparation. To ignore these realities lays Slow Food open to criticisms of being a romanticised fantasy, compromising the authenticity that it lays claim to.

The long-term viability of Slow Food

Slow Food is often presented as a great success, spreading globally and increasing annually. Such enthusiasm needs to be tempered with the understanding that such a niche product may have issues with its long-term viability. A number of Slow Food festivals have failed, either being no longer run or changing their name and theme. Personal communication from organisers acknowledges that one of the factors is that the market was not sufficiently large to support these festivals. To survive the organisers had to broaden their appeal, making them more general food and wine festivals.

The appropriation and distortion of Slow Food

As Slow Food becomes more well-known and popular, there is a danger that it will be appropriated and modified by conventional commercial interests. This *commodification of dissent* may divert the impetus for real change in gastronomy and may lead to disillusionment amongst consumers. Pollan (2006) identified this as a major problem with the organic food movement, exemplified by the paradox of the marketing of organic TV dinners.

Similar developments are now occurring in respect to Slow Food. A major supermarket chain, for example, sells a boxed 'Slow Cooked Pork & Apple'. On the packaging is a prominent faux sticker which proclaims 'Save time! Already slow cooked for 4 hours'. The 'advantage' for the consumer is that the meal is already cooked – as with many frozen and canned dinners – and they just have to heat it in a conventional oven for 35 minutes. The charade is that heating a prepared meal is equivalent to slow cooking. Further concerns arise when looking at the ingredients. The sweet sauce is primarily composed of brown sugar, glucose syrup and corn starch. Furthermore, the corn starch has been imported from the USA.

Another example of the modification/commodification of Slow Food occurs on a variety of television cooking competitions involving the search for the best amateur or home chefs. The contestants regularly attempt to cook slow-cooked dishes. However, it is a common feature of such reality shows that there is limited time for cooking. Such a constraint is designed purely to introduce pressure and panic into the cooking challenges. Accordingly, attempts at slow cooking usually end in disaster, e.g. contestants failing in trying to slow cook pork belly in 45 minutes. Furthermore, these shows ignore seasonality owing to their production schedules. An episode highlighting fresh asparagus, for instance, might be filmed in spring, but not screened until autumn.

Beyond Slow Food: Recent Trends

In concluding this chapter, it is instructive to note some developing trends. The three we highlight have all been controversial, suggesting that the search for better quality food is being pushed to the extremes. Importantly, all three have developed with intense media interest, indicating that issues of food quality remain of major public interest.

The first example concerns American actress Shailene Woodley, star of films such as *Divergent* (2014). Woodley has been a regular guest on American talk shows, outlining her views on diet and health. These have included advocacy of foraging for wild foods and using a clay-in-water drink for detoxifying her system. Her consumption of clay has particularly led to ridicule in the media, provoking comments regarding drinking water from dirty puddles and eating the children's toy Play Doh. Woodley actually does not advocate such behaviour, instead utilising a commercial product based on bentonite available from vitamin and supplement suppliers. What is intriguing here is how the diet beliefs of Hollywood celebrities such as Woodley and Gwyneth Paltrow have entered into popular culture discourse.

The second example indicates a more worrying trend. Pete Evans, a chef and judge on the television show *My Kitchen Rules* (2010 onwards), has long been an advocate of the *Paleolithic* or *Paleo Diet*. The rationale behind this diet is that humans have not evolved to eat the common modern diet that is rich in processed foods and carbohydrates. This disconnection is argued to be the source of many medical and weight issues – a view held by Michael Pollan and discussed earlier in this chapter. The solution is to eat more like a palaeolithic hunter-gatherer. This diet includes meat, fish, eggs, fruit, nuts and vegetables. Excluded are processed foods, including anything made with flour, alcohol, coffee, sugar, legumes, grains and dairy products.

Evans has a strong online presence, including a series of short videos called *The Paleo Way*, which are often shown on daytime television. The paradox of being a television celebrity and his advocacy of the Paleo Diet has led to criticism of Evans via social media. As one of the judges of *My Kitchen Rules* he is critiquing and scoring meals made with ingredients that he not only does not eat, but which he feels are positively unhealthy. Furthermore, Evans endorses commercial products that do not fit the Paleo Diet, such as the Pete Evans Breville Pizza Maker.

In 2015, controversy arose when Evans announced his forthcoming book *Bubba Yum Yum: The Paleo Way for New Mums, Babies and Toddlers*. The area of main concern was the recipe for a beef broth as a substitute for breast milk. Professor Heather Yeatman from the Public Health Association stated that:

> There appears to be recommendations not to use either breast milk or an approved infant formula, but to provide other foods to infants under six months of age and that really is a big health risk ... There's been discussion about a beef broth with mashed up liver as part of a recipe. Now something like that might be appropriate for an older child, but under six months of age, really the best option [is] breast milk. (Quoted in Brennan, 2015)

Similarly, Rebecca Naylor from the Australian Breastfeeding Association said, 'all of the experts that you will speak to would say that feeding your baby anything other than infant formula or breast milk under six months as their primary source of nutrition is extremely dangerous' (quoted in Brennan, 2015). The Dieticians Association of Australia issued a press release warning of 'the food safety risks with the preparation of the DIY infant formula' and 'the use of ingredients that are not recommended for infants within the first 12 months of life due to microbiological risks' (Dieticians Association of Australia, 2015). In the face of this negative publicity, the publisher Pan Macmillan chose to not publish the cookbook.

The final example concerns Belle Gibson. In 2013, she launched a smartphone application called *The Whole Pantry*. Following its success, she wrote a cookbook of the same name, which was published by Lantern Books, a subsidiary of Penguin. Gibson claimed to be suffering from cancer and to have successfully managed her condition through diet and exercise rather than conventional medical treatment. As a young mother in her twenties, Gibson's story attracted great media interest and support.

In 2015, however, Gibson's story was revealed to be false. Initially, a newspaper investigation revealed that monies raised for charities had not been passed on, prompting court action by the government consumer affairs agency. This was followed by doubts about her illnesses, leading Gibson to reveal that in fact she had never suffered from cancer. In the storm of public discussion that ensued, Apple and Penguin tried to argue that it was not their role to check the accuracy of what they published. In the end, they withdrew *The Whole Pantry* application and cookbook from sale (Donelly & Toscano, 2015). In the age of New Media, this sorry tale illustrates the challenges to the reliability and ethical behaviour of media producers.

7   Food Gardens and Foraging

Escape to River Cottage (Hugh Fearnley-Whittingstall, 1999)

Hugh Fearnley-Whittingstall quits London having worked at the River Café and heads to rural Dorset. He moves into an old house with a third of an acre called River Cottage. Previously known for some extreme gastronomic television in *A Cook on the Wild Side* (1995–1997), this 1999 series charts Hugh's new life.

On his small plot, he is seeking a 'more direct and fulfilling contact with the land'. Growing food, fishing and foraging, this is 'more than a hobby, it's a vital part of my food supply'. Waking on a crisp morning, he addresses the camera directly:

> Now that I'm a Dorset Downsizer, the city smoke is a million miles away and there's not a cling wrap chicken in sight. I look forward to a day devoted almost entirely to my stomach.

Each episode follows a set pattern. Hugh works in his garden, focusing on seasonal produce. Then he pays attention to his livestock of pigs and chickens. Then he jumps in his groovy red car and motors through the Dorset countryside in search of free food. The conceit here is that struggling Hugh will go to great lengths to supplement the produce of his cottage through bartering or foraging. Examples in this first series include fishing for pike (generally seen as a worthless pest) and joining a gang of itinerant fruit-pickers on condition he is paid in raspberries and blackcurrants. Irrespective of how the food is gained, Hugh then cooks it up in his cottage kitchen.

The series pulls together two gastronomic themes. The first is the idea of becoming an *amenity migrant*, shifting from the city to the countryside. As the series title highlights, this is an *escape*. The second is the desire to produce one's own food, to gain back some sort of control over the quality of what we consume. For Hugh this is achieved through multiple production points – garden, chicken-pen, pig-sty, river, foraging – which all allow him to be involved in the production and to be assured of provenance and quality.

Following on from the success of this initial series, Hugh Fearnley-Whittingstall has produced a constant array of television series and specials. Over time, his base has changed, with moves to larger holdings and the development of a string of River Cottage Canteens, and a cooking school. Despite these changes, he has stuck to the same successful format and to the same theme of growing and cooking one's own food.

Introduction

This chapter focuses on the growth of food gardens. As the population increases globally, the demand for sustainable food options is becoming increasing apparent. In Western countries, interest in personal garden production is linked to the demand for fresh and nutritious food and a desire to minimise mass-produced food heavy in artificial chemicals and pesticides (Brown & Jameton, 2000). This chapter explores these developments through three sections. The first considers a range of examples of different types of food gardens, including community, school and private. The second section examines the role of chefs – particularly those with high media profiles – in championing small-scale personal production. The final section focuses on the trend towards foraging.

Developments in Food Gardens

Community gardens

Community food gardens are a worldwide phenomenon. This may be because they are increasingly recognised to have multiple benefits for participants and the wider community (Turner & Henryks, 2012). At one level, there may be concerns about food security and reliability, as 'urban gardening and urban social movements can build local ecological and social response capacity against major collapses in urban food supplies' (Barthel *et al.*, 2013). Los Angeles, for example, has 118 community gardens and 761 school gardens (Rehm, 2014). In this instance, food gardens are used for a food supply for the most vulnerable and a social activity for the wider community. In Omaha in the USA, the Dundee community garden helps feed low-income seniors in a housing complex and is seen as a necessity for good health and fresh food supply. In South Africa, organisations such as the Food Gardens Foundation assist the poor and the hungry by teaching the simplest, grassroots, virtually no-cost methods of restoring life and fertility to poor soil and producing food (Niland, 1995).

Community food gardens allows refugees and immigrants from traditional societies to continue farming the land whilst in new and unfamiliar surroundings (Schult, 2014). These programmes support groups of people to better integrate into society, but also enable them to maintain some traditional practices and familiarity that can be incorporated into their daily routine. In the Northern Territory in Australia a community group called Remote Indigenous Gardens is establishing gardens in isolated towns to introduce indigenous people to better health, wealth and well-being for both adults and children (Maddocks, 2014).

In some communities, so much additional food from small gardens is being produced that the surplus is being provided to others. Uxbridge Community Garden (UK) has built a food pantry designed for volunteers to make lunches for the elderly with excess food that the growers do not consume themselves and similar programmes have appeared in America (Drake & Lawson, 2014). This allows people to grow their own food for private use, sell it for commercial use (mainly restaurants) or to donate it to charity. The USA has introduced a Seeds for Change programme, which offers grants nationally to assist organisations with food supply. This enables schools, food and nutritional educational programmes, farms, urban food gardens and other community projects to start initiatives for nutritional food growth. Commercial businesses applying for a grant must commit 1% of their global net sales to be put back into community-based nutrition, gardening and farming programmes, which include small food gardens (Reese, 2014).

Even in wealthy capital cities, there are also many unproductive spaces available for food plots that are starting to be utilised. In the USA and Canada, government tourism advertising glamourises urban food gardens with slogans such as 'eat locally' and 'fresh is best' (Schnell, 2011). Initiatives such as the Chippendale Road Gardens in Australia – where food gardens are grown on 20 street blocks utilising the nature strip as a food plot – have sparked media interest, with other cities now replicating the initiative (Maddocks, 2014).

Roof tops on car parks and buildings are now seen as ideal for creating food gardens. In the central business district of Melbourne, a 140 plot garden has been established on the car park of Federation Square. Community members pay an annual fee to maintain their own individual plot. It is mainly utilised by people who live in city apartments and do not have their own garden space. There are also local food vendors and every restaurant and café located in Federation Square has its own allocated garden space (Figures 7.1 and 7.2). Daily menu specials are often created from the seasonal fruits, vegetables and herbs harvested on the day. There is even an on-site food stand to sell any additional produce. Not only does this attract locals living in the city, but it has also become a tourist attraction in its own right. Tourists can wander through laneways of converted apple crates, having a visual image of fresh produce in a concrete, city setting. This idea is being replicated in other cities worldwide and is often referred to as 'pop-up' vegetable patches.

Figure 7.1 The Melbourne Food Garden – *Pop up Patch* at Federation Square (photo P. Strickland)

School gardens

The idea of school gardens educating children and instilling civic and national pride dates back to the 19th century (Kohlstadt, 1997). In recent years, the focus has shifted to using school gardens for teaching children about nutrition and alternatives to fast food (Schult, 2014). Instrumental in this change has been chef Alice Waters (discussed in Chapter 6). In 1995, she started the Edible Schoolyard Program in Berkeley, California and it has since spread across the USA and to other countries.

The Edible Schoolyard grew out of conversations between Waters and Principal Neil Smith of the Martin Luther King Jr Middle School at Berkeley. The school had a disused cafeteria kitchen dating from the 1930s and extensive grounds, albeit asphalted. Why not grow some food and serve it as part of the school lunch programme? Within two years, an acre of asphalt had been removed and replaced with a garden and the kitchen had been refurbished.

The programme went further, beyond just growing food. It sought to educate the children and change their behaviours. Accordingly:

> The mission of the Edible Schoolyard is to create and sustain an organic garden and landscape that is wholly integrated into the school's curriculum and lunch program. It involves the students in all aspects of farming the garden – along with preparing, serving and eating the

Figure 7.2 Bokchoy Tang's vegetable patch – Bokchoy Tang is a pop-up restaurant in Federation Square (photo P. Strickland)

food – as a means of awakening their senses and encouraging awareness and appreciation of the transformative values of nourishment,
community, and stewardship of the land ... Garden classes teach the
origins of food, respect for all living systems, and principles of ecology ... In the kitchen classroom, students prepare and eat seasonal
dishes from produce they have grown in the garden. Students and
teachers gather at the table to share food and conversation during each
class. (Murphy, 2003: 4)

While confident that the programme was a success, one of the funding
bodies was keen to quantify its impact. They commissioned a study by

Figure 7.3 Stephanie Alexander (photo S. Griffiths; source: Stephanie Alexander http://www.stephaniealexander.com.au)

Harvard Medical School. This study found three main areas of improvement at the school (Murphy, 2003):

(1) grades were higher, particularly in science and mathematics;
(2) 'psychosocial adjustment' had improved significantly; and
(3) students had a higher level of ecological knowledge.

In Australia, this idea was taken up by chef Stephanie Alexander (Figure 7.3) and her scheme is now co-funded by the federal government. Alexander aims to create a more healthy food environment for children from the 'paddock-to-plate'. This means actively encouraging children to participate in every aspect of food production from planting, growing and harvesting to preparing, cooking and serving food, not only at school, but at home (Alexander, 2009). An evaluation concluded that the 'results showed that some of the program attributes valued most highly by study participants included increased student engagement and confidence, opportunities for experiential and integrated learning, teamwork, building social skills, and connections and links between schools and their communities' (Block *et al.*, 2012: 419).

Whilst school gardens operate on school grounds, they are also complemented by a range of community operations that cater specifically for school visits. Such operations are typically run by not-for-profit organisations and

Figure 7.4 The orchard at Collingwood Children's Farm, a community operation where school children can visit and work in the gardens (photo P. Strickland)

developed in an ad hoc manner either to preserve open space or to make use of disused rubbish dumps and industrial lands. In recent years, some of these community gardens have developed extensive programmes for visiting school groups (Figure 7.4). In addition, many stage farmers' markets and other semi-commercial activities.

Commercial and tourism ventures

The end food product itself is not the only selling point as it was decades ago. Today, an entire food experience is essential in agritourism, a distinct tourism market (Schnell, 2007). Consumers are willing to 'get their hands dirty' before being wined and dined in a restaurant. The industry is responding by allowing customers to literally pick their own ingredients for salads that will then be served to them in the restaurant. Food gardens are gaining popularity in the backyards or gardens of restaurants that have the ability to offer this experience. Other examples include gathering produce from nearby community gardens, roof tops or even laneways, giving the consumer a food experience.

The availability of local and seasonal food is also a drawcard for tourists wanting to dine in regional restaurants. Having a food garden specifically for a restaurant enhances the overall dining experience for the guest. Based on the philosophy that food gardens are essential for the health and well-being of many cultures and communities, it is no surprise that the positive feelings that food gardens can bring can be transposed as a promotional tool for restaurants.

Potager gardens (as edible gardens were previously referred to) are gaining momentum as many restaurants highlight the use of their food gardens through local media publications, their menus and websites. Blue Hill at Stones Barns is a working farm and restaurant that opened in Tarrytown in upstate New York in 2004. It has a simple concept of no menu; instead there are simply tasting plates and the chef brings out what has been harvested, displaying the raw ingredients to the customers before preparation. According to a count by Yonan (2010: 46), '67 items had been harvested from the farm outside, 35 had been grown within 175 miles, and 24 had come from ocean, river or simply beyond'.

There is a growing trend of wineries (typically found in rural locations) not only opening restaurants and accommodation facilities but also establishing food gardens (mainly vegetables and herbs) to supply fresh produce for their customers. In South Africa, Babylonstoren, a combined 5 star hotel, winery and restaurant, is an example of this trend: 'for traveling gourmands, some cottages offer kitchens, glassed-in cubes facing an eight-acre garden from which you can pick your own herbs, fruits and vegetables, the same produce used by the chefs at the restaurant, Babel' (Rogers, 2011). Hotel guests and restaurant customers are encouraged to venture out into the garden and select items to be prepared for them by the chef. Not only does this give the customer a sense of engagement, but it also adds to the overall dining experience.

In Australia's King Valley, most of the wineries are owned by Italian families. Originally they were tobacco farmers, but since the late 20th century they have transitioned into wine. The Italian theme is strong, with their restaurants sourcing produce from kitchen gardens and chicken-pens that are prominent and visible to the customers (Laing & Frost, 2013). We interviewed one operator, who noted that visitors 'can walk around our wineries, they can stick their heads in barrels, they can meet the families'. Another observed, 'we take pride in that you know we make our own salamis, we do salami [making] classes, my mother-in-law makes Torrone, which is an Italian sweet, and that's what we like'. And a third winery operator stated:

> You literally see Nonna – you know the grandma – and grandpa all there [and] the kids running around. In some of them, it's quite literally walking into little Italy … and they've got the huge veggie garden. That's what they're making all the food from … I've done [visitor] surveys. They all say about how wonderful the atmosphere is and how authentic it is.

Creasy (2013), highlights the niche market of growing edible flowers solely for garnishing plates in local restaurants, arguing that the overall customer experience is enhanced when linked to a story, feeling or emotion. His philosophy is that a simple garnish of edible flowers, herbs, fruit or vegetables can stimulate the customer's emotions in a more positive way. Sutherland-Smith (2015) suggests that the best way to experience food gardens is to: 'Wander down the paths lined with many varieties of thyme, visit the checkerboard herb area and taste some of the fragrant herbs, see the varieties of olive and fruit trees mingling with dozens of roses and learn about companion planting'. In this case, this involves stirring up emotions of the five human senses whilst providing information about companion planting.

The increased demand for garden food has led to some interesting hybrids that blur the lines between public, community and private. A concept termed *kitchen crowd-sourcing* allows local gardeners to barter their excess produce for meals and drinks at cafés. Either by word of mouth or by signs in their windows, café proprietors seek out locally grown seasonal produce. Apart from reducing food-miles, this builds a sense of community identity, which is important to the success of such local businesses. As one café owner described the system, 'all our figs are crowd sourced, but then [only] about 50 per cent of our quinces. At the moment we have Jerusalem artichokes from an elderly gentleman we have built up a relationship with who is a phenomenal gardener' (quoted in Lewis, 2013). Another collaborative programme is the Pop Up Garlic Farmers programme. It is aimed at young people who want to get into horticulture, but who don't have much capital or any connection to a family farm. On small blocks on the peri-urban fringe they are sowing garlic crops, with the produce being sold to local shops or at farmers' markets. The use of the land has been donated, either by community groups or by sympathetic farmers (Green, 2015).

There are issues with the sustainability of supplying a restaurant with local garden produce. Toensmeier (2013) believes that growing food for restaurants in a city or small farm setting is very difficult as the quantities of food demanded are far greater that what some food gardens can supply. He suggests perhaps selecting only niche offerings or seasonal (perhaps even weekly) produce to still be able to promote, fresh, local and seasonal food grown in the restaurant's own garden, albeit a garnish or a few items on the daily specials board. This has also been highlighted on reality cooking shows such as *Local Food Hero* (2006–2008) and *Market Kitchen* (2007–2010) in the UK, which have both argued that relying solely on local produce is not sustainable.

Chefs and Food Gardens

There are many media champions of food gardens who can be seen in a variety of books, magazines and increasing number of cooking shows that are transmitted on a global scale. Jamie Oliver is one such example; having his cooking programmes broadcast into 100 countries worldwide making him one of the most well-known chefs on the globe. His website claims 'Jamie has inspired people to spend more time enjoying cooking delicious food from fresh ingredients and even start growing their own food' (Oliver, 2015). He has included his own personal garden in his shows, highlighting the seasonal produce that he cultivates.

Jamie Oliver, among other celebrities, has had a massive impact on the sales of cookbooks and advertising through their television series. However, Ketchum (2005) argued that television shows in particular have a history of creating stories that invite viewers to create a fantasy and do not necessarily reflect the daily routine that most people follow. Ketchum highlighted that this is particularly true for cooking shows when she wrote about the Food Network:

> This nonfiction media relies on a similarly fictitious construction of consumer realities in an attempt to build a viewer base beyond the traditional cooking show audience. The network offers the possibility of pleasure through creating the fantasy of an intimate connection to viewers and the promise of satisfaction through consumption.

These programmes are a medium to create a food fantasy and lifestyle that the average viewer can adopt but generally does not. This includes showcasing celebrity chefs in food gardens offering suggestions regarding cultivating herbs and vegetables and the benefits of fresh produce. The visions of fresh produce grown in the backyard are something that the audience would most likely like to emulate.

However, not having the time, space or finances to create a food garden, viewers may purchase other promotional items that are aimed at the viewing audience. These items include cookbooks, DVDs, cookware and appliances that are almost entirely based on trying to recreate the cooking fantasy that they have viewed. The food fantasy concept put forward by Ketchum (2005) does support the popularity of television programmes based on food as indicated by the seemingly large numbers of the viewing audience and sales of related merchandise.

Hugh Fearnley-Whittingstall (as detailed at the beginning of this chapter) has had a similar impact. His website claims that 'our hard-hitting campaigns have changed the eating habits of a nation and improved the welfare and sustainability of animals and fish'. Sage (2014) observes that Fearnley-Whittingstall is an advocate and celebrity campaigner for sustainable farming and the need to have the right balance between farming fruit, vegetables and animals. The television series showcases the essence of sustainable farming, with emphases on health, nutrition, community engagement, farm-to-plate harvesting and leaving a low carbon footprint.

Food writer Annabel Langbein presents the New Zealand show *The Free Range Cook* (2010). It is set in the South Island resort town of Wanaka, where she has a holiday home, and she draws on produce from her own garden and nearby farms. Langbein is a strong advocate of reducing the use of fertilizers, pesticides and chemicals in all food production, including smaller food gardens for restaurants and home use. Through Langbein's website (2015) she said:

> Eating home-grown, home-cooked food is part of the way we live as a family today. It connects us, even if only in a small way, to the rhythms of nature. Wandering around my garden at the end of a busy day to find something to serve for our evening meal is incredibly satisfying. So, too, is the daily ritual of setting the table, lighting some candles and sitting down together to enjoy simple, freshly cooked food.

The involvement of chefs in food gardens is not simply a television phenomenon. Rather it is an example of the common occurrence where the media has picked up and popularised a trend, reinforcing it and extending it to a wider group. Many chefs talk about having an epiphany, sometimes stimulated by the media or travel, where they realise that they want to change what they are doing. For example, Annie Smithers recalls that:

> for a long time I had a little voice in my head that said you've got an acre of land at home that you don't use, and you're a cook and you have a restaurant ... so do you want a provisioning budget, or do you want a garden? And I chose a garden. (Quoted in Speed, 2014: 2)

Naomi Ingleton established a café in a disused butter factory. Over 100 years old, it presented the right sort of ambience for a rural gastronomic fantasy. One day a customer asked her if the butter with his meal was made in the factory. When she replied that it was imported, 'he looked at me like I was crazy'. For Ingleton, this was the moment she realised she had to make her own butter (Wood, 2015).

James Viles spent six years as a chef in Dubai and Oman. He became disillusioned that: 'everything you cook in the Middle East is imported. It has travelled thousands of miles, and gone through 40 pairs of hands before it gets to you, so for me there was no connection with the food and in one way I was lost as a cook' (quoted in Speed, 2014: 2). By the time he was ready to return to Australia, he had visualised what he wanted. Employing his mother as the full-time gardener, he developed a restaurant with two adjoining gardens (herb and vegetable) that supplied 55% of what the kitchen needed (Speed, 2014).

Resurgence of Foraging for Food

Before agriculture was developed, early humans had to either hunt animals or gather food. Indeed, the gathering of edible leaves, tubers, berries, fruits, nuts and shellfish, was usually the most reliable source of food (Mathewson, 2000; Watson & Caldwell, 2005). Although this practice has occurred for a very long time, with advances in agricultural food production, the need for food foraging has significantly declined in most cultures. However, with a growing interest in healthy eating, organic food and offering different food products, some well-known chefs are actively foraging for food in cities, forests, beaches and public gardens to offer in their restaurants (Duram & Cawley, 2012).

The resurgence of food foraging is gaining momentum especially with the assistance of the media. Award winning restaurants and talented celebrity chefs are showcasing foraging for food to distinguish themselves from other food establishments. Ben Shewry, head chef of Attica in Melbourne, forages for food along the beach, railway tracks and urban alleyways and then serves what he finds in his restaurant. Mike Eggert from Pinebone's restaurant in Sydney also forages for food and 'the chef had foraged it himself, picking the young, tender dandelion leaves from the grounds of an old, abandoned mental asylum where they don't spray pesticides, and everything is left to get a little wild: no cars, no chemicals' (Rigby, 2013: 17). Eggert explains that it is really just getting back to the roots of finding food for cooking.

Robinson (n.d.) suggests that 'urban harvesting benefits on all levels. It saves money (free food!), reduces waste (all that fruit isn't rotting in the gutters), and builds community (both by encouraging interaction between strangers when asking permission and within foraging groups themselves). We can also get some exercise, eat fresh food and reduce agribusiness demand'. Eric from Wild Food UK has a similar view; 'living off the land and sustainable foraging are part of his family tradition and he himself has many years' experience of farming, foraging and eating from the wild' (Wild Food UK, 2015). In Europe, it appears that the most popular food obtained from foraging is mushrooms, whereas in North America it is more likely to be edible weeds and flowers (Edible Wild Food, 2015).

Arguably the most famous celebrity forager is actor Shailene Woodley (see also Chapter 6). Woodley advocates foraging for mushrooms and leaves in New York's Central Park, which is interesting given that such activities are specifically forbidden by park authorities. The problem of damage caused by foragers also occurs for food gardens and producers in urban and peri-urban areas (Figure 7.5).

As foraging continues to attract media attention as a desirable activity, it is not surprising that it is now featuring in destination marketing. A

Figure 7.5 Sign outside the orchard at Collingwood Children's Farm (photo P. Strickland)

recent travel article (McCabe, 2012) presents Marlborough New Zealand – previously known for its wine – as now 'perfect for the hunter-gatherer experience' and 'custom-made for a spot of 21st-century foraging'. This article outlines how the writer accompanies a number of chefs as they go foraging and hunting. It is an attractive picture, although at the end it becomes apparent that there is no such tour or experience on offer for prospective tourists. There might be foraging in these hills, but there is no clear way for the visiting tourist to participate.

8 Farmers' Markets

Parks and Recreation (Season 6, Episode 12, 2014)

This series is set in the fictional small US city of Pawnee, Indiana. Leslie (Amy Poehler) is initially in charge of the Parks and Recreation Department, but by series 6 she is an elected councillor. Her latest achievement is the opening of the local farmers' market. As she puts it, 'it's good for the economy, it's good for families and it's good for promoting a healthy lifestyle, which Pawnee desperately needs'. Indeed, it seems to be doing some good, for Pawnee residents who don't recognise a broccoli or a cauliflower are now being exposed to fresh food.

However, the rural ambience is disrupted by the antics of the owner of the stall selling chard. He is using scantily clad dancers and loud music to sell his chard. Lesley is outraged. The farmers' market is a community meeting place and having these half naked dancers negates its purpose, she asserts. Her husband Ben (Adam Scott), who also happens to be the City Manager, is not convinced that the selling technique being used warrants banning the chard vendor from the market. The couple speak with the chard vendor, only to find that he recently inherited the chard farm from his father and that his reasoning behind his selling technique is, 'chard is disgusting, you try selling it without sexy dancers'. The husband and wife team, after struggling to set work/home boundaries, eventually come to an agreement. There will be no sexy dancers during the family-orientated farmers' market, but after 5 pm there will be 'Farmers' Market After Dark', with a more adult emphasis.

This episode highlights a range of issues concerning farmers' markets. As originally conceived, there are community benefits – including the education of urban customers and sales opportunities for local farmers. However, in this new competitive market, one farmer goes to extreme lengths in making claims about his produce. Being a comedy, this is not that his crop is more organic, but rather that it is sexy. Finally, much of the episode focuses on the love of bureaucracy, epitomised by the need to have policies that will regulate who can sell at the market and how they can approach selling.

Introduction

Farmers' markets are a fundamental part of the urban–rural linkage and have experienced a recent resurgence in many parts of the world (Buman et al., 2014; Coster & Kennon, 2005; Guthrie et al., 2006; Murphy, 2011). An appropriate definition of a farmers' market is:

> a predominantly fresh food market that operates regularly within a community, at a focal public location that provides a suitable environment for farmers and food producers to sell farm-origin and associated value-added foods and plant products directly to customers. (Coster & Kennon, 2005: 6)

Most farmers' markets are not-for-profit and support local community initiatives (Guthrie et al., 2006); however, there are others that are operated privately or by regional food groups (Coster & Kennon, 2005). The 'farm to fork' or 'farm to table' movement, whereby consumers are more concerned about the origin of their food in connection with the environment and a healthy lifestyle, has received renewed interest worldwide. Farmers' markets provide the opportunity for consumers to access farm fresh produce, and to know where and how the food is grown. Regular farmers' markets date back to ancient times and were a feature of many cultures around the world (Basil, 2012). Many European markets today reflect this traditional market concept, as exemplified in the French market that is central to the feature film *The Hundred-Foot Journey* (2014). However, in the last few decades farmers' markets have grown in number, spreading well beyond traditional agricultural communities.

The reasons for this resurgence in farmers' markets are varied and complex; however, all emphasise the benefits to both producers and consumers (Guthrie et al., 2006). There is growing demand for locally grown organic fresh produce (Buman et al., 2014). Farmers' markets are an educational, often cost-effective and social way for consumers to shop. They also serve as an important direct sales outlet for producers who cannot compete effectively through economies of scale production and provide the farmers with the opportunity to introduce new produce and develop a personal relationship with their customers (Hunt, 2007). Destinations are increasingly using gastronomic experiences as a draw card and farmers' market may serve as a great source of destination competitiveness.

This chapter discusses the history of farmers' markets, factors contributing to their recent resurgence, including media influences, producer and consumer benefits (economic, social and environmental), both farmer and consumer profiles, and market associations along with future challenges facing farmers' markets.

History of the farmers' market

Traditional farmers' markets date back to the beginnings of agriculture, where farmers often would sell their produce within a market square at the centre of a town. (Basil, 2012). This traditional market concept may be traced in concepts as diverse as the Middle Eastern Grand Bazaar, African spice markets, medieval fairs, the market day and the European market cross (Basil, 2012). Wet markets in Asian countries – distinguished by a wide array of live animals and fish for sale – are also examples of traditional markets continuing into the modern day and are still particularly common in both Hong Kong and Vietnam (Basil, 2012; Goldman *et al.*, 1999; Maruyama & Trung, 2006).

The introduction of supermarkets saw the disappearance of these types of markets in countries such as New Zealand, Australia, the UK, Canada and the USA, although many European and Asian countries have maintained them in continuous existence (Guthrie *et al.*, 2006). The resurgence of the new generation of farmers' market movement in the USA began during the 1970s, with restaurateurs such as Alice Waters taking a leading role (see Chapter 6). Farmers' markets continued to grow in popularity during the 1980s and 1990s, especially following the passage by the US Congress of Public Law 94-463, the Farmer to Consumer Direct Marketing Act of 1976 (Brown, 2002). The United States Department of Agriculture began publishing a national directory in 1994, which listed 1755 farmers' markets; this figure had grown to 8144 in 2013 (United States Department of Agriculture, 2014).

The first new generation of producer-only farmers' market to formally operate in the UK began in 1997 following a visit by Harriet Festing to the USA (Festing, 1998). According to the National Farmers' Retail and Markets Association (FARMA) (2014), approximately 500 farmers' markets operate in the UK today.

In Australia, the first farmers' market to operate was in Victoria's Yarra Valley in 1998. Similarly to the UK, the catalyst was a visit by advocate Jane Adams to the USA. Between 2004 and 2011, the number of farmer's markets doubled to over 150 nationally (Victorian Farmers' Market Association, 2014). The first farmers' market to operate in New Zealand was in 1998 in Whangerei. Markets followed in Hawkes Bay and Hastings in 2000 and others in Marlborough and Dunedin in 2001 and 2003, respectively. Farmers' Market New Zealand Incorporated (FMNZ Inc.) was established in November 2005.

Factors contributing to the rise in popularity of farmers' markets

The growth in popularity of farmer's markets is a worldwide phenomenon. Changes in consumer demand, along with changing economics of agriculture, are major factors contributing to this regeneration (Brown, 2002;

Brown et al., 2006; Guthrie et al., 2006). Increasingly discerning consumers are demanding better food with consumers gaining a greater awareness and concern of what is in their food (Brown et al., 2006; Guthrie et al., 2006). There is growing demand for locally grown organic fresh produce and farmers' markets may be used as a strategy to improve access to this fresh local produce (Buman et al., 2014).

Shoppers are also seeking a more social, educational experience that provides the opportunity for cultural exchange (Murphy, 2011). Meeting the farmer or producer provides the consumer with the opportunity to discuss the product in more detail, where it is made, the production methods, preparation and cooking instructions, and even to taste the product before purchase. An increased awareness of sustainable agriculture, climate change concerns and communicated benefits of investment into local resources may be additional contributing factors. The focus on healthy production and eating also leads to linkages with sponsors keen on communicating health messages. In Davis, California, the local health group sponsors the farmers' market in order to promote a message of healthy eating of fresh food (Figure 8.1). Also in the USA, the insurer Kaiser Permanente has allowed over 20 farmers' markets to set up in the carparks of its health clinics (Morales & Kettles, 2009).

In rural areas, farmers' markets play a key role in destination marketing strategies. They both directly attract visitors and promote a regional tourism image that may be focusing on creativity and rurality (Hede & Stokes, 2009; Jolliffe, 2008; Smith & Xiao, 2008). This complementarity leads to partnerships between farmers' market organisers and tourism marketers, with an increasing emphasis on the use of the media. Hall (2013) found that the media was highly influential on how visitors understood farmers' markets. In a survey of 361 attendees, he found that 76% cited television as influential and 21% identified food magazines (note: multiple responses). In a study of regional tourism guides in the USA and Canada, Schnell (2011) looked for changes in what was promoted between 1993 and 2008. What he found was, 'an enormous expansion in promotion of local food and agriculture to tourists as a means of experiencing the "authentic" or "true" nature of a place' (Schnell, 2011: 281). Such an idealised view of lifestyles and food production has also been noted in other studies of tourism to rural areas (Connell, 2014; Frost & Laing, 2014; Sims, 2009).

Much of the media coverage of farmers' markets comes over as organic rather than induced. Celebrity chefs emphasising the use of local fresh seasonal produce in their cooking often advocate farmers' markets. Hugh Fearnley-Whittingstall is a patron of FARMA and often promotes the importance of farmers' markets. He once held a stall at the Winchester Farmers' Market (UK) and recently opened a River Cottage Canteen in the same city, promoting a menu using Hampshire-only ingredients wherever possible (Curtis, 2011). Celebrity food producers may also contribute to increased

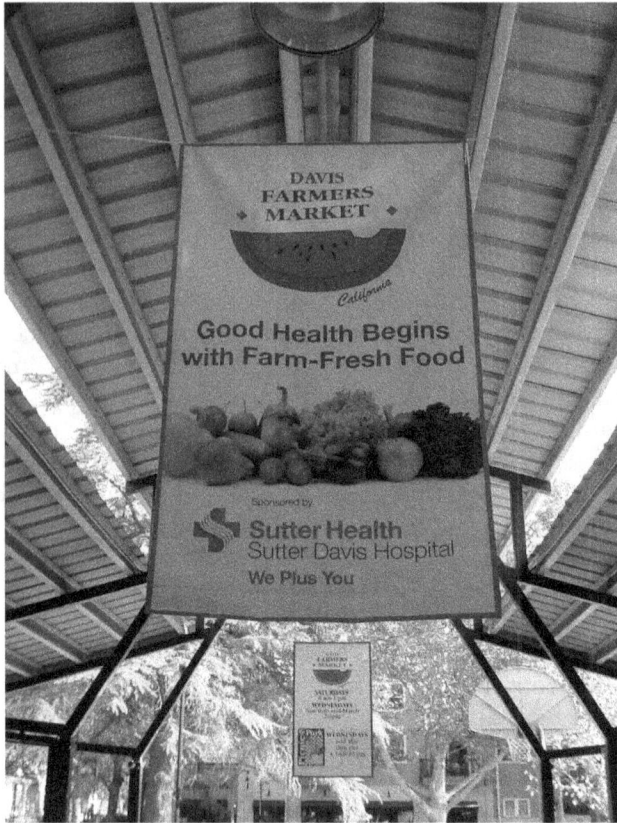

Figure 8.1 Good health begins with farm-fresh food. Sutter Health Group sponsors the Davis farmers' market in California (photo W. Frost)

attendance at local farmers' markets. Actress Elizabeth Hurley has a stall at the Cirencester Farmers' Market (UK) and has been seen serving behind her own stall on a Saturday morning (Mackenzie, 2011).

Kylie Kwong, celebrated Australian chef, holds a stall at Eveleigh Farmers' Market in Sydney where her regular cooking demonstrations serve as a highlight for many visitors. She launched her latest cookbook at the market in 2012 and often shops at the market for her own restaurant produce (Australian Technology Park, 2014). The Eveleigh Farmers' Market was also featured on *River Cottage Australia*, increasing not only its own profile but that of the farmers' market movement in general. Matthew Evans, former editor and restaurant reviewer for the Sydney Morning Herald, relocated to Tasmania (Australia) and, along with friends and fellow producers Nick Haddow and Ross O'Meara, appears in *The Gourmet Farmer* (2010–2015). Episodes feature Hobart's Salamanca Market and Hobart's Farmers' Market, where each of these 'gourmet farmers' has held stalls in the past selling their produce and promoting cookbooks. Poh Ling Yeow, another television cook, set up a stall at the Adelaide Farmers' market, with the results being broadcast in the show *Poh & Co* (2015).

Benefits for Producers

Owing to changes in the agricultural industry over the years, many small- to medium-scale farmers are forced to seek alternate methods of production and or sales outlets in order to remain a viable business (Pollan, 2006; Weaver & Fennell, 1997). While some farmers/producers selling at farmers' markets do so as a hobby or venture once they have retired, many others do so as a potential for increased farm income (Brown *et al.*, 2006; Guthrie *et al.*, 2006; Hunt, 2007; Jones *et al.*, 2007). Bloomfield farm, for example, sells its organic produce directly to consumers at the St Helena Farmers' Market in California (Figure 8.2). Overproduction has threatened the viability of the small-scale farm economy and few of these farmers are able to 'take advantage of the economies of scale that make extensive agriculture viable' (Brown *et al.*, 2006: 20). Instead, some farmers are seeking to remain viable

Figure 8.2 Bloomfield Farm selling organic produce at the St Helena farmers' market, California, USA (photo W. Frost)

through becoming smaller and avoiding conventional sales distribution chains.

A major attraction for participation in farmers' markets is the direct sales aspect, enabling the farmer to retain a larger proportion of the normal retail price. Those selling produce at farmers' markets are more likely to be either small-scale farmers whose produce output is too small to sell through larger supermarket type outlets or those retired from other occupations (Brown, 2002; Guthrie et al., 2006). A farmers' market may be the best, and often only, market channel available to producers. It provides a cost-effective direct sales outlet, eliminating the middle man in supermarkets and therefore maximising profit to the producer (Brown, 2002). Being a direct sales outlet, reduced transportation is required resulting not only in reduced associated costs but also in reduced fuel emissions into the environment. Less packaging material is also necessary (Festing, 1998). Farmers' markets complement local existing businesses with increased spending in nearby shops often recorded on market days (Brown, 2002). This increased spending in the local economy provides a multiplier effect and may act as an incubator role for many supporting industries (Coster & Kennon, 2005). The opportunity also exists for increased networking and knowledge sharing between local producers/businesses. Employment growth involving both family members and external employees is an additional advantage. Farmers' markets also provide the opportunity for producers to access new markets, enabling small-volume producers to directly serve specialised or niche markets (Brown, 2002; Govindasamy et al., 2003).

Many producers will use these markets as an opportunity to showcase their produce and build exposure (Coster & Kennon, 2005; Guthrie et al., 2006). New products may be introduced and tested in a low-cost market, business confidence may be improved and this may result in increased sales (Coster & Kennon, 2005). Radical changes may also be implemented within the production process or marketing strategies (Coster & Kennon, 2005; Govindasamy et al., 2003). Farmers' markets enable a producer–consumer relationship to develop while promoting social interaction between farming and non-farming communities. These markets provide an opportunity for farmers to gain consumer feedback instantly and may also encourage consumer loyalty (Guthrie et al., 2006). Having more control over their market is a major advantage to producers of participation in farmers' markets (Woodburn, 2014). Also, often it is an opportunity for business and personal growth, where the aim is to become too large to continue selling at the market (Coster & Kennon, 2005; Guthrie et al., 2006).

Farmers' markets also provide an alternative to other forms of direct selling. One producer recounted to us how government authorities had encouraged them to open a farm shop catering for passing tourists. They quickly found that they hated this. Visitors could arrive at any time, disrupting farm work, and they were disappointed by the low sales. Furthermore, they found the questions about their lifestyle and personal life quite intrusive. When a friend suggested a farmers' market, they were initially apprehensive. However, when they sold all their stock in one morning they were jubilant. Switching to farmers' markets allowed them to focus all of their sales effort into one day of the week. Similarly, other producers see farmers' markets as a viable alternative to online mailing lists and sales.

Farmers or producers attending farmers' markets have been researched extensively with reasonably consistent findings (Brown, 2002; Brown et al., 2006; Griffin & Frongillo, 2003; Guthrie et al., 2006). Those selling produce at farmers' markets are more likely to be either small-scale farmers or those retired from other occupations seeking a part time farmer income. Most are small-scale fruit and vegetable growers receiving modest profits from their produce sales (Griffin & Frongillo, 2003). Many vendors have arrived at the markets as an indirect career route and often from a non-farming background. Large-scale farmers often find the lack of economies of scale unfavourable for participation in farmers' markets (Brown, 2002; Guthrie et al., 2006).

Brown et al. (2006) indicated in their research into vendors participating in farmers' markets in West Virginia, USA that the majority of respondents were over 50 years of age, with 20% of respondents being over 70 years of age. Slightly more males than female vendors (58%) participated and females were slightly more likely to have pursued higher college or university education. Vendors indicated they attended a market at least two days of the week and, on average, vendors attended 1.6 different markets. Vendors travelled on average 10–12 miles (16–20 kilometres) to sell at a market, with some travelling larger distances of 50 miles (80 kilometres) or more (6%). The median range of reported sales was between $1500 and $2999. 39% of the 300 respondents indicated that at the farmers' market they offered free samples, 34% offered bulk discounts, 34% used a business card for advertising and 57% used price comparisons with other vendors.

Research conducted into four farmers' markets in New Zealand found that 70% of stallholders were selling fruit and vegetables, 12% herbs and spices, 10% flowers/plants and 10% sauces/preserves. Only 12% of market vendors relied on the market as a sole distribution outlet with almost half indicating that they traded through other small local retailers; 36% had their own farm shop or gate sales (Guthrie et al., 2006).

Benefits for Consumers

Consumers are increasingly searching for locally grown fresh produce (Figure 8.3). Farmers' markets connect people to their rural heritage and provide the opportunity for social interaction (Brown, 2002; Brown & Miller, 2008; Guthrie et al., 2006; Woodburn, 2014). Providing an intimate connection with the producers of food allows consumers greater satisfaction and

Figure 8.3 Fresh produce in an uncomplicated setting at the Pakenham farmers' market, Australia (photo J. Laing)

feelings of well-being (Sidali *et al.*, 2015). The markets are also an educational and often a more cost-effective way to shop. Consumers attend markets because they enjoy the shopping experience and feel that they provide high-quality produce at a reasonable price. The direct sales access allows consumers to obtain fresh local produce at more competitive prices (Guthrie *et al.*, 2006). Meeting the grower is also a major motivator for attendance at farmers' markets, with shoppers more often than not able to talk to the farmer about the produce they are buying, which makes for a sociable and educational experience (Baber & Frongillo, 2003; Brown, 2002; Guthrie *et al.*, 2006; Sidali *et al.*, 2015). Consumers are becoming interested in where their food is coming from and seeking alternative food outlets as a result of concerns relating to public health scares, food production methods, environmental impacts and quality of ingredients/additives (Woodburn, 2014). The opportunity also exists for consumers to learn more about environmentally sustainable growing practices from the growers. Less wastage often occurs as more focus is often placed on the flavour of produce rather than appearance (so produce can be sold which may not meet supermarket specification grades) (Coster & Kennon, 2005). Finally, farmers' markets provide the potential to revitalise local rural communities and facilitate rural and urban links.

Despite the dramatic growth of farmers' markets in recent years, there has been little conclusive research conducted into the profile of farmers' market shoppers. In addition, a variety of factors influence the reasons why consumers shop at farmers' markets, many of which are complex and interrelated.

Wolf *et al.* (2005) found in their research into the profile of farmers' market shoppers that they are inclined to be female, married and have a postgraduate-level education. No significant differences existed between income levels, age and employment status when compared with the non-market shoppers surveyed.

Meanwhile, a review of research studies conducted by Byker *et al.* (2012) concluded overall that more research needs to be conducted in order to accurately determine a shopper or consumer profile and their motivations. There is, however, some convincing evidence to suggest that the typical farmers' market shopper is female, middle-aged (over 40 years of age) and living in proximity to the market (Baker *et al.*, 2009; Conner *et al.*, 2010; Elepua *et al.*, 2010). Research also indicates that females are largely responsible for food shopping and preparation and have strong attitudes towards local produce, which may affect this finding. Hunt (2007) suggests a connection between age and frequency of social interactions; in other words, older people attend a farmers' market for the social interaction as well as the local food produce purchases. Further research into age characteristics and possible connections with income is required. In terms of shoppers' education level, some contradictory results also exist between research studies conducted on-site (primary) vs off-site (secondary). Some research results show that farmers' markets attract highly educated consumers (with some level of college/university education), while others have found no major differences. There is often high repeat patronage with consumers inclined to shop at markets that they are familiar with and which are convenient to access (Brown, 2002). Very few studies have researched the location of the farmers' markets in relation to the shoppers' residence; however, the general radius of trade can be considered to be approximately 32 kilometres or 20 miles (Brown, 2002). Shoppers are more likely to travel longer distances to attend a better quality farmers' market or one located in a more rural isolated location.

Motivations for shopping at farmers' markets identified in the literature include the opportunity to purchase fresh high-quality produce, variety, access to organic and chemical/pesticide free food, price, value for money, access to specialty items, ability to buy direct from the farmer, which supports local agriculture, the opportunity to taste produce prior to purchase, social aspects, entertainment and the ability to combine with shopping at stores in the local area (Brown, 2002; Byker *et al.*, 2012; Hall, 2013; Wolf *et al.*, 2005). Interestingly, some shoppers listed convenience as a major motivating factor for attending farmers' markets and therefore, not surprisingly, inconvenience was identified as the main reason shoppers didn't shop at a farmers' market. Inconvenience was considered when markets were held at inconvenient times or locations (Wolf *et al.*, 2005). Further research into consumer behaviour and motivations relating to farmers' markets is required overall.

The role of famers' market associations

Farmers' market associations are often established to represent their members in areas regarding food policy delivery, accreditation and certification and sustainable development, and may also assist with promotional activities. Some examples of farmers' market associations existing in Australia, New Zealand, the UK and the USA are provided below.

The Australian Farmers' Markets Association (AFMA) was established in 2003 to provide a 'framework for best practice farmers' market operators to exchange information, coordinate policy and promote producer farmers' markets across Australia'. The AFMA is a voluntary-run, not-for-profit organisation dedicated to the sustainable development and growth of a national famers' market sector (Australian Farmers' Market Association, 2014). Farmers' Market New Zealand Incorporated (FMNZ) is a membership organisation of approximately 25 independently owned and operated farmers' markets and over 1000 small food businesses. Their mission is 'to promote and support the development of Farmers' Markets in New Zealand' (Farmers' Markets New Zealand, 2014). This organisation seeks to facilitate the growth of a farmers' market network, support sustainable development of markets by sharing and providing appropriate resources, act on behalf of its members on issues affecting farmers' markets, promote fresh local food benefits and facilitate communication between members and stakeholders (Farmers' Markets New Zealand, 2014).

FARMA is a cooperative of approximate 500 businesses across the UK. FARMA assists its members by providing expert advice regarding new business ventures and management, supporting and promoting local direct sales and maintaining high standards within the farm retail sector through its highly successful farmers' markets certification scheme (National Farmers' Retail and Markets Association, 2014).

The National Farmers' Market Association (NFMA) is a volunteer-run organisation in the USA aspiring to connect people with opportunities to access fresh food. The NFMA relies on public donations and a Board of Directors oversees and guides the association and its volunteers. This organisation promotes health awareness and health standards in food eating, aims to keep local businesses thriving and educates the public on the benefits of being part of a farmers' market.

Challenges in Future Farmers' Market Development

Although there are a number of benefits to both the farmer and consumer for participation in a farmers' market, future challenges within the industry exist and need to be addressed.

Finding and maintaining a niche amongst changing consumer demand and increasing competition is a major challenge for those participating in farmers' markets. Competing with larger farms or producers and vendors selling similar produce at a much cheaper price is also a challenging issue for participants (Griffin & Frongillo, 2003). Consumers feel that farmers' markets provide high-quality produce at a reasonable price and, therefore, the integrity of the produce must be assured. A quality assurance programme must be established to ensure that a consistent quality product is delivered to the consumer (Coster & Kennon, 2005).

There is often a high reliance on volunteers in managing farmers' markets and it is vital that these personnel are supported with appropriate training. Organisers devote a large amount of time to communicating with and recruiting stall-holders and this raises issues of 'burn-out' and the need for succession planning (Hede & Stokes, 2009). High-quality leaders to 'champion' the market and a supportive local community are required. A lack of local support, poor management and inexperience with private entrepreneurship and marketing remain major obstacles to broader involvement in farmers' markets (Syrovatkova et al., 2014). Maintaining grower commitment to the market, ensuring a year-round supply of produce and overcoming a lack of product diversity may also be major challenges for market organisers (Coster & Kennon, 2005; Griffin & Frongillo, 2003; Guthrie et al., 2006). Balancing the mix for the market requires time and effort and includes both a broadly attractive mix of stall holders and the programing of additional activities such as entertainment and demonstrations (Smith & Xiao, 2008). Funding and costs remain an issue for future market development as does securing appropriate market infrastructure, especially relating to covered market space (Griffin & Frongillo, 2003). A coordinated approach to public liability insurance, health regulations and local by-laws must also be considered in future market development and operations (Morales & Kettles, 2009).

A major factor contributing to the resurgence of farmers' markets is the increased demand for locally grown produce. Tapping into this local demand (those consumers seeking fresh local produce) is a major challenge for farmers and producers, especially when local supermarkets are selling produce labelled 'local' and 'home grown' (Griffin & Frongillo, 2003; Hunt, 2007). Further research needs to be conducted into the operations of best practice markets and communicated to assist in successful market development.

9 Food for Nutrition

2001: A Space Odyssey (1968)

Stanley Kubrick's masterpiece provides an insightful understanding of how mankind has moved from hunter-gatherer to consumer in an age of technological revolution. It conjures up themes of some great stages of life, namely 'Eating, Killing, Reproducing, Dying and Evolution' (Agel, 1970). Reviewing only the eating scenes in the movie, there is a clear evolution of humans and the food they eat and how they eat it. At the beginning, the proto-humans are foraging for scarce resources and competing with others tribal groups while under the threat of being eaten by feline predators. This reflects what we know about the human fight for survival, which 'depended on an ability to learn about and use the environment in the search for food as well as for protection from threats' (Crouch, 2013: 5). The appearance of the mysterious alien Monolith affects the evolution of the proto-humans sleeping nearby. They are transformed, using primitive weaponry to kill their competition. Food becomes a symbol of status in this prehistoric group, as well as a focus for envy (Crouch, 2013).

Fast forward millions of years and humans are shown flying in Pan Am shuttle spacecraft to space stations (Crouch, 2001), where they wait to catch connecting flights to the Moon. These passengers are passively seated, consuming processed food through a straw whilst deciphering pictures to determine their flavour. These humans are as far removed from the origins of their food as it is possible to be. They have neither gathered nor cooked their food and what they consume seems stripped of fibre and texture. On the spaceship *Discovery*, food is served as multi-coloured pastes on a segregated plastic tray reminiscent of American television dinners. The first space station scene shows Dr Floyd sitting in a lounge consuming fake sandwiches which he comments are 'getting better all the time'. It is a bleak vision of a future in space that is bland and without visceral stimulation.

Introduction

Despite the excitement that greeted the film at the time, space travel – and eating in space – is still not a commonplace event. As John Pike, former space policy analyst for the Federation of America Scientists, noted in 2001, the year in which the film was set: 'Pan Am went bust, there are no bases on the Moon, and the (International) Space Station doesn't have a Hilton' (quoted in Davidson, 2001). Yet the media coverage and general interest that greeted the news of the first lettuce grown on the *International Space Station* (Kitson, 2015) suggests that future space tourists will not be content with eating pills to ensure adequate nutrition. Food is a sensory pleasure, not just a means of staying alive. This is one of the paradoxes that this chapter confronts.

There is a growing interest in nutrition, which may be traced to the strong influence of celebrities promoting nutritional food, an increase in 'healthy' food programmes through educational initiatives and the impact of government policy. Given we know so much these days about nutrition and food is so much more plentiful than ever before, why are people generally eating worse diets than their parents and grandparents, and what can be done about it? The facilitation of informed choices about food and improving general health through what we eat is one of the great challenges facing contemporary governments around the world. A particularly vexed issue is the provision of food in institutional settings, where merely ensuring adequate nutrition might have a deleterious effect on morale and well-being.

This chapter includes an investigation of two high-profile chefs who encourage the eating of healthier food, one being Jamie Oliver in the UK and the other being Stephanie Alexander in Australia. They are focusing on children in particular, in the hope that good food habits learnt while young will last a lifetime and be passed on to their children in turn. Others are concentrating on parents as role models for their children. We also mention the relatively new concept of celebrity endorsement of superfoods.

We conclude with a case study of space tourism as an instructive example of the challenges of ensuring adequate nutrition in an extreme environment. Not only will food need to be provided for lengthy trips, but it will also have to be nutritionally balanced and served appropriately for space travel. This initially means that the food offered in space may forfeit taste for nutritional value and convenience. However, there are also issues in that taste buds are dulled in space (thereby requiring more heavily seasoned food) and coping with boredom will be a key factor in the experience. It will also be important to establish self-sufficient food sources such as gardens when humans eventually colonise the Moon and Mars. We discuss how television programmes such as *Star Trek* (1966 onwards) and *Lost in Space* (1965–1968) have influenced our perceptions of eating in space and how the reality will compare with the imaginary version.

Food, Glorious Food

The key message is not to overeat. But why do we eat at all? Food is necessary for the survival of humans, providing nutrients and energy. Water, minerals, fibre and vitamins are essential but provide little to no energy, whereas carbohydrates, fats and sugar provide energy. All are necessary for the structure of body cells and for the body to function properly. However, it is widely acknowledged that there are good and bad nutrients (Scrinis, 2013). It is also known that, for good health, humans should consume the amount of calories required to satisfy their needs, although overconsumption of food is becoming problematic in many cultures.

Realising that food is essential for survival and the proper functioning of the human body, why do people choose foods that are not nutritionally sound? The answer is not as straightforward as it seems. Mankind has evolved from the hunter-gatherer way of acquiring food to mass production of refined foods through technology. Through each era of food production advancement, sometimes the nutritional aspects of natural food has been lost, changed or genetically modified to suit the changing tastebuds of modern humans (Tapsell, 2013). We are also increasingly removed from the source of our food. It may be difficult to know what we are eating and how nutritious it really is. This situation is only exacerbated by meal plan services, where ready-made meals are delivered to the home and promoted as a convenient way to access a nutritionally balanced diet. These meals might also form a cornerstone of a weight-loss programme, such as the meals that have helped to build the Jenny Craig empire. Yet they are a costly substitute for eating and preparing fresh food and don't give people an understanding of the right food choices when they eat outside the home. They also don't provide the satisfaction of cooking a meal from scratch and knowing exactly what ingredients and produce went into it and why.

The finding, producing and acquisition of food is only one consideration of the modern food palate. For a start, human beings often eat for emotional reasons, and associate food with comfort or a reward. Television programmes such as *The Biggest Loser* illustrate this graphically. Its taste, smell, sight and sound can appeal as well as repel. People may eat out of boredom or habit, rather than hunger. Alternatively, food can be enjoyed as a social ritual, and for its links to personal identity and culture. Australian chef Kylie Kwong makes this point:

> The combination of 'multi' and 'culture' brings to mind a beautiful, blended images of large, close-knit families, delicious food and markets, exotic religion and ritual, different skin colours and tones, intriguing customs and traditions, textures and layers within the world of art, literature, drama and music; a richness and a diversity of people and life. (Kwong, 2003: 6)

Kwong is trying to articulate the complexity and symbolism of food in a multicultural society. Her recipes and dishes served to diners at her Sydney restaurant Billy Kwong are created based on ethnicity, tradition, culture, family, geographical location and seasonal availability. This cannot always be communicated in a cookbook. In 2003/2004, a television series featuring Kwong aired on Australia's ABC network titled *Heart and Soul*. Through this series, Kwong tried to showcase the nutritional value of the dishes she was preparing, but also the history of the dish (albeit in different locations, with local specialities and customs). She showed that nutritional considerations need not be ignored in order to achieve a satisfying and delicious meal.

As influential as celebrity chefs are, there are other powerful organisations that influence our food consumption patterns. These include food standard associations, corporations and government. In this next section, we investigate the influence of government policy and how it affects people relying on government-supported meals.

Government Food Policy

Research into food and nutrition is a topic of interest to governments when it is of public concern. This could be due to an increase in overall public health issues, pressures on hospitals or the rising statistics of diet-related diseases and ailments such as diabetes and heart attacks (Duff, 2004). Studies have found that humans will generally choose a balanced diet if the produce is available; however, *freedom of choice* of foods is paramount in Western cultures (Fischler, 1981; Tapsell, 2013). Fischler (1981) argued that a human omnivore will naturally select a variety of foods within each food category but will base much of their decisions on taste. That could lead to selecting appropriate or inappropriate food choices without taking into account nutritional value. He argues that the way food is being consumed is also changing. It is common for the standard three meals a day in Western society to be ignored, with an individual perhaps only consuming one of the traditional breakfast, lunch or dinner meals owing to time pressures of work and/or family life. This has led to an increase in *snacking*, which is dominated by processed foods high in sugar, fat and additives (Warin, 2011). Celebrity chefs might be selected to promote these snack foods, effectively endorsing a product that may not be nutritionally focused. This can be controversial. Australian chef Darren Simpson developed a burger range for KFC in 2011 and ran the gauntlet of social media. According to fellow chef Colin Fassnidge: 'If you read Twitter, he's destroyed – he's a laughing stock' (quoted in Halliwell, 2011). Interestingly, American chef Rachael Ray's recent endorsement of iced coffee at Dunkin' Donuts was criticised and later pulled, not on health grounds, but because of concerns about the ethnic origins of her scarf (Bukszpan, 2015).

Tapsell (2013) argued that nutrition from food needs to be constantly assessed as problems can be identified at various levels including individual, community and institutional levels. She asserted that food choices are up to the individual and therefore individuals have responsibility for their own health. At a community level, it may be a function of the food products that are available in local gardens, food markets, supermarkets and other food stores. In some cases, *urban food deserts* have become apparent, being neighbourhoods with no fresh food available in retail outlets. At an institutional level, governments and/or non-government agencies shape the food standards that suppliers must follow including food additives, food handling and labelling laws. As there are many food stakeholders, this can be difficult to monitor but it is viewed as the government's responsibility to try and do so. It is acknowledged, however, that differing cultures, traditions and religions may influence food choices, which government food policy may not be able to influence (Duff, 2004).

Food stakeholders include health services, government organisations, nongovernment organisations (e.g. the National Heart Foundation of Australia), professional societies (e.g. the American Society of Nutrition or the British Nutrition Foundation), schools, universities, research and development sectors, food-related primary industries (e.g. farms), food manufacturing industries, retail and other food outlets. All have an input into food and nutrition policy and all have separate agendas. Some stakeholders are monitoring the health of the population based on nutritional intake, while the main priority of others is to make a livelihood or extremely large profits. Tapsell (2013) and the 17 contributors to her book advocated that there needed to be a balance between all stakeholders and that this can only be achieved through constant monitoring and reporting to form strong food policy.

According to Duff (2004), the overall creation of food policy at a government level tends to be based on a cost–benefit analysis, given that it is difficult for governments to influence every person's food intake decision at every meal. Continued and improved education programmes about nutrition at an early age are likely to shape individual preferences in later life (Gormley *et al.*, 1987). This equates with the work of chefs such as Jamie Oliver discussed in this chapter. There is, however, a growing recognition that parents also need to be educated to assist their children in making healthy choices. As American chef Nikki Shaw noted at the launch of the Healthy and Nutritious Meals Awareness Campaign by the National Childhood Obesity Foundation of America on 14 August 2014, 'Making smart food choices starts at the grocery store. If the adults don't buy junk food, it won't be available to the children at home'.

Nutrition Education Through Celebrity Status

English born Jamie Oliver is a best-selling author and television cooking show presenter who has been an advocate of 'home cooking' for over a decade. He is a well-known food campaigner trying to change government food policy in schools to tackle childhood obesity in the UK, America and Australia. Another food campaigner for children's health is the highly respected Australian chef Stephanie Alexander. These two celebrity chefs will be used to illustrate the power of the media in changing food policy at a government level.

There are many examples of where food and nutrition can be intrinsically linked to the health of individuals and it has been suggested that heath education should start with children. Through the media and various television programmes, Jamie Oliver has been the face of tackling the growing obesity problems of children and adults, including educational campaigns such as *Jamie's Ministry of Food* (2008). The name alludes to the Ministry of Food established by the UK Government in the Second World War to educate the British public about nutrition during a time of food rationing (Hollows & Jones, 2010; Warin, 2011). In Jamie's opinion, a similar campaign is needed in modern-day UK and Australia: 'By teaching people to start cooking for themselves once again and equipping them with some simple skills and knowledge, the campaign aims to inspire and empower change in the way people eat and think about food' (Jamie's Ministry of Food, 2012).

Despite the pioneering work of Alice Waters to improve school lunches in the USA, which she argued teaches students that 'good food is a right in life' (Bryant, 2014: 27), Oliver incurred much resistance in the beginning to radically changing the food offering in school canteens, as illustrated in his television series *Jamie's School Dinners* (2005). He did, however, successfully obtain the backing of many governments in many countries to invest money into at least trialling better food and funding ongoing nutritional initiatives. As Oliver observed:

> Everything we do is about improving lives through better knowledge of food, where it comes from and how it affects our bodies. Whether it's training disengaged young people to give them careers in the restaurant industry; campaigning for real food in schools; teaching kids how to grow and cook food; or teaching adults who have missed out on those skills how to cook from scratch, we want to show that making simple choices can make a big difference. (Oliver, 2014)

However, there is debate over whether Jamie Oliver promotes contradictory messages. He can be seen as a 'moral entrepreneur' fighting obesity and high sodium intake (Hollows & Jones, 2010) and he is studying for a degree in nutrition at St Mary's University in Twickenham, because he 'wanted to have proper knowledge' to pass on to his audience (Roberts, 2014). Unlike most students, his tutors travel to him to deliver their classes, but his intentions are good.

Clawson (2010) wrote a book highlighting Oliver as a powerful media figure who has morphed and re-invented himself to continually remain relevant and, more importantly, to protect the strong personal brand that Jamie's empire now relies on. Oliver has successfully campaigned in the UK and America to secure government funds to showcase nutritional cooking that is easy and affordable in designated cooking schools across the countries.

Another celebrated restaurateur, chef, and food writer, Stephanie Alexander, spearheaded the campaign to create kitchen gardens in Australian primary schools to get kids 'back to the garden', growing fruits and vegetables that can be served in the school canteen (Figure 9.1). More importantly, these food programmes educate children about where food comes from and its nutritional value, so that, as the children become adults, they can make more informed decisions about their food intake. It has been so successful that it has been implemented in over 180 Australian government-funded schools, giving students the 'opportunity to plant, nurture, harvest, prepare and share fresh, nutritious, and seasonal food' (Block et al., 2012: 420). It is also intended to promote a return to communal family meals. Stephanie Alexander shared the philosophy behind the campaign and what she hoped it would lead to:

> I believe absolutely in the importance and power of the shared table. In many cultures, eating together around a table is the centre of family life. It is the meeting place, where thoughts are shared, ideas challenged, news

Figure 9.1 Stephanie Alexander and children from the Kitchen Garden programme (source: Stephanie Alexander Kitchen Garden Foundation)

is exchanged and where the participants leave the table restored in many ways. (Alexander, 2014)

The *rules* for the Stephanie Alexander Kitchen Garden Foundation programme are simple and direct (Alexander, 2009):

- Encourage fun, flavour and texture through experiences that engage all the senses.
- Model good food choices without resorting to pyramids or labels of 'healthy' or 'unhealthy' food.
- Reinforce techniques repeatedly, providing the confidence to plant seeds or cook simple dishes at home.
- Plan menus around the fresh, seasonal produce growing in the garden.
- Use ingredients at their peak – seasonal herbs, crisp vegetables, fresh fruits.
- Expand culinary horizons, presenting cultural differences as fascinating rather than strange.
- Expand vocabularies for describing foods, flavours, textures, plants and processes.
- Food should be delicious and the cooking of fresh fruit and vegetables should be timed with great care.
- Come together at the end of the cooking to share a meal around the table.

It is clear from these guidelines that the philosophy of food should not solely be focused on nutrition. There are many elements to encouraging children to eat healthy food and that includes making it fun, getting the children involved and making eating a social and *slow* experience, rather than grazing or grabbing food on the run. Stephanie Alexander has plans to continue to expand the programme to all kindergarten and primary schools Australia-wide, but knows that to remain successful and relevant, funding by the government is essential as well as the backing of teachers, parents and children alike.

There are other programmes worldwide that offer similar gardens in schools and community gardens, often helping the disadvantaged and poor tackle obesity (Castro *et al.*, 2013), as it is clear that these types of programmes assist in disseminating nutritional knowledge through education and changing food choices (Gibbs *et al.*, 2013). These programmes all have educational and nutritional benefits as a theme but generally exist without any celebrity or broad media exposure.

Feeding People in Government Institutions

Having the media focus on school food programmes that uncovered mass production of unhealthy food made the general public pay attention. However, there does not seem to be the same focus on food served in our jails and hospitals. For example, findings relating to nutritional foods in jails have been published that have linked low nutritional intake diets to inappropriate behaviour problems such as aggressive behaviour and rule-breaking in adolescent males in prison (Zaalberg *et al.*, 2010). This is thought to be associated with the increased amount of fat and sugar levels available with reduced food choices and the spikes associated with only consuming food at designated meal times. Additionally, it appears that there are some differences based on gender and race but overall there seems to be a higher sodium intake in jails, leading to increase risks of cardiovascular disease and diabetes (Trexler & Sargent, 1993). Prisons do have a recommended dietary intake and portion sizes; however, it is up to the individual to choose the type and quantity of personal food consumption.

While prisoners are generally aware of their daily dietary intake as directed by dietary guidelines, owing to boredom and depression, the majority will consume additional food, adding to a higher risk health problems (Eves & Gesch, 2003). This phenomenon is not limited to adolescent males. A study conducted by Shaw *et al.* (2008) suggested that female prisoners also had acceptable dietary guidelines for calorie intake; however, the majority of women put on weight owing to boredom and reduced exercise spaces.

Hospitals are also not immune to the issues of nutritional intake of patients. Dupertuis *et al.* (2003) highlight that eating offers comfort to patients and food is necessary for their recovery and ultimate survival. These authors, however, conclude that two-thirds of hospital patients do not receive the necessary nutritional needs during longer hospital visits. This could be for a variety of reasons, including inadequate food provision, inadequate food consumption, the underlying disease or illness or simply because patients have a suppressed appetite when feeling unwell. Other authors suggest that it may be due to clinical practice having insufficient nutritional knowledge, a low priority given to nutritional needs, unclear feeding procedures, lack of time or lack of responsibility to assist in feeding patients (Kondrup *et al.*, 2002). Whatever the reason, it causes many ill patients to lose weight in hospital and a large amount of food wastage.

Although these problems exist in jails and hospitals, there have been no celebrities or even the general media drawing attention to these issues. These problems are just as real for government-funded institutions as they are for schools, so why do celebrities and the media choose to ignore the issue? Berry (2011) suggests that there is no real benefit for the media to intervene or no opportunity for the private sector to make money and therefore these sectors are overlooked. In the case of jails, the lack of attention given by politicians to prison food might result from concerns that this will be unpopular amongst voters or constituents, akin to making jail a holiday resort. There may also be an element of treating the incarcerated as *scapegoats*, where they must suffer 'as a repository for our fears and aggressions about crime and violence and those who are accused of committing such acts' (Gould, 2015: 180). It takes a lurid tale in the media to cut through this indifference, such as the recent exposé about a convicted drug-dealer who argued that prison food made her hair fall out (Crawford, 2015).

However, positive media coverage is often given to programmes that assist the elderly in maintaining independence and receiving at least one meal a day with high nutritional content. For example, the *Meals on Wheels* programme started in Britain during the Second World War, to assist service personnel, and has subsequently been adopted by Australia, Canada and the USA. It is based on a volunteer workforce, and nutritious meals are prepared and delivered to people's homes (Tapsell, 2013), allowing the elderly to remain in their homes with someone checking up on them daily and giving a 'good' meal. This also allows for social interaction, which is important in many people's lives.

It appears that the media can play a role in highlighting the nutritional issues associated with institutional meals, such as celebrities bringing attention to schools and securing government funding for educational programmes. However, with little to no media reporting on jails and hospitals, unless it is a *feel good* story or based on such sensational material that it can't be overlooked, inadequate nutritional concerns remain unpublicised by mainstream media outlets even though there is a shift by nutritional organisations to move away from mass-produced processed food to have more nutritional and 'fresh' food choices.

Superfoods

Jamie Oliver and Stephanie Alexander have both referred to superfoods on their cooking shows. Superfoods are generally classified as delivering large quantities of select nutrients that assist the human body with its daily functions and are generally linked to good health. Examples include blueberries, salmon and almonds. Additionally, Pratt and Matthews (2004) also suggest that superfoods can actually change the individual biochemistry in your body and stop damage by preventing diseases at a cellular level. The trend to increase the superfoods in people's diets is obvious when looking at the marketing of produce. Television advertisements, testimonials selling food preparation equipment and nutritionists on specific television segments all highlight the benefits of consuming superfoods. Both Jamie Oliver and Stephanie Alexander have endorsed the international supermarket chain Woolworths. Images of Jamie and Stephanie holding superfood items such as avocadoes are at the register checkout of Woolworths in Australia, with slogans referring to 'healthy eating', 'superfoods' and 'affordability', and featured in their in-store magazine titled *Fresh*.

Although consuming these superfoods can have positive benefits, far too much emphasis has been placed on nutrition alone. To be healthy overall, there needs to be a balance between genetics, the environment, lifestyle and diet, known as the *health cycle* (Gormley *et al.*, 1987). It is interesting to note that diet is only one-sixth of a human's health cycle, which is affected mainly by lifestyle and then the environment. Although consuming super-foods does have an impact on the nutritional intake into our bodies, it is only one of four elements and the least significant. It would be of greater benefit to the public if the media highlighted superfoods as a subset of lifestyle and environment, which people can also control.

Food in Space

Computer – bacon and eggs!
(Captain Kirk's command, *Star Trek* television series)

After these words were spoken, the computer initiated a *food synthesiser* aboard the spaceship *Enterprise* in which Captain Kirk's bacon and eggs mate-rialised out of nowhere. This fictitious technology was designed to assist the on-board chef with food preparation. Characters in the television series sug-gested that the food was similar to 'natural food', but they could tell the difference between the two. As *Star Trek* gained popularity, the next advance-ment in fictional food technology was *food replicators* that reputably tasted the same as the order that was placed – 'the ultimate solution to the world food crisis' (Yeoman & McMahon-Beattie, 2015: 29). The third advancement for humans was a *protein re-sequencer* that beamed natural and organic food from a distant source to their location, in which the food was deemed exactly the same as if grown on the planet. Interestingly, the Robinson family in *Lost in Space* combined high-tech meals that simply emerged on pressing a button (and protein pills on occasion) with the luxury of vegetables grown in a hydroponic garden, set up on the surface of one of the numerous planets across the galaxy. The viewing audiences of both these television series were fascinated with the novelty of eating in space.

Leaving fiction behind, food in space is 'the final frontier of nutritional research offering unlimited challenges in an environment with the most unknowns' (Boyce, 2011: 45). This author referred to the fact that, even though human consumption of food in space has already occurred, there are still many aspects that still need to be explored as space exploration contin-ues and expands. From the first space travel in the 1960s 'the development of space food has evolved from tubes to cubes to near Earth-like cuisine over the past 30 years' (Bourland, 1993: 271). Bourland further suggested 'there are unresolved problems related to space food such as nutritional require-ments, the variety required, and methods of preservation for long-duration missions' (Bourland, 1993: 271).

Initially, food was initially designed for purely nutritional purposes and consumed from tubes that were not well received by the first astronauts and cosmonauts owing to the lack of taste and smell and the unusual texture. Bite-sized cubes, freeze-dried powders and semiliquids were developed next that were still too bland for the recipients. The powdered orange juice Tang was used on some of the Mercury and Gemini flights, and was also available commercially, much to the delight (or not) of children growing up in the era of the Moon landings. It is still available today. Buzz Aldrin, the second man to walk on the Moon, was less than complimentary, observing 'Tang sucks' (Memmott, 2013).

Kerwin and Seddon (2002) documented two astronauts' perceptions of space food whilst on mission, describing the difficulties of eating, the terrible food and the inevitable complications of using the toilet facilities. Many astronauts opted to reduce their consumption of food based on these concerns. Bourland (1993) suggested that space food only has nutritional value if it is consumed, and the first space missions indicated a dislike for the food products as much of it was returned to Earth unopened. This made nutritionists develop other food offerings assisted by advances in technology. There is now a large variety of food items that can be reheated and consumed in circumstances that mimic meals prepared on Earth.

The primary goal of future space flight with respect to meals is to develop food systems that are palatable for the crew, nutritious and safe, with minimal size and volume and able to withstand long-duration space travel (Perchonok & Bourland, 2002). There are some 'out of the box' ideas that are currently being tested, such as the silkworm moth, which can offer good protein through larvae and live off inedible biomass that can provide food for people living in extreme conditions such as other planets (Tong *et al.*, 2011). The recent publicity given to the growing of a lettuce on the *International Space Station* is a step forward. As Kitson (2015) noted, 'growing vegetables and fruit can have a positive effect on an astronaut's mental well-being', as well as allowing them to be somewhat self-sufficient, rather than relying completely on supplies from Earth.

However, the bulk of an astronaut's diet is more likely to be drawn from a variety of products that have extended shelf-lives, providing the nutrients required for good health, as well as being palatable and acceptable to astronauts (Cooper *et al.*, 2011). A recent NASA-funded team of six researchers spent four months living in a dome on a Hawaiian lava-field to examine the optimal foods and cooking techniques for a long-duration space mission. They concocted several dishes using the tinned meat product Spam, for example. The researchers were pleased with the taste of the freeze-dried products provided to them, which replicated the real thing back home. Problems occurred, however, when using non-perishable ingredients, as they were generally 'highly processed, and lacked fibre' (Associated Press, 2013).

There are serious consequences of inadequate nutrition for these long missions. For example, monitoring levels of calcium and vitamin D will be vital to help minimise the loss of bone mass or *osteopenia*, which occurs when the human skeleton is not subjected to the Earth's gravitational forces. This is a major health concern inherent in a long flight at *zero-g* to reach Mars. Other potential health problems during long-duration space flight include muscle atrophy and the risk of exposure to radiation (White & Averner, 2001).

Any missions to the Moon and certainly Mars will require long periods of time to be spent on the surface and there may also be plans to set up a permanent base in the future. It will not be possible to rely totally on food supplied from Earth (Zubrin, 1996). The Martian regolith appears to be devoid of biological material and may even be toxic in places (Murphy, 2010). While it could be treated to make it more Earth-like, the early Martian settlements are more likely to grow their food hydroponically in enclosed greenhouses, where soil is not needed and external temperatures can be controlled. This is the method used to grow vegetables in Antarctica at the various bases (Murphy, 2010), which is a partial analogue for the extreme environment of the Red Planet. Sources of animal protein might be limited to the cultivation of small creatures such as fish, seafood and insects (Murphy, 2010; Zubrin, 1996). The variety of food available to settlers might increase over time, as Mars is *terraformed* (made more Earth-like), either naturally or intentionally (Cockell, 2007; Zubrin, 1996).

Boredom will be a problem with a potentially monotonous diet (Koerth-Baker, 2013). On long stays down in Antarctica during expeditions, leaders such as Ernest Shackleton and Robert Falcon Scott understood the importance of providing special food to boost morale. On Scott's 1912 expedition, the men celebrated mid-winter with a decorated Christmas tree, jokes, whistles and plum pudding (Cherry-Garrard, 1922). In the NASA-funded study mentioned earlier in this chapter, the researchers living in isolation found that comfort foods were vital, such as stores of the hazelnut and chocolate spread, Nutella. According to the commander, Angelo Vermeulen, the researchers were forced to ration it, to ensure that they all were able to satisfy their chocolate cravings (Associated Press, 2013).

Whatever eventuates from technology designed by humans, it is clear that food in space has had a long continuing evolution. People in general are fascinated with these technological advances, which are a staple of science-fiction films and television series, although it remains to be seen how readily these innovations will be transferable back on Earth and how they might affect human nutrition in the future (Cockell, 2007).

The Future for Nutrition

If we accept that there are *good* and *bad* nutrients, it is only through education that individuals can be better informed about the food-related decisions they need to make. This can be done through educational campaigns and food labelling rather than relying on profit-driven food manufacturing companies that use mainstream advertising as enticements for selecting so-called 'bad nutrients' (Scrinis, 2013). A key assumption in promoting good nutrition is that stakeholders will be ethical in their representation of labelling and marketing individual food products.

Celebrities play a major role in the promotion of nutritional food in today's society, with Jamie Oliver and Stephanie Alexander being exemplars. It is also apparent that both of these celebrities endorse individual products such as superfoods and promote supermarkets, which might influence their ability to remain totally impartial.

Looking to the future, food in space has been depicted in books and television for over half a century. Science fiction such as *Star Trek* and *2001: A Space Odyssey* showcase how food storage, preparation and consumption have morphed and changed over time; however, this revolutionary process is actually what is happening in real space travel. Although current space food techniques have not quite replicated how food is consumed on Earth, advances in technology make it more and more plausible in the future. When we eventually travel to and inhabit the Moon and Mars, it will be imperative that we are able to grow food and be self-sufficient. Through technology transfer, these experiments may help us to grow food back on Earth in the most unlikely and unhospitable of places and to improve the nutritional value of the food we eat.

10 Food Trucks and Pop-up Restaurants

Chef (2014)

The movie *Chef (2014)* depicts a number of life challenges for Chef Carl Casper (Jon Favreau) who suddenly decides to resign from his job at a renowned Los Angeles restaurant after refusing to compromise his creative integrity concerning the restaurant menu selection. Returning to his home town of Miami with his ex-wife Inez (Sofia Vergara), and his son Percy (Emjay Anthony) for a short break, he is convinced to launch a food truck enterprise. His friend Martin (John Leguizamo) joins him in this venture and Carl, Martin and Percy drive the food truck across America from Miami to Los Angeles.

In the opening scene of the movie, chef Carl is found in a commercial kitchen preparing mise en place for the next meal session. He is a passionate and creative chef who has been stifled by the restrictive restaurant manager Riva (Dustin Hoffman). Riva is only interested in having a chef churning out dependable but prescriptive recipes that have been on the bill-of-fare for too many years. The restaurant menu is now very passé. A food blogger, Ramsey Michel (Oliver Platt), who respects and admires the work of Carl, comes to critique the restaurant. Carl is forbidden by Riva to develop a new and edgy menu and is instructed to follow the true and tried pedestrian menu of the past years. Carl follows the manager's instructions, but then receives a very damning review via cyber space. He naively responds to the review, believing it is a private message to the blogger, inviting him to return and sample an exciting new menu. This plan is once again fought by the restaurateur and Carl decides to resign his position and uphold his personal culinary creativity and integrity.

The next confrontation between Carl and Ramsey (the food blogger), occurs when the critic pays a second visit and is served similar food. After his resignation, Carl also visits the restaurant that night, determined to clear his name. A confrontation occurs and escalates to an uncontrollable rant from Carl that becomes a raucous public video going viral via YouTube.

Carl's cooking career is now in ruins and employment prospects have disappeared. Without any job offers, he decides to take a trip to Miami with his ex-wife Inez and son, Percy. He is convinced to take on the resurrection of a food truck, and calls it El Jefe (Spanish for 'the chief' – chef and chief share the same etymology). He decides to sell Cuban-style food, (especially Cuban sandwiches), influenced by his ex-wife's family heritage. With his old colleagues from the last establishment joining him, he and his son make a road trip across America taking the truck home. They stop to sell their mobile food truck delights along the way, testing the market for this type of cuisine. Percy, who is social media savvy, actively engages with Facebook and Twitter. Before their arrival at each destination, his social media outputs have provided the food truck with prior marketing and promotion exposure to the locals. The truck is a roaring success in all the locations they visit, selling out of all their delicious wares in no time and this reinvigorates the chefs with a passion for what they are doing.

The movie ends with the establishment of a new restaurant El Jefe, now owed by Chef Carl Casper. It is financially backed by Ramsey (the food blogger), after he has sampled and been very impressed with the Cuban-style food at a popular food truck location in Los Angeles. The last scenes depict a remarriage celebration for Chef Carl and his ex-wife Inez. There is a happy ending for all.

This movie illustrates the power of social media to alternatively promote or defame both bricks-and-mortar dining establishments and also the rising phenomenon of pop-up businesses such as food trucks. This cinematic experience provides an excellent example of the growth of food trucks and their connection and the benefits that are able to be gained from new social media platforms.

The Pop-up Concept

Life in the 21st century has taken on the mantle of uncertainty. The societal bonds and support networks of the past have diminished. Globalization has introduced new challenges and has intensified the pace of life, suggesting we now live in a *liquid* society where life is unpredictable and forever changing (Bauman, 2007). The concept of temporary or rather pop-up establishments reflects this phenomenon, providing surprising and unexpected food and beverage purchasing experiences, moving the consumer from stable and familiar circumstances to what might be called the cutting edge of industry practices (Surchi, 2011; Yeoman & McMahon-Beattie, 2015).

In the present commercial arena, pop-up retail has been embraced by the business sector across the globe as a strategy to provide an experiential shopping environment that is now desired by the adventurous consumer. It is a way to attract the attention of new customers, while developing a brand image and identity. This combines to provide an exciting, if only temporary, shopping experience (Niehm *et al.*, 2007).

Bergqvist and Leinoff (2011) indicated that pop-up retail can complement and augment online retail. The pop-up provides a vehicle for consumers to personally access and sample products unexpectedly for a short period of time. This has the capacity to extend and develop an online company's promotional mix. This strategy can provide a boost for sales owing to the temporary nature of the pop-up outlet's existence. Trust and confidence can be low when dealing with online vendors and the establishment of a pop-up outlet – even for a limited time – can go some way to assist with these issues. Online retailers can utilise pop-up outlets to overcome distrust and difficulty in making quality judgements concerning products and assist in developing loyalty from consumers in the market place. Pop-up shops assist in testing the potential of the market and also aid in obtaining direct reactions from the consumer, enabling the retailer to make modifications and alterations to the product mix based on this valuable feedback.

Pop-up outlets in the retail sector allow the public to connect with knowledgeable brand representatives and provide a feedback loop, while also hopefully generating positive word of mouth concerning the company's products (Kim *et al.*, 2010). Mulvihill (2010) further explained that a pop-up shop is a way for sellers to introduce a brand to the market without the usual long-term rental contracts and large financial commitment. He also suggested that there are valuable benefits for retail property owners in accepting this short-term arrangement. An example of this was in New York, where building owners in 2010 embraced the concept because it was a vehicle to fill, at least in the short term, valuable vacant space that had appeared because of the downturn in the American economy. Another benefit of the short-term leasing transaction is the ability to show off or showcase your retail space at its best, thus improving the possibility of attracting another potential rental client for a long-term lease.

An Innovative Dining Phenomenon

The pop-up concept has been readily adopted and can work equally well for enterprises in the hospitality sector, gaining many benefits similar to those mentioned for the retail sector. Numerous pop-up eating establishments have emerged in a variety of different locations worldwide, including the USA, Cuba, the UK, Germany, South Africa and Australia, to name some of the most popular locations.

Pop-up culinary businesses materialise in a variety of guises and can be either static or roving. Food trucks, underground supper clubs that operate from a private home, former factory sites, underutilised or vacant commercial catering sites or outlets set up during a festival can all be classed in this genre. The one feature they all have in common is that they are temporary, springing up unexpectedly and then vanishing. In general, they may be open for business at any one location from as little as one day to possibly as long as 12 months.

Along with the temporary nature of this venture, there are tangible and intangible benefits from this style of enterprise. As with pop-up retail – but even more so because of the expensive equipment required for catering operations – there is a lesser financial risk compared with setting up a standard bricks-and-mortar hospitality business. However, operators must also consider that it might be difficult to build loyalty and a long-standing reputation with such a transitory business.

A restaurateur or chef can often take advantage of underutilised kitchen and dining spaces within a city and provide a pop-up on a night when the kitchen would normally be closed (Dicum, 2010). This strategy can assist in saving money because there are limited set-up costs for specialised equipment and there is no long-term lease arrangement required.

A major incentive or motivation is the possibility of greater personal control over presentation and service protocols, allowing more creativity to experiment with new ideas for the chef and restaurateur (Strand, 2010). Dicum (2010) concurred with this notion and also suggested that the flexibility of the pop-up establishments allowed for creativity, experimentation and the application of seasonal and fresh produce. This quite often translates into a multi-course, fixed price menu, which may be at lower price points for the customer than a similar feast at an established fine dining restaurant, owing to the lower overheads and the desire to attract clients.

Pop-up ventures have brought vitality to the hospitality industry by providing something novel. The adventurous food explorer of the 21st century is looking for distinctive and adventurous experiences that will provide memories and possibly one-upmanship to impress their peers (Laing & Frost, 2015b, see also Chapter 3). Interesting and well-designed food vendors can thrive because they provide a supply of this type of service, a demand which might not be met by the traditional bricks-and-mortar catering establishment, whilst utilising otherwise empty spaces (see Figure 10.1).

The following discourse will explore a variety of the most popular pop-up enterprises models in the culinary arena. Specific examples from across the globe will be utilised to illustrate this phenomenon.

Food Trucks

As illustrated in the movie *Chef* (2014), gourmet food trucks are a popular type of pop-up catering enterprise that has appeared in many cities across the globe. Food trucks have been on the road and stationed at late-night venues for many years; however, there have been some radical changes to create the

Figure 10.1 Espresso Base pop-up tent in the forecourt of a London church (photo J. Laing)

contemporary food truck. There has been a change in how they look, when they sell, what they are selling and how they promote their business enterprises. The contemporary food truck is no longer just serving up greasy hamburgers or hot dogs, but rather delivers a fresh and innovative gourmet offering. The hamburger has not completely disappeared, but it has been dragged into the healthier era of the 21st century. Carter (2013b) points out that other distinctive dishes are appearing on the gourmet food truck's bill-of-fare, such as pastry dumplings filled with kangaroo or sambal chilli tiger prawns with water spinach, both complemented with a ponzu and white truffle sauce.

Bainger (2013) reported a number of conversations with food truck operators. These interviews revealed that many of these operators are taking this new enterprise very seriously by producing food that will appeal to foodies and is adventurous and quirky, while also using local produce. Many have made substantial investments in equipping a well kitted-out food truck, which is visually attractive and commercially inviting. These types of changes and the passion for interesting, high-quality food items were illustrated in the movie *Chef* (2014) discussed earlier, with Cuban-style food being sold from El Jefe.

Food trucks can also enliven and re-invigorate urban landscapes. Whyte (1980) suggested that people are attracted to public spaces because of the presence of others and a sense of 'buzz', and this has been specifically applied to food truck sites by Wessel (2012). Three examples are considered.

USA and Canada

While lunch trucks have long been part of the urban landscape in the USA, recent developments have been more up-market. Their rise may be seen as a product of the financial downturn in the USA, 'at a time when consumers are cutting back on restaurant spending, a food truck selling inexpensive lunches and snacks can be an easier sell to diners … new trucks are rolling in as many restaurants report steep declines in their lunchtime traffic' (McLaughlin, 2009). Some trucks are operated by established restaurants as a way of extending their market reach. One owner of an Austin restaurant had experienced a revenue drop of 20–25%, but this was matched by sales from a new food truck (McLaughlin, 2009).

Across the USA, there is widespread variation in regulations for food trucks. In Seattle they must be on private property, whereas New York issues permits for public parking spots (McLaughlin, 2009). Alexandria, Virginia bans food trucks as out of place with the city's historic character, whereas they are perfectly legal minutes over the border in Washington, DC (Vanessa Harvey, personal communication). In Vancouver, local laws meant that sales were originally restricted to hot dogs. This was dropped in the lead-up to the 2010 Winter Olympics, but there is still tight policing of food trucks. Would-be operators have to be approved by a panel of judges and then there is a lottery to award spaces (McCabe, 2015). In Dallas, San Jose and Phoenix there are restrictions of one hour at a time and no more than three hours at the same location within a 24 hour period. In Los Angeles, a local rule requiring movement every hour was overturned by the courts (Morales & Kettles, 2009). Such easing of regulations suggests that food trucks are now more widely accepted.

Certainly, food trucks seem the epitome of modernity. Their marketing – as in the film *Chef* – is intrinsically linked to social media, particularly Facebook and Twitter. The use of social media is particularly important for interacting with established customers – a form of relationship marketing. In a study of a San Francisco food truck location, Wessel (2012) found that nearly all patrons initially found out about the trucks by word of mouth, but later used social media to keep updated on developments. In addition, there are strong linkages with green concerns. It is common to see businesses marketing that their fish is sustainably harvested and that they use free-range chicken and heritage pork, and the vehicles may be fuelled by vegetable oil or electric powered (McLaughlin, 2009).

Clustering is apparent. At the wonderfully named DUMBO in Brooklyn (Down Under the Manhattan Bridge Overpass), the trucks are contained within a converted parking lot. A video feed accessible by an internet site allows potential patrons to observe how long or short the queues are. Houston has started a For the Love of Food Trucks Festival on Saturday mornings. Interestingly, it charges admission ($1 pre-sale, $5 on the day).

In Vancouver, there is a daily World's Best Food Truck Tour, which includes food at nine trucks (McCabe, 2015).

A host of television shows feature food trucks as part of a media fascination with Dude Food. Two are worth noting. The first is *The Great Food Truck Race* (2010 onwards), a reality show in which contestants set up their food trucks in various US cities. The second is *Diners, Drive-Ins and Dives* (2006 onwards). Its host is Guy Fieri, a restaurateur who had won the reality show *The Next Food Network Star* (2006).

Paris, France

In 2011, Paris, a city renowned for exemplary food and the wonderful pleasures of consuming gastronomic delights, welcomed the first American-style gourmet food truck. Le Camion qui fume ('The Truck That Smokes') was initiated by an American, Kristin Frederick. In 2014, there were two food trucks. Both engaged the promotional advantage of being located at different locations at separate meal times across the city. It was observed that each truck had its own distinctive marketing aspect and was well patronised by the French luncheon consumer because of the cost, service speed, novelty value and quirky food offerings.

The first Paris food truck visited was Le Camion qui fume (Figure 10.2). On that day, the truck was situated at a fresh food market in the Place de Madeleine. One of the food truck staff members was taking orders from a

Figure 10.2 Le Camion qui fume, Paris, France (photo K. Williams)

pre-printed display and allocating each client with a numbered ticket to be called for food dispatch, which took approximately 20 minutes. This system allowed each customer to feel confident about their anticipated wait for their order. The food came in a branded bag. There were no tables for the customers to consume their purchases on site, so customers did move away quickly once they received their food purchase. The pre-printed board had a number of hand written alterations which made it look a little scruffy and did not provide a fresh and up-to-date impression for the customer. This temporary food truck enterprise provided a 'buzzy' atmosphere and added to the ambience of the public space, as suggested by Whyte (1980), and furthermore complemented the fresh food market at Place de Madeleine. In addition to the bill of fare, Le Camion qui fume also promoted a cookbook entitled *Burgers Les Recettes du Camion qui fume* containing recipes from the food truck's wares.

The second food truck was Cantine California, which was located at Marche Raspail, a very popular, traditional open-air market (Figure 10.3). Our first impression of this food truck was that food ordering appeared to be less systematic, even though the truck was also very busy with a waiting queue of potential customers. The food selection of predominantly burgers, tacos and house desserts (especially cupcakes) was on a blackboard menu, which allowed immediate update and alterations of what was available. The side of the truck advertised organic meat and hand pressed tortillas. Unlike the other truck, there were standing tables for the customers to socialise and eat at. This kept a crowd around, increasing the sense of popularity. However, there were no branded bags, as was the case with Le Camion qui fume.

Figure 10.3 Cantine California, Paris, France (photo K. Williams)

Cantine California had also published a cookbook, providing recipes to their customers; however, this was not on display at the food truck.

Both food trucks were identified after conducting a quick search of the internet. The website listed the forward locations and the times of service for the next few days of that week. Recently, both of these trucks have started their own Facebook and Twitter pages, providing extra information, photos and feedback from patrons and staff.

Melbourne and Perth, Australia

Melbourne is considered by many Australians to be the food capital of Australia. The diversity of cuisines is outstanding, with over 178,000 seats in restaurants and cafés available for the public to select for a dining experience (City of Melbourne, 2012). Therefore, how could food trucks compete? It could be suggested that, like so many innovative food ventures, food trucks have been embraced by this city because they represent another inviting aspect of the catering arena. In addition, they are fun, casual and unpretentious.

It was only recently, however, that the City of Melbourne lifted a ban on food trucks operating in the central business district outside of special events (Carter, 2014). Twelve food truck operators were involved in a three month trial in the latter part of 2015 to assess the feasibility and appropriateness of including this type of food outlet in the central city area. In the inner suburbs, there has been a tendency towards permanent or regular clusters. These include the Coburg Drive-In Cinema Food Truck Festival, the Richmond Food Truck Park and the Welcome to Thornbury Food Truck Park. Food trucks are also being utilised at festivals (see Figure 10.4) and even private events such as weddings.

As in the movie *Chef* (2014), marketing and promotion are conducted via social media such as Facebook and Twitter. Food trucks also featured in the television series *Rachel Khoo's Kitchen Notebook Melbourne* (2015). There are, however, some interesting diversions from the American model. Whereas most food trucks in the USA cater for the lunch market, in Melbourne the focus is on evening meals. Furthermore, there is a greater emphasis on alcohol, with food trucks either parking next to bars or clustering in truck parks with purpose-built bars.

Food trucks have become a popular, novel and temporary way to offer a number of different food cuisines at one spot. Higher education institutions such as William Angliss Institute, situated in the central business district of Melbourne, invited a number of food trucks to be on campus during their 2015 orientation week. This provided an extra vibe on the campus during this time.

Similarly, Curtin University in Perth trialled a six month invitation to 10 different gourmet food trucks to come on campus and provide dining

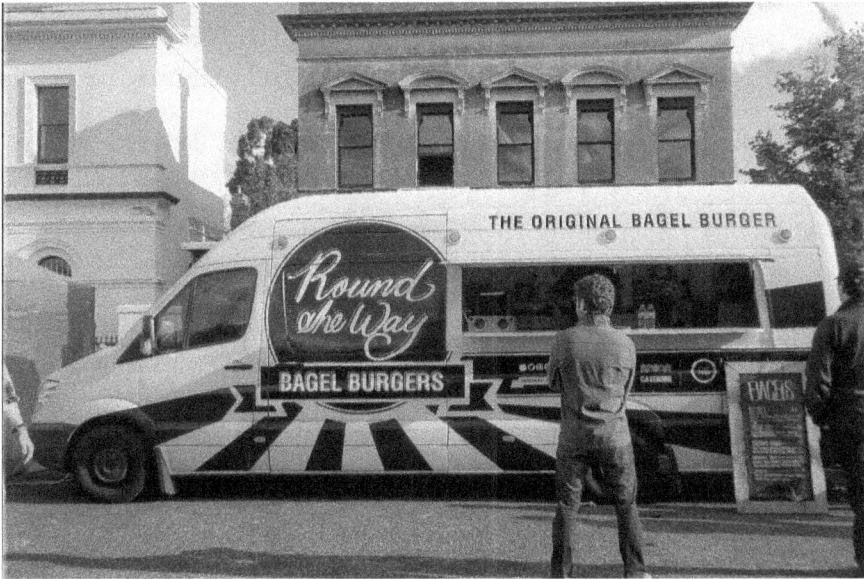

Figure 10.4 Round the Way Bagel Burgers Food Truck, Clunes Booktown Festival, Australia (photo J. Laing)

opportunities for students. Carter (2013b) reported that the trucks operate on different days and at different locations. As with all pop-ups, they are promoted to the students via social media and also the University website. At a similar time to Melbourne, the Perth City Council decided to trial food trucks at 15 locations within the city boundaries. To try to protect against and minimise any financial impact on existing venues, there are restrictions on these traders. For example, their trucks must be parked at least 50 metres from an established restaurant or café.

Pop-up Hospitality Establishments

The pop-up hospitality establishment can provide social interaction for guests in an informal, intimate and exclusive dining environment, especially if conducted in the lounge room of a residential home. The diner of the 21st century is now seeking innovative and unique eating experiences that go beyond the standard restaurant model.

Pop-up restaurants or supper clubs in private homes

Pop-up restaurants have been established in private homes and this underground movement provides a diner with a novel and intimate experience. These establishments may have a slight edgy quality because they may not strictly abide by all the legal requirements of a standard restaurant, adding to the entire escapade. The customer is invited to dine by the internet or by word of mouth. The patrons arrive at the abode and are usually provided with a number of courses prepared in the domestic kitchen. There might be a set price or the payment could be a discretionary contribution decided by the guests. There might be alcohol provided; however, in an attempt to limit legal risk, guests may be requested to supply their own. A desirable aspect of this encounter is that guests are able to socialise freely because there is a predominantly casual and comfortable mood, owing to it being situated in a private home.

Rachel Khoo, the author of *The Little Paris Kitchen* (2012), established a very intimate restaurant in her tiny apartment in Paris. Her motivation for this underground enterprise was to test and trial recipes for her forthcoming cookbook. Khoo opened her home on Wednesdays and Saturdays – linked to the opening of the fresh food markets – and preferred to offer a luncheon menu. She did not charge full price because she decided this was a good way of not wasting food and gaining feedback about her recipes (Wilmoth, 2015). There was only room for just two diners at a time since her abode was so very tiny. Khoo (2012: 10) declared that 'people from all over the world (including the French) booked in and came for lunch … no matter what nationality they were, the thing they loved most was the fact that it was simple home-cooked food'. Her cookbook and culinary adventures are discussed later in Chapter 12.

Tyler (2009) suggested that the customer's attraction to home pop-up restaurants could be connected to the contemporary decline in dinner parties in a domestic setting and the limited opportunities for a person to dress up. Pop-ups restaurants in the home provide a channel for those who are excited about informal dining with friends, even if in this case, one has only just met them that night. This occurrence of meeting and mingling with strangers could also heighten the excitement of this type of dining experience. In addition, there is the attraction of spending some quality time at a stranger's home, providing an entrée into someone else's life and lifestyle, which can be a fascinating experience in itself.

Commercial sites and former factories

Unused or underutilised factories or commercial sites can provide a perfect venue for a fleeting food and beverage venture. They are large enough to accommodate a range of customer group sizes, additionally delivering an interesting atmosphere to the audacious customer looking for an extra-adventurous and stimulating meal experience. Usually these locations are secret and difficult to find for the customer, thus increasing the anticipation for a more captivating and memorable feasting encounter that can be shared with companions on the night or as a dinner table story in the future. These secret sites may disclose the final details concerning location and meal times shortly before opening via an in-the-know social media platform.

Celebrity and/or television ventures

Celebrity chefs are also becoming involved in the pop-up trend even if they suggest they are not. In 2015, Heston Blumenthal opened the Fat Duck in Melbourne, while his restaurant in Bray, Berkshire (UK) was closed for six months for a major renovation. To take advantage of this down-time and to keep the team working together productively and effectively, Blumenthal decided to relocate the restaurant across the world for the duration of the renovation. The entire team, including Blumenthal (when he was not attending other business and media commitments), took over a space in the Melbourne Crown Casino.

A ballot system was applied to obtain a booking since the space only had the capacity to seat 45 diners a night. The online ballot booking system was reported to have been scammed by a number of financial professionals, securing over 100 reservations under false names (Hawthorne & Wright, 2014).

The Fat Duck's degustation menu is not cheap even for the most discerning diner. At a price per head of more than AU$525 for 10 courses (beverages additional), the menu and pricing reflect a one-off dining experience, rather than creating repeat business. To maximise sales, the ballot system captured potential diners' contact details so that disappointed customers could be contacted later if there were any cancellations.

Warhurst (2015) deliberated about whether this venture could be classified as a pop-up, especially when the dining experience was set at a premium price and the establishment was booked out before opening. Keen and Gardener (2014) additionally reported that Blumenthal stated 'this is not a pop-up restaurant'. This assertion is possibly true because Heston plans to continue a restaurant called Breeze in the space once the Fat Duck is relocated back in the UK.

Another famous celebrity chef, Jamie Oliver, and his friend Jimmy Doherty embarked on a television series called *Jamie & Jimmy's Food Fight Club* (2014–2015). Their pop-up café was located at the end of Southend Pier in the UK. The pair invited celebrity guests and other foodies to be part of the television programme at the café. The theme was to celebrate to the viewing audience what is great about British food and how it compares with other cuisines. The café was only a temporary home for the duration of the filming of the series, but it produced a tourist destination where the general public hope to sight a celebrity or two.

Continuing this trend is the Australian television series *Restaurant Revolution* (2015). This culinary virtual reality programme allows the general public the opportunity to attend a restaurant of the dreams of each contestant. Temporary restaurants are established in shipping containers in major Australian cities and the contestants are required to establish a viable restaurant business. This television concept could be considered as another pop-up venture with the added aspect of five minutes of fame for staff. For diners, there is also the prospect of appearing on television – perhaps even being asked to critique a meal – and of parasocial interaction with the contestants and judges.

Festival on-site pop-ups

Festivals also make an ideal setting to showcase a pop-up venture. Up and coming and even well-known chefs have the opportunity to experiment with menus and increase their own brand awareness with a captive market of festival attendees. Producers can display their fresh products at festivals and market spaces.

In 2013, the Urban Coffee Farm and Brew House hosted a coffee plantation for 17 days at the Melbourne Food and Wine Festival. This pop-up was staffed on a rotational basis by renowned Melbourne baristas and bartenders. The coffee plantation offered a unique coffee consuming experience to Melbournians, which also included master classes to discover more about the coffee story (Russell, 2013).

In 2015, for the fourth time, Queensbridge Square in Melbourne hosted a creative one-off pop-up project. This time the festival showcased an artisan bakery, a workshop space and a coffee and wine bar providing baked goods prepared by bakers from all over the globe. Justin Gellatly, a renowned British baker, headed a team of local and international guest bakers staging a baking exhibition and also hands-on workshops for the public.

Pop-up hotels have also appeared in this temporary festival landscape. In 2011, at the Glastonbury Music Festival, the largest greenfield festival on the globe, the first appearance of the lavish Pop-up Hotel was witnessed. The hotel's 150 canvas bell tents and facilities provided guests with a luxury accommodation experience located a walking distance from the festival site. In 2015, guests could purchase a range of accommodation packages for the duration of the festival starting from £1999 and ending at a whopping £8950 (Travelmail Reporter, 2014). The Pop-up Hotel also provided their customers with a range of other facilities including food and beverage options and an on-site spa to complement the luxury accommodation.

On a more controversial note, pop-ups at festivals can produce hostility from traditional bricks-and-mortar establishments and hospitality association members. The Adelaide Fringe Festival in South Australia has received some unfortunate press and media coverage. The media reported that the pop-up venues located on the festival site had led to a decline in revenue for traditional food and beverage properties during the four week festival period (Templeton, 2015; Carter, 2013a).

Pop-ups and guerrilla marketing strategies

Levinson's (1984) guerrilla marketing concepts are associated with innovative, creative, unusual and flexible promotional activities, making a significant impression in the market place, while being conducted on a very low budget. There are a range of guerrilla marketing techniques available for the savvy marketer, including viral (Van der Lans *et al.*, 2010), buzz (Siefert *et al.*, 2009) and ambush (McKelvey & Grady, 2008). Guerrilla marketing is a customer-oriented approach with the media and/or customer spreading the advertising message. Thus, these marketing promotions rely on a surprise or diffusion effect produced by the participation of the potential patron and the rapid and immediate capability of social media platforms such as Twitter (Hutter & Hoffmann, 2011). Traditional marketing communication tools (advertising, personal selling, sales promotion and public relations) can also incorporate guerrilla tactics (Ay *et al.*, 2010).

Pop-up outlets can be considered as a type of guerrilla personal selling strategy where the sales personnel connect directly with the customers on a short-term, fleeting basis. Marketing for pop-up catering enterprises is commonly done via the internet, using Facebook, Twitter and Blogs to attract 'guerrilla' diners who might be looking for a cutting-edge gastronomic experience and also wish to be able to brag that they had dinner at a soon-to-be-famous chef's restaurant when they were just starting out (Strand, 2010; Tyler, 2009). The marketing approach for these businesses is concentrated on word-of-mouth communication via social networking sites where the consumer is the one who promotes the enterprise and assists in building brand loyalty by providing the pop-up dining experience with credibility and desirability (Castronovo & Huang, 2012). This style of advertising can create an attendance-motivating hype for the adventurous customer wishing to engage with this opportunity.

Castronovo and Huang (2012) further suggest that consumer buying decisions are often influenced by others and the recommendation of a friend or even a stranger can provide some reassurance that the product or service is considered to be value for money and in the case of a pop-up a worthwhile and pleasurable dining experience. Adding to the culinary adventure, the locations of many of the pop-ups, especially the private home dining, and unique one day/night events, are very often secret until the day of opening. Thus, owing to the very short lead time, social media platforms give a just-in-time aspect to providing the potential customer with specific secret pop-up details just before opening.

Fad or fixture?

The question remains whether food trucks and pop-up restaurants are merely a short-term novelty, or are heralding a new way of dining that is less stuffy and puts the food centre stage. Hipsters who shun the likes of McDonald's and other fast-food franchises appear to be comfortable with quickly prepared food, eaten with fingers while seated outdoors in a public space. Pop-ups appeal to our love of novelty and authenticity, but this might be a short-term craze, especially if home dining regains its popularity. More research is needed to explore the phenomenon further, particularly the variations around the globe.

Part 3
Media and Gastronomy

11 Food Pioneers and Champions

Julie and Julia: My Year of Cooking Dangerously (Julie Powell, 2005)

Julie Powell is a secretary who works by day at a government agency involved in developing the memorial site for 9/11. By night, she is a blogger, who is working her way through all 524 recipes in *Mastering the Art of French Cooking Vol. 1* in a year, a book which was, as she notes, 'a cultural landmark' (Powell, 2005: 14). One of its three authors and the person who was most identified with the tome, Julia Child, had been directionless until she discovered cooking and her desire to expose Americans to the delights of French cuisine. The Julie/Julia Project is a similar transformative opportunity for Julie Powell, as she tries to work out what she wants to do with her life. Her blog posting expresses how she feels about Julia: 'She wants you to remember that you are human, and as such are entitled to that most basic of human rights, the right to eat well and enjoy life' (Powell, 2005: 41). Julie swings between despair and euphoria at times, but attains her goal in the end. Julia Child's influence thus extends beyond the techniques of cooking, to the idea that there is a joy attached to becoming proficient at something that is difficult. As Julie concludes:

> I didn't understand for a long time, but what attracted me to MtAoFC [*Mastering the Art of French Cooking*] was the deeply buried aroma of hope and discovery of fulfilment in it. I thought I was using the Book to learn to cook French food, but really I was learning to sniff out the secret doors of possibility. (Powell, 2005: 305–306)

Introduction

Throughout history, there have been a number of individuals, often charismatic and/or eccentric, who have led public opinion and contributed to the development of gastronomy. The term *champion* is often used to refer to 'an individual who encourages or is an advocate of a particular cause or way of thinking' (Mair & Laing, 2012: 686). We use it with reference to those people who have been instrumental in developing gastronomic tourism within a particular destination, sometimes through a signature restaurant or shop, which may have contributed to the image that this destination has in the minds of potential tourists, often heightened through the involvement of the media (Fields, 2002). It can also be applied to those who have been influential by highlighting or introducing the food heritage of one country or region to another, thus transforming the culinary landscape.

This chapter focuses on five individuals and how they have transformed the way that people think about food and its preparation, and played a part in the worldwide love affair with regional food. Julia Child and her English counterpart Elizabeth David are rightly considered to be food pioneers post-Second World War, and are both immortalised through the cookbooks they have written, which remain in print and are enduringly popular, despite the fact that neither woman ever ran nor worked in a restaurant. Julia Child also enjoyed a high profile as one of the first celebrity cooks on television and Rick Stein continues this tradition in the present day, with his influence helping to stamp Cornwall as an important culinary region. Another television chef, Antonio Carluccio, has developed a chain of Italian café restaurants with an attached food retail business across Britain. He is also known for popularising the pastime of foraging, based on his childhood experiences back in Italy. In Australia, Italian-born Stefano de Pieri extols the benefits of slow food and using regional produce, and has been instrumental in placing the country town of Mildura on the culinary map. We consider the influence of these individuals on both food movements and the development of *gastronomic destinations*, as well as the role of societal changes and the media in this process.

Elizabeth David

Elizabeth David, famous for the visceral sensuality of such works as *A Book of Mediterranean Food* (1950), *French Country Cooking* (1951) and *Italian Food* (1954), promoted the beauty of simplicity, local produce and fresh ingredients to post-war Britain, still in the grip of rationing. While most people had enough to eat, it was food as *fuel*. David offered them food as fantasy (or *food porn*), with many of the ingredients unable to be procured, too expensive for the average pocket or in limited supply (Humble, 2002). David's travels to the Mediterranean had opened her eyes to what food could be like: 'it was not only her body which had been nourished, stimulated and soothed, but her emotions and spirit too' (Chaney, 1998: 45).

In contrast, she felt that the English had turned their backs on their food heritage and needed to return to their roots, which she encouraged through books such as *English Bread and Yeast Cookery* (1977). In this, David was not a trailblazer – Jane Grigson's *English Food* (1974) had preceded her – but

Grigson had already acknowledged the debt she owed to David's books, in the introduction to *Charcuterie and French Pork Cookery* (1967), which stated, 'Nobody can produce a cookery book these days without a deep appreciation of Elizabeth David's work'. While Chaney (1998: 93) argues that David is an example of the trope of an English traveller motivated by a 'dislike of home', it is perhaps fairer to observe that part of what she was running from was the stodgy nursery food she was served as a child growing up in the patrician surrounds of Wootton Manor. She felt that English food was and could be so much better if it returned to its authentic roots (Jones & Taylor, 2001). David explained her love–hate relationship with English food in *Italian Food*:

> There is no lack in England of talented and experienced cooks. English cakes, jams, jellies and preserves are first class; we are good at pastry-making and at roasting meat and game. During the last twelve years or so we have been obliged to exercise ingenuity and patience to the utmost limit, but we have perhaps become too accustomed to accepting third-rate travesties of good food. (David, 1954: 2)

David's other passion was for kitchenware, in which she opened English eyes to 'the beauty of functional objects and an appreciation of the social traditions of rooted cultures, still connected to their non-industrial past' (Chaney, 1998: xxiii). David thus continued her role as a taste maker or arbiter of taste (Lane, 2013), but moving beyond food to the *cultural products* that accompany it. Her specialty kitchen shop in South Kensington, Elizabeth David Ltd, was a revelation in 1965, and created a demand for provincial French staples such as wooden draining racks, glazed enamelware, copper pans and ramekins – a trend that continues to this day and was readily copied (Chaney, 1998). She never quite forgave Sir Terence Conran for his Habitat homewares store, which opened the year before her shop and which she felt borrowed the ideas that she had espoused in her books.

David was a difficult character at times. This might have been part of the reason why she never took to the medium of television, or radio for that matter. She was too self-conscious and sharp-tongued to come across sympathetically (Chaney, 1998), unlike the quirky charm of a Julia Child, or the easy-going enthusiasm of a Rick Stein. David's influence was purely based on her books and her shop, which makes their longevity even more remarkable. Her written work is scholarly, but never dry, not content with simply providing readers with recipes (although these were superb), but 'describing a world which could be imagined and summoned up amidst the cooking pots' (Chaney, 1998: 347). Her descriptions of ingredients are painterly in their detail, as this extract from *Italian Food* (David, 1954: 3) shows:

> The beautiful colours of [Italian] food is one most characteristic point. The vivid scarlet dishes of the south, the tomato sauce and the

pimientos, the oranges and pinks of fish soups, the red and white of a Neapolitan pizza, contrast strikingly with the unique green food of central and northern Italy; the spinach gnocchi of Tuscany, the lasagne Verdi of Bologna, the green pesto sauce of Genoa, the green peas and rice of the Veneto, green artichokes in pies, in omelettes, in salads; the green and yellow marbled stuffings of rolled beef and veal dishes – such food can scarcely fail to charm.

She was also ahead of her time in her fight 'against mass-production and standardization. However instinctive and unarticulated it may have been she understood the dubious benefits of industrialization on the long-term quality of food' (Chaney, 1998: 386). David extolled the pleasure that could be gained from making things by hand, getting one's hands dirty, and using the best quality ingredients. She would have understood the contemporary preference for using regional produce and 'fresh is best', which modern chefs such as Jamie Oliver and Rick Stein promote to their television audiences. It is no surprise that restaurants at the forefront of slow food such as Alice Waters's Chez Panisse owe a debt to her vision (Chaney, 1998), and the inspiration continues even in contemporary times. Australian chef Kylie Kwong, of the Sydney restaurant Billy Kwong, explained the practical benefit of David's work:

> I actually never went to technical college for cooking 'cause I was actually too old, or I felt too old. I just sort of gained all of my knowledge from working on the job and reading such cookbooks by Elizabeth David and so on. (Kwong, 2004)

Julia Child

Julia Child's influence on culinary tastes, in her case the American public, through her tome *Mastering the Art of French Cooking* (1961) and her television appearances, allowed a generation of cooks to appreciate the allure of France and French cuisine. She had an unlikely beginning, however, in her chosen career. Child liked to eat, but before living in France with her husband Paul, who worked for the US Information Service, her culinary experiments were limited. With her eyes now opened to the delicacies Paris had to offer, and armed with a copy of the *Larousse Gastronomique*, a birthday present from Paul, she decided that she wanted to learn how to cook *à la française* at the age of 37.

Enrolled at the famous L'École du Cordon Bleu, she studied under some of the best chefs in Paris, and her growing confidence is documented in her biography *My Life in France* (2006):

> I was in pure, flavorful heaven at the Cordon Bleu ... I suddenly discovered that cooking was a rich and layered and endlessly fascinating subject

... I fell in love with French food – the tastes, the processes, the history, the endless variations, the rigorous discipline, the creativity, the wonderful people, the equipment, the rituals. I had never taken anything so seriously in my life. (Child, with Prud'homme, 2006: 67–68)

This gave Child the idea of providing cooking classes from her Paris apartment, so she could pass on her knowledge and love of French cuisine to others. She teamed up with two French women – Simca Fischbacher and Louisette Bertholle – an auspicious partnership. They mentioned to her a cookbook they had been working on for the American market, with their own French recipes, and asked Child to help them with it. She worked tirelessly at making sure that the recipes worked, using American ingredients and measurements, and the work continued even when Paul was posted to Marseille and later to Norway and Germany. The original manuscript morphed into *Mastering the Art of French Cooking* (1961), a massive tome of 732 pages, which is still in print today, along with its companion volume (1970).

A number of companies had considered publishing the cookbook, only to drop the project when they became nervous at the scale of the undertaking and the depth to which the subject-matter was to be covered. Their disquiet is understandable, given some of the culinary exports of the USA in the early 1960s – TV dinners, jell-o, whipped cream and string cheese in cans, and the emphasis on fast food and new labour-saving devices. It was an age when women began to rail against the 1950s ideals of homemaking (Humble, 2002), finding their voice in Betty Friedan's *The Feminine Mystique* (1963). That people (i.e. women) would try to create *feuilleton de boeuf en croûte* or *bouillabaisse à la marseillaise* from scratch was difficult to envisage, but Child never gave up on her vision. The level of detail was her idea: 'I was basically writing these recipes for myself. And I was the type of person who wanted to know everything about a dish' (Child, with Prud'homme, 2006: 277). She was fortunate, however, that her vision coincided with a boom in Americans travelling overseas, with France a popular destination, and the fact that 'the Kennedys had installed a French chef, René Verdon, in the White House' (Child, with Prud'homme, 2006: 267). Jacqueline Kennedy was an acknowledged Francophone, having lived in Paris as a young woman. The other auspicious element was Child herself. Without her involvement, it is unlikely that the book would ever have seen the light of day, let alone had anywhere near the impact that it did. Her co-authors needed assistance with English and were not blessed with her charisma and drive. Neither enjoyed the same level of celebrity as Child – to their chagrin, it must be said (Riley Fitch, 1997; Spitz, 2012).

Child became an instant star when promoting *Mastering the Art of French Cooking*. She was difficult to overlook – 6 foot 3 inches tall with a voice that would 'unexpectedly drop down, slide up, gasp, and pitch forward with a whoop – covering a full octave in the course of one recipe' (Riley Fitch, 1997: 296). Audiences loved her bloopers and bonhomie in the face of kitchen disasters, as well as the double entendres she rattled off during the live shows. She was eventually offered her own show – *The French Chef* (1963) – which ran for a decade (Figure 11.1), followed by other programmes that included her name in the title, evidence of her fame, such as *Dinner at Julia's* (1983).

While Child was not the greatest technical exponent of French cooking, which she did not deny, her work on her cookbooks was painstaking, aimed at demystifying French cuisine. For that alone, she must be applauded. However, it was her fizzing personality and charismatic presence on television that really made her stand out amongst her polished and plastic TV peers:

> The irrepressible reality of Julia Child was a combination of spontaneity, candor and wit, which is why her passion for cooking bore unparalleled results. She not only brought fun headfirst into the modern American kitchen, a place that housewives equated with lifelong drudgery, but used it to launch public television into the spotlight, big-time. (Spitz, 2012: 7)

The kitchen set of three of her shows, created specially by her husband to accommodate her height, was donated to the National Museum of American History in Washington, DC in 2001, and featured as a crucial scene in the film *Julie and Julia*, where Julie leaves behind a pat of butter in the museum

Figure 11.1 Julia Child in *The French Chef* episode #231: Flaky Pastry (photo Paul Child; source: The Schlesinger Library, Radcliffe Institute, Harvard University)

kitchen in homage to her idol. In a neat coda, Columbia Pictures donated some artefacts from the movie to the Museum in 2009, such as an outfit worn by Meryl Streep as Julia Child and an annotated film script. While Child wasn't a huge fan of the movie, it undoubtedly shone a contemporary spotlight on her achievements, and the legacy she left to a new generation of television chefs, as well as winning her a new group of fans.

Rick Stein

Rick Stein's family's business involved distilling and he grew up on a farm, which he noted, during a recent guest appearance on *Masterchef Australia* (2015), 'gave me a unique insight into where food comes from'. His first job was an entry position as a larder chef at the Great Western Royal Hotel at Paddington Station. This move was mainly because he felt a failure and 'catering seemed to me to be just about what I was capable of, bearing in mind that catering was not the sort of job that the career master at my public school would have advised' (Stein, 2013: 54). If nothing else, it taught him basic skills such as making salads, hors d'oeuvres and sauces. This was followed by a restless few years travelling, starting a university degree at Oxford and running a mobile disco. Food was a theme running throughout, but one would hardly predict at this stage that he was destined to become such an important influence on gastronomy internationally (Figure 11.2).

Stein liked to throw parties, and was running a nightclub in Cornwall when he began serving food to patrons to comply with his liquor licence. While his hamburger bar didn't last long, the fish restaurant proved to be an

Figure 11.2 Rick Stein (source: Anna McCarthy, Press Centre, www.rickstein.com/press-centre/)

inspired idea. Stein did the cooking, mainly because he couldn't afford to pay anyone else. His philosophy was 'Fresh, local and simple' (Stein, 2013: 175), and his presentation of English fish and seafood as the star of the menu spearheaded a renaissance in these items as more than just the basis for 'fish and chips'. The name of his establishment – The Seafood Restaurant – put them centre-stage. A lot of his success came from his restaurant's strong association with place. Stein's intense love of Cornwall, where he grew up, came through in what he served his customers – Cornish lobsters, salmon from the Camel estuary, local mackerel, sea bass and mussels. Many of the vegetables came out of his own kitchen garden. This gave his menus great authenticity, an attribute that can be lost if 'a particular dish is removed, or disembedded, from its indigenous locale and recreated in an alternative location' (Jones & Taylor, 2001: 180).

Stein paid homage to a previous culinary luminary in his menu design, which featured a drawing from Elizabeth David's *A Book of Mediterranean Food*, one of his food bibles (Stein, 2013). This was prescient, in that he was to become an important food champion in his own right. In his television series *Rick Stein's Food Heroes* (2002) and *Rick Stein's Food Heroes: Another Helping* (2003–2004), he highlighted those individuals who were doing their bit to ensure the high quality of British cuisine, and thus continued Elizabeth David's quest:

> I have always had a mission to show people, not just at home but every-where, that Britain is a place of really good-quality food. I've always wanted to dispel the idea that our cooking is bland and that our meat and vegetables are invariably overdone. (Stein, 2013: 269)

Stein discovered that he had a flair not only for cooking, but also for *promoting* the love of food to others. It began in 1984, when The Seafood Restaurant was voted the best restaurant in England. At the time, he had been writing a monthly cooking column in *Women's Realm* magazine, focusing on fish, which led in due course to his first cookbook, *English Seafood Cookery* (1988). A journalist mentioned Stein's restaurant to a colleague who was producing Keith Floyd's TV series *Floyd on Fish* (1984) for the BBC. Floyd, a dishevelled roué of a chef known for his 'slurps' of wine between cooking, filmed a segment alongside Stein in his restaurant. Stein had caught 'the TV bug' (Stein, 2013: 228) and was thrilled to be offered a series of his own, *Taste of the Sea* (1995). It changed his life. As his then-wife Jill discovered: 'The day after the show came out ... I can remember manning the phones. They never stopped' (Adams, 2015).

He became one of the new brigade of television celebrity chefs, travelling around the world and often publishing tie-in cookbooks. Stein's shows, like Floyd's, began by showcasing the best of British seafood, but then moved on to the cuisines of France, Spain, the Far East and more recently India and Germany. Stein has made these cuisines more accessible to the home cook, showcasing the ingredients that make them special and demonstrating how they should be prepared and incorporated into dishes. His programmes educate us on the origins of much of the food we eat. *Rick Stein's Indian Odyssey* (2013), for example, makes it clear that the menus that many British diners were exposed to and thought of as 'Indian' were in fact largely Bangladeshi in origin (Frost & Laing, 2016). He also uses his media profile not just to promote cooking, but also to argue for sustainable fishing practices, helping to make people more aware of 'less well-known species of seafood which are plentiful but under-used' (Stein, 2013: 265–266). Stein let slip in his *Indian Odyssey* that his restaurants have never received a Michelin star, as he didn't care about 'all the bullshit' that goes with the territory. His pleasure comes from educating the public rather than being at the cutting edge of gastronomy, even though it could be argued that one influences the other.

Stein's role in creating the association of the Cornish town of Padstow with good eating is now ubiquitous, so much so that the town is often known as Padstein (Busby *et al.*, 2013), a nickname coined by a journalist, which he acknowledges has had its advantages (Stein, 2013). His television programmes reinforce this geographical link, such as *Rick Stein in Du Maurier Country* (2007), a tribute to his favourite writer Daphne du Maurier, and *Rick Stein's Cornish Christmas* (2010). Stein now runs four restaurants in Padstow, alongside accommodation, a cooking school, a gift shop, a delicatessen, a fishmonger and a patisserie. He also runs the Cornish Arms in St Merryn and restaurants in Falmouth and Porthleven. One of his goals in the creation of these businesses was to 'attract more people to Padstow' (Stein, 2013: 239) and it appears to have worked, complementing the image of the destination. According to research undertaken by Busby *et al.* (2013), 71% of visitors considered Rick Stein to be a major influence on tourism to Padstow, while almost 12% of visitors cited Stein as the reason for their visit. Thus, 'in the modern world of celebrity, when a particular chef is juxtaposed with the location and cuisine, it is argued that a certain iconic status is achieved'. This study also identifies, in the case of Stein, a new form of film-induced tourism 'influenced by cookery programmes' (Busby *et al.*, 2013: 579).

Not all locals have been supportive of Stein's presence in their midst. In 2007, some residents took umbrage at the development of accommodation next to his St Petroc's Bistro, with the building works said to have led to the cancellation of bookings at other local establishments (Salkeld, 2007). Stein was incensed, arguing in an email which was picked up by the *Cornish Guardian* that these local businesses had benefitted from the spotlight he had trained on the town:

> I would have been charmed if those other businesses that have benefited from the rosy glow of publicity, particularly those whose letting season has been considerably extended, could have shown some sort of recognition for the work done. (Salkeld, 2007)

This inflamed matters and led to threats from Cornish separatists, who argued that the global fame of his restaurants and subsequent tourism boom had led to house prices spiralling and raised the cost of living in the region. All the windows were smashed at the front of his restaurant one night (Stein, 2013).

Stein could have offered additional rejoinders to this abuse. His businesses employ '290 people all the year round, and up to 400 in the summer months' (Stein, 2013: 304). In addition, 'the standard of other restaurants in Padstow has increased, as other employers have identified the increase in demand and tried to compete with the TV chef' (Busby *et al.*, 2013: 576; see also Jackson, 2010), an example of the clustering effect that a destination champion brings in their wake. Jamie Oliver opened one of his Fifteen restaurants in Newquay in 2006, a decision that was arguably influenced by Cornwall's growing 'foodie' image. Stein's story, however, is the classic one of tourism development being a two-edged sword; while it has brought clear economic benefits to Padstow, it has also changed the character of this once sleepy town, perhaps irrevocably. The same effect might also be seen in the small Australian seaside town of Mollymook, in New South Wales, where Stein and his Australian wife run Rick Stein at Bannisters. His menu is based on the same ethos as he has promoted elsewhere – fresh and local is best. Mollymook has received less publicity than Stein's Cornish associations, which might change if he films a future television series in the region. At the time of writing this book, he had plans to return to Britain, which might also be a factor in the long-term development of Mollymook. It would make an interesting comparative case study to the rise of Padstow.

Antonio Carluccio

Antonio Carluccio had the perfect childhood for a future chef and restaurateur. He grew up in in an Italian family where his mother made everything from scratch, and lived in a number of different regions, including Sicily during the Second World War with his grandmother, where he was surrounded by farmers and artisans, and Piemonte in the north, close to the Swiss and French borders. The family ate well, mainly because of their ability to forage for what was freely available growing wild, such as berries, mushrooms, figs and nuts. As Carluccio reminisces: 'Really, when it came for fresh foods, we were spoilt for choice even during the war' (Carluccio, 2012: 42). It was a lesson he never forgot – the way that nature's bounty could be used in many different dishes and for very little cost. He also learnt the seasonal rhythms of food production, commenting as an adult: 'When you live like that, outside whatever the weather, playing, or foraging for fruits or nuts or mushrooms, you become very aware of the changing seasons – spring, summer, autumn and winter – all marked by distinct variations in climate and vegetation' (Carluccio, 2012: 54). In winter, the family ate dried or preserved fruits, in spring and summer they ate what was fresh. Nothing was available all year around, and foods were thus made even more special for being eagerly anticipated.

Like Rick Stein, Carluccio took on a number of different occupations as a young man, including as a naval cadet, a salesman, a crane operator, a journalist and a worker on the assembly line at Olivetti. His journey towards a gastronomic career started when he began working in the wine industry, but he also found that he instinctively turned to making food at difficult times of his life, such as when his young brother died. The preparation of food, using his mother's old recipes, and serving it to others was a comforting ritual 'and this process was to become a source of solace to me again many, many times in the future' (Carluccio, 2012: 101).

Moving to London in the mid 1970s and working as a wine merchant, Carluccio discovered that a bounty of mushrooms could be gathered during his frequent walks in the English countryside. He started to provide them to his restaurant clients, who trusted his experience and knowledge about fungi. At the time, Italian food was fashionable, particularly in London's Soho area, and pizza chain restaurants such as Pizza Express and the American Pizza Hut were opening across Britain (Carluccio, 2012). It wasn't however an era of high integrity in terms of Italian cuisine, with dishes often adapted from the original or simply 'unheard of in Italy' (Carluccio, 2012: 164). As Carluccio observed: 'It was what I came to call Britalian food' (p. 163). The restaurants who bought his mushrooms, however, were keen to produce food that had a heritage, using recipes that their family had cherished down the years. This resonated with Carluccio: 'It was a sentiment I applauded, and reflects the same love of authenticity that I brought to bear when developing the first menus for the future Carluccio Caffè' (p. 164).

Carluccio married Priscilla, the sister of Terence Conran (*bête noire* of Elizabeth David) and owner of the Neal Street Restaurant in Covent Garden, which Carluccio joined as Managing Director in 1981. The same year, he was a finalist in the *Sunday Times* Cook of the Year, and his food philosophy at the time was to become the cornerstone of his restaurants and the *mofmof* (minimum of fuss and maximum of flavour) message he tried to get across to British diners at a time when nouvelle cuisine was on the rise (Carluccio, 2012: 191):

> I was innately convinced of the value of good ingredients and of working with them, rather than disguising them with fancy techniques or sauces ... keeping things simple and allowing the food to 'speak' for itself. This was rather at odds with the fashion in cooking in the early 1980s, which had become massively over-complicated to my mind.

At the Neal Street restaurant, Carluccio looked after the 'culinary direction', the style of the place and the promotion, which suited his *bon-vivant* personality.

Nothing escaped his notice; even the process of making coffee was scrutinised. His influence can be seen on his most famous apprentice, Jamie Oliver, who has made the use of fresh ingredients and understanding where food comes from a personal mantra. Regional Italian dishes began to pepper the Neal Street menu as experiments, to see how they were embraced by patrons, particularly those with mushrooms when in season. It was television, however, that helped spread Carluccio's philosophy on food to a wider audience.

Carluccio's first cookbook, *An Invitation to Italian Cooking* (1986), led to a series of appearances on the BBC's *Food and Drink* programme. His television shows such as *Antonio Carluccio's Southern Italian Feast* (1998), *Two Greedy Italians* (2011) and *Two Greedy Italians: Still Hungry* (2012) (the latter two with Gennaro Contaldo) showcased regional Italian food, and placed the produce centre-stage. He received a number of awards and honours, including the Order of Merit of the Italian Republic in 1998 and the Order of the British Empire (OBE) in 2007, while his food business was given a Royal Warrant as Supplier of Italian Food and Truffles to HRH Prince Charles, the Prince of Wales (Carluccio, 2012). The television exposure also made Carluccio a household name in Britain, assisting with his next venture – a series of café-restaurants bearing his name across the country.

The Carluccio Caffè concept included an attached shop and delicatessen, selling things like good olive oil, fresh pasta, focaccia and sun-dried tomatoes, which were not then readily available in supermarkets, as well as freshly prepared food and hard to find kitchen items. The first Carluccio shop/deli had been opened next door to the Neal Street Restaurant in 1991, and its success was due to 'years of experience and expertise and knowledge of both Italian food and how to market it' (Carluccio, 2012: 221).Unlike Elizabeth David Ltd, it went beyond being a kitchen shop. While other chefs had opened their own delis/shops, such as Rick Stein in 1982, the trail-blazing twist of Carluccio's 1990s version was to roll it out nationwide, and piggyback it with a restaurant, providing a place where people could both dine and shop. There are now over 80 Carluccio Caffès throughout Britain, which are generally open all day, allowing diners to drop in at their convenience and enjoy European-style café culture. Carluccio's contribution to gastronomy is to give people a sense of what good and authentic Italian food can be like, as well as the edible bounty that is available from nature.

Stefano de Pieri

Stefano de Pieri has had a similar impact to his countryman, Antonio Carluccio, but in Australia. Starring in the television series *A Gondola on the Murray* (1998), helped to make chef Stefano de Pieri a well-known personality. It also made the town of Mildura a magnet for foodies for the first time in its history. De Pieri migrated to Australia from Italy in the 1970s, at a time when Australia was just starting to embrace a greater variety of ethnic cuisines, although it is fair to say that culinary excellence was not then part of Australia's brand image internationally. After getting married, he moved to his wife's home town of Mildura and became involved in the running of the Grand Hotel, which was owned by his parents-in-law. The hotel restaurant, Stefano's, has won numerous awards, but it is not the only business that he runs in Mildura. De Pieri has his own micro-brewery (Figure 11.3), as well as selling a range of wines and preserves under his own label.

In an interview with the authors, de Pieri made it clear that he always intended to make a splash with his restaurant: 'We thought we'd repaint the picture of Mildura – I feel like a pig in creative shit!' Yet his innovations took a while to be accepted in what was a conservative country town. His first venture around 20 years ago was a breakfast outlet with tables on the footpath, coffee and newspapers, which was ahead of its time and pre-empted the coffee culture which is now a feature of Melbourne in particular (Frost et al., 2010). As de Pieri notes: 'Australia leads that globally in some ways'. The isolation from major cities was a challenge, but he was excited at the array of produce at his disposal and thought Mildura was a place 'full of possibility and energy – you just have to see it and embrace it'.

While the original idea was simply to write a cookbook, which was an emotional exercise for de Pieri ('trying to remember what was the food of the Veneto'), the television documentary gave him much greater exposure. *A Gondola on the Murray*, 'grabbed the public imagination', his wife Donata

Figure 11.3 Stefano de Pieri's Mildura Brewery (photo One Idea)

believes, because of its 'authentic elements – we showed where the food grows and that what we were able to provide is real – which meant that people started to make this pilgrimage to Mildura'. It was also a time, she recalls, when shows like *Two Fat Ladies* (1996–1999) were popular and television networks were keen to find the next big thing to satiate viewers' demands for new programmes.

De Pieri balks, however, at the suggestion that he is a destination or food champion: 'It's a collective thing, not just us', although others we met in Mildura described him as a leader of the community. While modest, he does at least acknowledge the influence he has had on the industry: 'Anecdotally, I get letters from a guy who started a café in Albury because he was inspired by us'. We would argue that he has had a far greater impact than this, helping to create a new identity for Mildura as a place that is no longer a cultural desert. The food scene has been augmented by various festivals and artistic endeavours, but they may have been more difficult to justify or even support without the trailblazing efforts of de Pieri to raise culinary standards and 'make the place vibrant'. This is not to say that the town is without its challenges on the food front. De Pieri recently took back his restaurant from a local chef who failed with a concept which was too ambitious: 'The restaurant was a bold and exciting venture that attempted to develop a cuisine of place. But punters weren't going in sufficient numbers'. He is not willing to give up on his dream: 'Mildura needs a destination restaurant. People have always enjoyed my food in the past. I hope they will continue to' (Grundy, 2015).

Meet the Chef: Changing Roles and Influence in the Digital World

A number of destinations have a long history of being celebrated for their food, some spanning many centuries. Cities like Paris, Florence and Venice have a history of aristocratic patronage and a tradition of restaurants and fine dining (De Jean, 2005; De Vooght, 2011; Dickie, 2008). Other destinations have enjoyed more recent renown for their gastronomic excellence. This is in some cases due to an influx of migration (New York, Melbourne) or the discovery of the local cuisine once the destination is opened up to tourism after war or the advent of greater political freedom, such as Barcelona or Phnom Penh. The media may also have a strong influence on this destination image or destination branding through the messages that they promote via channels such as films, guidebooks and magazines (Bhattacharyya, 1997; Mercille, 2005). In more recent years, there has been a growing interest in the role that social media may play in this process (Hays *et al.*, 2013; Lim *et al.*, 2012).

In this chapter, we focused on how the growth of food tourism in some destinations can be linked to the existence of a *champion* or taste maker.

The image of France as a centre for gastronomic excellence, for example, has been shaped by a number of factors, including the writings of individuals as diverse as Escoffier in the 19th century and Julia Child and Elizabeth David in the 20th century. Padstow's reputation as an object of gastronomic pilgrimages has grown steadily since celebrity chef Rick Stein opened his restaurants and cookery school in the small Cornish fishing village (Busby *et al.*, 2013). In a similar vein, Stefano de Pieri, through the establishment of Stefano's restaurant and encouragement of local producers, has spearheaded the transformation of the town of Mildura in regional Victoria, Australia into a gourmet getaway. Apart from writing cookbooks, a number of these people have used television as a medium for promoting a particular gastronomic destination, including highlighting their *personal* links with that place.

This *place association* is an important hallmark of the gastronomic champion. The fact that the chef has either lived in or continues to live in a particular destination, and/or runs a business there gives their championship an *authenticity* or veracity that makes it highly persuasive in the eyes of the general public. They thus have an authoritative platform from which to speak, although it could also be argued that they 'profit from their identity' (Cherro Osorio & Best, 2015: 348). There is also the frisson inherent in the thought of potentially encountering that person in that destination or meeting someone who knows or knew that person or might have been trained by them.

The networks created by the gastronomic champion are an outcome of their presence *in situ*. They often attract a critical mass or clustering of high-quality restaurants, cafés, producers and accommodation to complement their own offerings. For example, after Rick Stein started his restaurant and associated businesses in Padstow, other businesses moved in, including Paul Ainsworth at Number 6 restaurant, which has a Michelin star. In other cases, staff trained by the champion branch out on their own to open a new establishment. According to Stefano de Pieri, some of his former employees have started food-related businesses in Mildura, such as former Stefano's chef Jim McDougall, who runs the Black Stump Bistro, providing competition that de Pieri sees as a positive development for Mildura.

Another way to characterise some of these individuals is to label them *culture brokers*, being those who 'act as intermediaries between their society and the external world by representing their culture to the outsiders' (Cherro Osorio & Best, 2015: 347), thus helping to bridge the two cultures. In a tourism context, this terminology has been applied to tour guides and tour operators (Cherro Osorio & Best, 2015; Reimer, 1990), and extended to those who promote their own ethnic cuisines to outsiders, known as *culinary brokers* (Cherro Osorio, 2013). The gastronomic champions we highlight in this chapter might also be characterised as engaging in a form of *cultural mediation*, which might be heightened through their association with the media and resultant high profile.

Culture brokers need not necessarily be born within the culture that they promote to others, as highlighted in this chapter. While Antonio Carluccio and Stefano de Pieri are Italian born and bred, and Rick Stein grew up in Cornwall, Elizabeth David and Julia Child popularised cultures and cuisines which they had only been exposed to as adults. All five individuals discussed in this chapter have lived between two cultures, and like many culture brokers, most are bilingual, which allows them to 'communicate effectively and translate knowledge and skills from one culture to another' (Cherro Osorio & Best, 2015: 348). Julia Child eventually mastered the French language but one would never say that it came easily to her: 'Her trademark warble, a curse to even the most gifted linguist, strangled any hope of developing a decent accent' (Spitz, 2012: 177). Yet like her cooking, she worked diligently to improve her language skills and took every opportunity she could to practise what she had learnt. This provided Child with an entrée to the French way of life and the secrets of their cuisine.

A hallmark of each of these individuals studied in this chapter is their passion for food and for passing on that love to others, which squares with the notion of a culture broker deriving 'personal satisfaction' from their work as a catalyst for social change (Cherro Osorio & Best, 2015). These five have all altered the way we understand the food of other cultures, but also the role and importance of food in our lives, including the types of food we eat and the way we select, prepare and present it. This has not changed in a world of new media, where an online presence may provide the modern food champion with an even more powerful platform for sharing their views and opinions with the world.

12 A Recipe for Travel

The Little Paris Kitchen (Rachel Khoo, 2012)

Paris, the city of culinary dreams and quaint tiny apartments, sets the scene for Rachel Khoo's first cookbook and television series. *The Little Paris Kitchen* is a six-episode series depicting Khoo's time in Paris, trialling recipes, visiting fresh food market spaces and entertaining diners at her home pop-up restaurant. Rachel Khoo was drawn to this capital city by her desire to study French *pâtisserie* at Le Cordon Bleu.

The series features classic street views of Paris with Khoo visiting a *fromagerie* (cheese shop) and a *boulangerie* (bread shop) before she arrives in her petite, make-do kitchen, typical of what is found in many Paris apartments. She prepares a *Quiche Lorraine* showing how simple it is to make and she discloses her modern interpretation of *coq au vin* – a barbeque version. The key to these dishes is that they 'are not snobby, which a lot of people think French food is and they are a pleasure to eat and enjoyable'. Khoo combines all her talents to be a captivating cook, food and travel writer and a culinary television celebrity. For the audience, the series and matching cookbook kindle the desire to travel to Paris and have similar experiences.

Food, Cookbooks and Travel Writing

Travel writing and travelogues are not new in the literary arena. This genre of narrative nonfiction has been consumed by readers for many centuries, allowing the less fortunate to vicariously experience another person's travel encounters. While travel and food narratives date back to the classical period, it was in the 19th century when they became more accessible. The rapidly expanding middle classes were voracious readers and their interests extended to a wide range of food topics. Society ladies started to advise other women on how to run an effective and efficient household, with a wide range of cookery manuals and columns in the popular press (Sage, 1999). In more recent times, the cookery book has increasingly included narratives of the travel experiences of the author, providing the reader with a cultural culinary context. Humble suggests that:

> even the most conventional cookery book is now far more than a mere collection of rules for dishes. Alongside the recipes we may find narratives, anecdote, travelogue, history, anthropology, political diatribe and science. (Humble, 2002: 323)

Cookery books engage the reader on a wider variety of travel and cultural matters and discourses than ever before, helping to stimulate a desire to further investigate this cultural arena. This chapter will explore the present-day relationship between travel, the media and gastronomy through the aegis of the cookbook. It discusses the potential influences of travelogues contained in contemporary cookbooks upon consumers, while reviewing the cultural interpretations provided by the cookery book author. In addition, many of the chefs/authors who have written gastronomic travelogue literature have also filmed corresponding television programmes depicting their travel experiences. These television programmes assist the reading audience to unravel their own personal interpretations of the cookbook narrative by providing extended visual and virtual travel representation. Therefore, it could be asked, when is a cookbook not just a book containing a set of recipes? The discussion within this chapter will examine the rapidly changing format of the cookbook, which has progressively metamorphosed into a vehicle for both entertainment and education.

Throughout the generations, cookery literature has provided a window into the lifestyle of the time and therefore provides a depiction of what were cultural issues of that era. The cookbook has been able to be re-conceived in line with modern inclinations, and thus it has single-handedly been one of the publishing successes in the last century (Humble, 2002). Many provide not only a cookery manual but also a configuration of culinary history (Jones & Taylor, 2001). The cookery book has been a medium to reveals trends, taste habits and practices of a specific bygone era, as well as the present. Neuhaus (1999: 536) argued that, 'every cookbook, more or less consciously is a work of social history ... [offering] vivid examples of what we might appropriately term a cultural text: recipes are loaded with meaning particular to their time and place'. Tobias (1998: 3) supported this notion, observing: 'cookbooks contain not only recipes, but hidden clues and cultural assumptions about class, race, gender and ethnicity. They reflect many of the dramatic transformations that have come to define the boundaries of the modern public sphere'. Thus, the cookbook has been able to reflect and define different roles in society. Hooper (2010: 123) further suggested 'writing about food and travel, which can be found in the modern cookery book, are derived from sensual pleasures, providing the reader with actual experience of consuming good food and going to new or familiar places that are both reacted to by our senses'. The cookery book seduces the reader to enjoy and consume the pleasures of the presented cuisine and its *terroir*.

Adema (2000) suggested that the buying and reading of a cookery book becomes a pleasurable end in itself and the actual cooking and eating of the dishes is secondary or may not even occur. Modern foodies can purchase numerous volumes to display in their personal culinary library, which may indicate to others the owner's cooking prowess. In addition, a cookbook is an acceptable and common gift for those who enjoy the culinary arts and the consumption of food. Indeed, one of the authors of this book would consider herself as an intuitive cook and seldom uses a recipe to produce a meal; however, this same person owns over 100 culinary volumes and obtains great delight in owning a small remnant of others' travel and culinary cultural interpretations. She and many other consumers can take great pleasure in having this genre of books on the shelf without any desire to cook a meal from them. A similar perspective is voiced by media chef Poh Ling Yeow, who writes of possessing, 'a comprehensive collection [of cookbooks] which she finds utterly beautiful as objects to love and hold but she too has never cooked from many of them' (Yeow, 2010: 9).

Bower (2004b) considers the contemporary cookbook to be akin to a novel in many ways. The cookbook allows the reader the escapism of consuming recipes, travel stories and history, with the addition of lush and opulent photographs of the author's travels and the gastronomic delights they are presenting to the cookbook consumer. Do these travel focused cookbooks inspire and motivate their audience to travel further or does the dialogue remind them of where they might have been in the past? More radically, will this form of infotainment be a replacement for the physical travel experience and connect or relate to the concept of virtual travel? One could assume that the answer is 'yes' to all of these questions, but it will also be dependent on the individual and their personal capacity to obtain fulfilment and satisfaction from someone else's experiences. Many of the general public may be satisfied to be only part of the virtual travel experience, especially when time has become a highly prized commodity and the world has become a riskier place to venture out into and explore.

The authors of cookery books containing travel narratives are selling the consumer more than a preparation technique, also incorporating the experience and engagement of the writer in the culinary transaction of both entertainment and education. As a consumer, we are buying a story, a glimpse into someone else's world of travel. The consumer can then superimpose these experiences onto their own travel memories from the past, or the anticipation of what they might experience in their future travel adventures. Owing to the fact that many consumers are influenced by the media, the reader of this genre of culinary literature desires to be able to trust the cultural and gastronomic experience of the author, who in many cases is a celebrity chef. This trust can be translated into the belief that the recipes are authentic because the author has visited and immersed themselves in the culinary culture. Thus one might consider that the consumer can be swayed by the cookery books and complementary cooking shows when reviewing options and selecting travel destinations.

Gastronomic literature was defined by Mennell (1985: 270–271) in terms of its fascination with at least one of the four following concerns:

(1) to set out certain rules of etiquette or 'correct practice';
(2) to provide a dietetic (or nutritional) perspective;
(3) to provide 'a brew of history, myth and history serving as myth'; and
(4) to evoke nostalgically 'memorable meals'.

We suggest a fifth concern, to include travelogues by the cookery book author, which seek to detail the gastronomic experience of place and culture enveloping the food of a region.

Early Cookbooks

Originally, cookbooks were typically just a collection of recipes. Even Julia Child's *Mastering the Art of French Cooking* (1961) followed that formula. While the dishes, ingredients and techniques might stimulate the reader to dream of France, there was nothing in the text that went beyond cooking. Perhaps the first writer to make this leap was Elizabeth David (see also Chapter 11), with a cookery book entitled *A Book of Mediterranean Food* (1950). Whilst still primarily a book of recipes, it contained three important features. First, she linked the recipes to specific countries. Second, there were evocative line drawings of Mediterranean scenes by John Minton. Most of these were set outside in the sunshine and showed smiling people collecting, selling and cooking food. Third, each section was introduced with a travel narrative vignette by writers such as D.H. Lawrence, Lawrence Durrell, Compton Mackenzie and Robert Byron.

David's books in the 1950s are as much travelogues as they are manuals for the preparation of food (Chaney, 1998). They juxtaposed the austere war-time food rationing in the UK (which ran until 1954) with the image of the Mediterranean as a land of plenty with exotic ingredients, warm weather and tantalising aromas and flavours (Jones & Taylor, 2001). Humble (2002) argued that David developed a theme of adventure within her cookery books – telling stories of strange eating establishments, describing the waiting staff and the magical food they delivered to the table and evoking a better time that the British hoped and desired to see in the near future.

In the 1970s, new technology opened up the possibilities of cookbooks encouraging travel. Improvements in printing allowed many books to utilise numbers of high-quality colour photos. These could be dishes and ingredients, but could also be attractive landscapes and sights. An intriguing example was the use of colour photos in a tongue-in-cheek publication called *White Trash Cooking*.

White Trash Cooking (Ernest Matthew Mickler, 1986)

Ernie Mickler grew up in Florida. His father was a shrimper and his mother was a cook and gas station attendant. In the late 1960s he moved to San Francisco to study Fine Arts. There he entertained friends with stories of the Deep South. He developed a proposal for a television show, parodying conventional fare like *The Galloping Gourmet*, but with the twist that it would be all about old-fashioned southern cooking. Eventually he found a publisher who saw the potential in a retro-style ring-binder cookbook that would be the antithesis of the 1980s trends in nouvelle cuisine and health-conscious diets (Edge, 2011).

The result was a sensation, selling over 650,000 copies. Despite its jokey popularity – it was a common 21st birthday present – it was also critically acclaimed. Harper Lee, the author of *To Kill a Mockingbird*, praised it with, 'I have never seen a sociological document of such beauty – the photographs alone are shattering … [it] is a beautiful testament to a stubborn and proud people' (quoted in Edge, 2011: x).

The recipes celebrated a different view of Americana. They included Slum-Gullion, Jail-House Chili, Dirty Rice, Chicken Feet, Collard Greens, Chicken-Fried Steak, Home Fries and Mock Cooter Soup. Scattered throughout were observations from the people Mickler had gathered the recipes from (if he had not invented them). For Quick Fruit Cobbler, Ora May says 'it don't look or sound much, but you gotta taste it one time and you'll be hooked'. Mavis Drew suggests, 'if someone's eating corn pone for the first time, this is the one that'll make a believer out of 'em!' Mammy says of her Hush Puppies, 'if you got a yappin' dog or a hungry man this ought to shut'um up' (Mickler, 1986: 92, 115, 121).

What really caught readers' imaginations was the extensive section of vibrant colour photos capturing the imagery of the Deep South. These included the contents of fridges and pantries, stoves, weatherboard shacks, gas stations, churches, roadside fruit sales, shelling shrimps, pick-up trucks and people sitting on their porches. It was a reminder that there still was a very different part of America, one that could be imagined as authentic and could still be visited.

Television

In the 1980s and 1990s, Keith Floyd pioneered television cookery shows that travelled to exotic destinations. Often made with the cooperation and funding of destination marketing organisations, they were attractively shot, highlighting landscapes, people and experiences. Floyd's efforts became the template for a wide range of culinary productions (Hall & Mitchell, 2002a).

Conceived now as a spin-off from a successful television production, the recipe book has now taken on a new appearance. Many include descriptive travel narratives reflective of the author's experiences with the cuisine and the culture. Through the eyes of chefs such as Jamie Oliver, Rick Stein, Rachel Khoo, Stephanie Alexander and Poh Ling Yeow, the viewing audiences can take a cultural gastronomic journey to another land from the comfort of their own residential space. The media creations of some of these chefs will be explored and examined further within this chapter.

De Solier (2006) suggested that many cookery programmes are no longer concerned with teaching the viewer how to cook but have become pure entertainment. The inclusion of travelogues or travel narratives increases the viewer's engagement with the culinary experience. The influx of reality television has permitted gastronomic programmes to explode on our small screens, and for those of us with a passion for food and cooking, this may have also manifested into a collection of culinary books on our personal bookshelves. Now more than ever, the viewing audience and the retail consumer are encountered by instructions on how to cook, what to cook and why it should be cooked in a certain way: 'Walk through any large bookstore and you will find crowded shelves of cookbooks all busy wrestling to attract your attention and spending power' (Brownlie *et al.*, 2005: 7). These volumes of culinary manuscripts can be instructional, inspirational or even motivational to travel to new and exciting destinations.

The modern television audience can experience a daily assortment of gastronomic programmes, including cooking shows, cooking competitions, programmes which explain how to run a successful commercial kitchen and those which suggest where to go and what to consume while on vacation. Has this influx of gastronomic appearances improved the image of food establishments and our gastronomic choices or has it led us to believe that now anyone can be a celebrity or master chef and produce a successful product for the commercial retail sector?

Historically, a chef had to build a reputation over a long duration by consistently demonstrating their capabilities in a commercial venture to attract an appreciative clientele. Aspiring and influential chefs in the 21st century have also utilised cookery books as another vehicle to make the general populace aware of their skills, knowledge, creativity and possible originality in their cooking prowess feasibly acquired from their travel encounters.

With the advances in media, the reputation and the charisma of a chef can be created virtually overnight in our lounge rooms. International celebrity chefs, such as Rick Stein, Jamie Oliver, Nigella Lawson, Marco Pierre White and Heston Blumenthal have become household names and the audience trusts in their judgement. This has occurred because of the proliferation of media exposure, and even the competitors whom celebrities judge in television cooking show competitions have also acquired popularity and, similarly, their own programmes and cookbooks. Busby *et al.* (2013) argued for the existence of a new type of film tourist, who is influenced by cookery programmes and, in the case of this discussion, by cookery books. Similarly, Hall (2013) found through an empirical study that the main source of knowledge about farmers' markets was from television shows.

Cookbooks with Travelogues

The following case studies examines a variety of cookery books written by four culinary authors, the renowned celebrity chefs Jamie Oliver and Rachel Khoo from the UK, plus from Australia the well-known cook Stephanie Alexander and the lesser known Tania Gomes. Each of their cookery books are presented in different formats and styles, whether in the way the content is organised, the discourse or narrative style applied or the overall 'look' of the cookbook. The presentation might be formal and sophisticated or in contrast can be more playful and fun. It could even be similar to a lifestyle publication, which could also include a generous variety of glossy colourful images of the culture and the recipes described (Brownlie *et al.*, 2005).

Jamie Oliver (UK)

Jamie Oliver is a prolific author of cookbooks and among his range of culinary literature there are a variety of cookery books that contain detailed travelogues and descriptions of cuisines from other cultures, including anecdotes of encounters with colourful local individuals, which provide a touch of what might be considered authentic. Oliver has written and produced a collection of television shows and cookbooks, commencing with *The Naked Chef* in 1999. Byrne *et al.* (2003) suggested that Oliver became popular owing to his screen appeal; his approach to the audience was informal, friendly and easy-going, chatting to the audience as if they were also in the room with him to build a connection and a bond with the viewer. The consumer was able to establish a feeling of confidence in what Oliver was presenting. Believable and authentic travelogues require an element of trust and faith, otherwise the audience can perceive them as staged and not credible. Oliver has been able to establish this trust and generate a reading and viewing audience.

Since 2005, Oliver has generated a steady output of cookery books containing travelogues marketing the details of his adventures in Italy (*Jamie's Italy*, 2005) and America (*Jamie's America*, 2009), followed by a compilation, *Jamie does Spain, Italy, Sweden, Morocco, Greece and France* (2010), which provides accessible dishes that are presented as easy to make and inspired by his travels in these regions. These cookbooks additionally provide a captivating tour guide of a region similar to a travelogue or grand tour, as in the case of *Jamie does Spain, Italy, Sweden, Morocco, Greece and France* (2010). This cookery book could be described as a virtual 'grand tour' across a number of destinations. Two examples of how he entices the reader are worth noting. The first is how he describes the mountains of Andalucia in Spain as 'blessed with plenty of sunshine, so although the land is quite rocky and steep, all the classic crops like olives, grapes and tomatoes grow in abundance' (Oliver, 2010: 18). The second occurs in his introduction to Stockholm, Sweden: 'I know they'd [his friends] all love it. It is big enough to be interesting, yet small enough to feel welcoming and friendly. And the people are real characters, but sane' (Oliver, 2010: 125).

Oliver's cookery books and travelogues are designed for the home cook. His focus is to provide recipes that can be made in the domestic kitchen setting of the consumer, especially those in the UK. He aspires to introduce his reading audience to the warmth and hospitality of family and everyday life in the regions that he has visited. His premise is 'fun' and is about speed and ease of preparation, so that the major focus is on the enjoyment of communal consumption (Brownlie *et al.*, 2005). Oliver provides the reader with an infectious dialogue of persuasive motivation to travel. He talks of 'flight tickets', a 'cheap fare' (from the UK to Europe), 'being brave to escape the daily routine' and 'taking time out to discover new things', by actually making the effort in getting there. The content for many of Oliver's cookery books is focused on the cuisines from a region with stories that accompany this adventure. *Jamie's America* (2009) examines New York, Louisiana and Arizona to mention a few, introducing the reader to food produced from these regions. It is a story of his 12 months of adventures during a driving tour across the USA. In each section there is a personal reflection on the destination and why this region or city was chosen for his cookery book. In the introduction to the book, Oliver recognises that America is widely known for junk food, but he reveals to his reader how he was 'welcomed into homes and saw sides of America that he never dreamt existed' (Oliver, 2009: 10). The books from Oliver's collection are captivating and engaging because of the travelogue narratives, which allow the reader to imagine each step in this culinary journey.

Rachel Khoo (UK)

In *The Little Paris Kitchen* (2012) Rachel Khoo prepares simple French dishes in a tiny kitchen in Paris. This series, like others discussed earlier in this chapter, is complemented with a cookery book that reveals to her audience her travel exploits through a cultural exposure to the gastronomic wonders of French cuisine. The cookery book and the series provide travel visuals and gastronomic immersion into a tantalising and desirable Western food culture. Khoo (2012: 11) explained: 'There is much to be said about the daily eating habits of the French. Simplicity and *savoir faire* and an understanding of ingredients are key'. The consumer can be inspired by the cookbook and Khoo's engaging television programme about how she opened a two-diner restaurant in the tiny Paris apartment to test and perfect her everyday classic cookbook recipes.

Khoo is of Malaysian and Austrian ancestry, but was brought up in the UK. In her twenties, similar to Julia Child, she went to Paris and undertook a foodie's dream by enrolling in Le Cordon Bleu Cookery School. She studied pâtisserie and, also akin to Child, she stayed for a number of years, honing her culinary skills. However, unlike Child, Khoo opened her own establishment. She describes to her readers aspects of this culinary journey. Thus, her cookery book is focused on a culinary adventure to celebrate and reenergise the fabulous world of French everyday cookery. Khoo has a desire to provide her reading and watching audience with the confidence to generate French food at home. She states that 'this book is not another collection of classics but the story of how I discovered these recipes, adding a fresh and simple approach to French classics' (Khoo, 2012: 9). The book's contents are presented as a menu: 'Everyday cooking', 'Snack time', 'Summer picnics', 'Aperitifs', 'Dinner with friends and family', 'Sweet treats' and 'French basics', plus a few other valuable notes. These categories depict aspects of French cooking that Khoo indicates are representations of contemporary French culinary culture. The book is also bursting with not only photos of the recipes, but also a glimpse into French culture and the French lifestyle (picnics/gardens, wine, bicycles, art, cafés and food markets just to name a few). If the consumer has not been to France, or has memories of past visitations, this cookery book certainly provides a motivation to travel to this region in Europe or reminisce on time spent there.

Following on from her successes with France, Khoo has produced *Rachel Khoo's Kitchen Notebook* (2014–2015). These series take in a wide variety of attractive destinations, including Turkey, Spain, Italy, Sweden and Australia.

Stephanie Alexander (Australia)

Stephanie Alexander's *Cooking & Travelling in South-West France* (2002) is part travelogue and part cookbook. The book provides evocative descriptions of the region and an insight to the regional culture through the eyes and stories of locals, whilst also offering interpretations of tradition cuisine via originally inspired recipes constructed by Alexander. The cookery book has a traditional and elegant style and is larger than the customary A4 size, offering the impression of grandeur, while the pages are presented in olive and cream as opposed to the more traditional white. All these fine details assist in creating a refined and classic impression for the consumer, once again giving them a sense of trust and confidence.

Alexander presents this cookery book in a manner to engage her readers by sharing her personal history as well as her favourite dishes from the region, which allows the reader a glimpse into the life of the famous Australian chef. She describes to her readers an enthusiasm for France, dating it back to experiences of working there in her younger years:

> This book is a personal response to a beautiful part of France that deserves to be better known and has much to offer the visitor, especially the food-loving visitor. The person I am writing for will be uplifted by the incredible landscape, will love to explore the countryside – above and below ground, its awesome caves as well as its food markets – and will delight in its savoury and satisfying cuisine and listen carefully to stories of times long gone. (Alexander, 2002: 5)

Alexander's cookery book is not structured in the same way as many generic cookery books with entrée/starters, meat, pasta and desserts. Instead she develops a story via the contents that will appeal to the culinary and travelogue reader. The chapters of topic headings speak of a journey travelled and cooked by the author. The appearance of the cookbook includes wonderful photographic imagery not only of the dishes but also of the region. There is an abundance of visual experience beholden to her travels of this region, similar to the colourful visual style widely utilised in lifestyle magazines (Brownlie *et al.*, 2005). It is noteworthy that she dedicates the first 43 pages of the book to descriptive text referring to her travel and consumption of food adventures with no recipes included. It is only after this extensive introduction that she introduces her readers to the selection of food recipes.

Tania Gomes (Australia)

Australian born Tania Gomes's *Flavours of Portugal* (2005) discusses her Portuguese background and introduces the cooking enthusiast to wonderful visions of Portugal. The recipes presented bring Portuguese cuisine to life, to be enjoyed at a dinner table anywhere in the world. The book is written in both English and Portuguese, reflecting the fact that Gomes is a child of a Portuguese family that migrated to Australia. Similar to Alexander's volume previously discussed, Gomes dedicates the first 38 pages of this cookery volume to explaining Portuguese cuisine, with a special emphasis on those members of the Portuguese diaspora who have carried their homeland traditions to a new host country. This is not only about her travel experiences to Portugal, but also about how 'memories, emotions, culture ... the Portuguese spirit carries on, across oceans, through the heart and minds of the thousands of Portuguese scattered across the globe' (Gomes, 2005: 13). The focus of this cookery book is traditions, heritage and history. With family photos inserted throughout (dating back to the mid-1950s), it provides via recipes and photographs an insight into Portuguese cookery and culture. This equates to Mennell's (1985) third concern of food writing being a mix of myth, history and story. This cookbook provides a slight contrast from the others because the travelogue is situated partly in the past rather than the present, providing the reader with a nostalgic travelogue of family memories and homeland tradition.

Conclusion

The cookbooks highlighted in this chapter may help to inspire travel, which is an aspect of gastronomy that has been underplayed and under-researched. There is a need for future studies to explore this issue further, including the extent to which these types of travelogues are considered more authentic and authoritative by consumers than the guides and handbooks that have been traditionally available. A world in which social media is increasingly important and non-professional opinions about travel abound also offers ripe opportunities for research. Is the cookbook as travel narrative a dying genre, or will the popularity of celebrity chefs on television maintain or create a market for this type of book? The cookbook/travelogue fusion might also assist in research that seeks to understand the importance of food within the tourist experience.

13 Just Desserts: A Darker Cinema Gastronomica

Entrée

> Food is part of the way that, for over a century now, movies have been telling us who we are, constructing our economic and political aspirations; our sense of sexual, national, and ethnic identity; filling our minds with ideas about love and romance, innocence and depravity, adventure, bravery, cruelty, hope and despair. (Bower, 2004a: 3)

Cinematically, gastronomy has always been both a fundamental and conspicuous element of narratives and images, most often, but not always, in an incidental sense that has, over time, become much more of a focus for enthusiasts and researchers alike. From the earliest flickering 'movies' in penny arcades, film has presented compelling constructed perspectives of society in all its multiple forms and at all levels, its past and future promises all imbued with continuous, inevitable processes and promises of change. Just as the familiar reassures, that which counterpoints such reality with a confrontational dialectic unsettles the cinematic status quo and its loyal coterie of enthusiasts for whom challenge is anathema.

Historically, cinema has relied upon an institutionalised practice of representing, in many instances, gastronomic practices that frequently depict the consumption of food and drink in an incidental, utilitarian yet reassuring manner. These include modest meals that both anchor and perpetuate Hollywood's 20th century version of family values in orderly, homely settings as well as relocation to vacation destinations that may necessitate reinvention, reassessment and reconfiguration of entrenched social values and practices. The construct of the tourist/innocent abroad has also frequently relied upon consumption as a narrative device that may confirm epicurean dreams or anxieties of a particular location, such as France in general, and Paris in particular. One obvious corollary, however, is when the gastronomic focus, often in a distinctive cultural and touristic setting, is given primacy, even to the extent of becoming a critical narrative driver.

The curative power of sumptuous, celebratory consumption in Gabriel Axel's *Babette's Feast* (1987) transcends the (imagined) austerity of remote 19th century Denmark and reconfigures, albeit temporarily, the drab palette of remote rural life with culinary French colour from the glowing, eponymous feast. The temptations of such romantic depictions tend to belie the larger reality of any given population's more modest patterns and practices of consumption. Brown asserts that 'the Danes have made eating their national pastime, both their sport and recreation' largely owing, it seems, to Denmark's lack of wild surroundings in which to climb and hike (Brown, 1969: 30). More recently there has been revived interest in traditional 'Nordic Cuisine', which has now morphed into 'New Nordic Cuisine' with its increased emphasis on healthy patterns of consumption (Micheelsen *et al.*, 2014). Health concerns, however, do not seem to have influenced those who in September 2014 voted for *Stegt flæsk*, a traditional roast pork dish served with parsley sauce, to become Denmark's new national dish (Wenande, 2014), not exactly Babette redux but certainly a counterpoint to 'New Nordic Cuisine'.

Lasse Hallström's film *Chocolat* (2000) has free-spirited Vianne and her six-year-old daughter opening a *chocolaterie* in a conservative French village. Despite ongoing confrontation with the mayor, Vianne and gypsy paramour Roux manage to transform the village animosity thanks to an indulgent mayoral chocolate epiphany. A similar motif of chocolate's allure is cited by M.F.K. Fisher (1968: 11), who fondly recalled an elderly French music teacher eating her mid-morning snack of warmed bread and melted chocolate. Apart from valid health concerns about excessive indulgence in chocolate's sugary, calorific content, its apparently benign role beginning as a childhood treat and culminating as a romantic, adult indulgence continues to consolidate in the minds of those with a 'sweet tooth'. Chocolate also enjoys many multinational cultural associations through long-established manufacturers such as Cadbury (UK, 1824) Lindt & Sprüngli (Switzerland, 1845), Leonidas (Belgium, 1913) and Whitman's (USA, 1842) to name but four.

One final curiously ambiguous chocolate motif is the multiple forms of gateaux and desserts collectively termed 'Death by chocolate'. Reviewing Santa Monica's then new PCH Grill on the site of former restaurant Les Anges, Perry observed 'that on windy nights you can still hear the ghost of *Les Anges* at this corner, making eerie whistlings in the rafters that sound for all the world like "in sea urchin sauce ... garnished with crayfish ... baby vegetables ... *la mort au chocolaaaat*"' (Perry, 1989: 1). Despite Perry's dismissal of passé *nouvelle* cuisine, his haunting, attenuated French moaning invests the dessert with much more mystique than the current clichéd oversupply of offerings that bear the same name. The term has also manifested in the title of at least six novels that offer mysteries related to death by chocolate, ranging from a chocolate-covered corpse (Moore, 2006), to strychnine-laced chocolates in 1870s Victorian Brighton (Jackson, 2012) and a murderous chocolatier (Nolan, 2011). Documented deaths by chocolate seem to be rare, but a 45-year-old French farmer faced 20 years in prison for murdering his parents after 'lacing their chocolate mousse with a highly toxic insecticide' (Australian Foreign Press, 2008).

Itami's *Tampopo* (1985) is a satirical Japanese moral fable of good ultimately trumping corruption in a number of food-oriented vignettes. Erotic food fun, the gratification of gourmet knowledge and the correct way to eat spaghetti inventively counterpoint darker visions of Japanese culinaria that flirt with notions of death and transcendence, the exemplar being a fondness for fugu fish. The Japanese fugu frisson may be aligned with 'La petite mort', the 'little death' where the post-orgasmic state flirts with unconsciousness, similar to that of auto-erotic asphyxia. According to Fox, the risk associated with fugu consumption tends to be offset by it being considered 'a prized delicacy despite the fact that it can be lethal if incorrectly prepared. Apparently the possibility of death shortly after dinner does not deter the Japanese consumer or diminish their enjoyment of this potentially dangerous comestible' (Fox, 2011: 75).

Baron's engaging overview of food and film notes that 'writing on food in film has often explored the use of cannibalism as a metaphor for colonialism or a corrupt society' (Baron, 2006: 102). The cinematic narratives that address a darker gastronomy, however, constitute a menu that few may choose to partake of. Cannibalism, culinary rebellion and being force-fed parts of one's own brain sautéed in butter are far from easy choices, not to mention such practices transgressing all that Emily Post promulgated.

Etiquette notwithstanding, the narratives and images of a darker cinematic gastronomy with unsettling depictions of culinary practices and forms of consumption, in a range of locations, constitute more of a voracious devouring than the usual discreet nibbling.

Main Course

I, for one, have always been fascinated by the forbidden ... I've never understood the incurious who draw the line at experimenting with different sensations. (Grescoe, 2005: 4)

The currency of cannibalism

The history of cannibalism, according to Avramescu, has three successive part historical and part conceptual stages. The cannibal was initially viewed as a creature from the perspective of natural law. The cannibal then became a form of 'diabolical retort', confounding theologians and metaphysicians alike. Finally, and currently, the cannibal is primarily understood as a creature of circumstances and education (Avramescu, 2003: 2). One significant challenge has been to conclusively establish a cannibal reality, particularly in light of imaginative, yet largely uncorroborated, travellers' 'reports' that have filtered back to 'civilization' over the last millennium.

Evert (2013) reported that 'French paleontologists located 100,000-year-old bones that had been broken by Neanderthals ... to extract marrow and brains ... tool marks ... suggested that tongue and thigh meat had also been cut off for consumption'. It is the act of human eating human that constitutes the greatest abomination, given that each human is so much more than the sum of their physical being. Cannibalism is the ultimate reductive act of consumption, whilst there may be times when it becomes a ghastly necessity, such as in times of famine, when a primal instinct to survive displaces philosophical moral reasoning. It is the latter, however, that usually informs the wider response to both the concept and the reality of cannibalism.

Despite a 14th century refutation of cannibals by a papal emissary to China: 'The truth ... is that no such people do exist as nations, though there may be an individual ... here and there' (Diski, 2009: 22), the monstrosity of the cannibal construct has not diminished since both Marco Polo and Columbus wrote of 'dog-headed men' consuming human flesh. In Columbus's case, MacCannell proposed that the explorer mistook local Indian warnings of 'Cariba' to mean 'cannibal'; owing to his assumption that the Indians were the guardians of the Great Khan's outer empire, Columbus only heard 'Khan-ibal' (MacCannell, 1992: 47).

In the 'New' world on the east coast of what would later become the USA, the harsh winter of 1609–1610 proved to be extremely challenging for the Jamestown colony, with its population experiencing what was called the 'starving time'. So desperate were the conditions that 'at least a half-dozen accounts, by people who lived through the period or spoke to colonists who did, describe occasional acts of cannibalism that winter'. Evidence suggests that corpses were exhumed and eaten, and that a husband killed his wife and then salted her flesh, presumably for later consumption (Brown, 2013a). Once again, the most primal human instinct is to survive; sociocultural conditioning is cold comfort when faced with starvation and imminent death.

Defoe's fictional, philosophical, eponymous desert island castaway *Robinson Crusoe* (1719) finds remnants of a cannibal feast in his 18th year on the island; more cannibals appear in his 23rd year, and he saves an escaped captive of the cannibals who becomes his man 'Friday' in his 25th year. Defoe's deployment of cannibals as a plot device emphasises not only the risk Crusoe faces of being murdered and eaten, but also his isolation and vulnerability. The saved escapee becomes Crusoe's 'man Friday', but the relationship is predicated primarily on servitude and echoes extant 18th century European approaches to race relations. The cannibal trope, however, serves to consolidate notions of the 'other' as well as the horror of primitivism, particularly in terms of Empire and its fundamental, spurious ethos of occupying in order to civilise.

Baker (1999), in his review of Sanborn's *The Sign of the Cannibal: Melville and the Making of a Postcolonial Reader* (1998), cited a Captain James Cook vignette from when his expeditionary ship, the *Resolution*, was anchored on the north island of New Zealand in Queen Charlotte Sound on 23 November 1773. A 'recently severed human head' was brought on board by one of the ship's officers, the reactions to which, not surprisingly, generated a lengthy discussion of 'cannibalism'. Despite no mention being made of either the source or the racial origin of the severed head, its totemic, trophy status is without doubt, in terms of both those who severed the head and those who were stimulated conversationally to locate it in a cannibal construct.

In March 1809, 90 years after *Crusoe*, the *Boyd* left London with convicts bound for Sydney, where the tragic human cargo was discharged. En route to New Zealand the *Boyd* was attacked then boarded by fierce Maoris, who killed and consumed the crew; 'Cannibalism excited particular horror, as it was one of the strongest European taboos' (Lummis, 2005: 27). Tourists visiting New Zealand these days may get a residual sense of such a Maori past when encountering the haka war dance, which is used these days to honour guests and forms part of ceremonies such as the official opening of sporting matches.

Cannibalism was also supposedly practised in indigenous Fijian culture but Banivanua-Mar identified that 'the reputed existence of cannibalism was also framed as an atavistic tendency capable of explaining acts of rebellion in ways that de-politicized and infantilized indigenous resistance' (Banivanua-Mar, 2010: 259). Banivanua-Mar's discussion distinguished between the upper-case discourse of 'Cannibalism' and lower-case for cannibalism's reputed existence, concluding that 'Because Cannibalism so effortlessly transmits the racialized relations of power between colonized and colonizer that formed its historical basis, its deployment today can be as disempowering as it was in the ... 1870s' (Banivanua-Mar, 2010: 281).

Facing challenges similar to those of the Jamestown colony in the early 17th century, the spectre of cannibalism manifested once again in late 20th century North Korea. Famine had wiped out almost 10% of the population and children who had left the barren countryside wandered into the towns; living rough and disappearances became commonplace, with 'dark rumours ... spreading, too horrifying to believe, too persistent to ignore' – 'at least one person in Chongjin was arrested and executed for eating human flesh' (Fisher, 2013). North Korea's continuing dire economic state coupled with the widespread hardship endured by most of its population is yet another appalling outcome of despotic exploitation.

Cannibalism in Pakistan is still legal, but that is about to change after two brothers recently robbed graves to make 'human curry'. Malm (2014) discussed the case, noting that a bill has been filed banning the exhuming of a corpse for consumption or 'use for magical purposes'. Convicted cannibal brothers Mohammad Arif Ali, 35, and Mohammad Farman Ali, 30, 'allegedly dug up more than 100 corpses from the local graveyard in order to eat them'. Neighbours complained about the stench coming from the brothers' home and when police arrived the head of a missing three-year old boy was discovered. Poverty and hunger constituted their defence which was, needless to say, unsuccessful.

In 2001, Armin Miewes, of Rothenburg, Germany, advertised for a dining companion on a Cannibal Café website. The catch was that Armin intended to dine on, rather than with, his companion, but that did not seem to discourage Bernd Brandes from replying, and eventually sitting opposite Armin at his table. It was to be Bernd's last supper, so to speak, but the beginning of lengthy litigation for Armin. Diski (2009) engagingly discussed a TV interview with Armin describing the meal: 'I sautéed the steak of Bernd, with salt, pepper, garlic and nutmeg. I had it with Princess croquettes, Brussels sprouts and a green pepper sauce'. Diski then wryly notes: 'you begin to see, as the suburban lace curtain drifts into place, that the reality of cannibalism could be far less interesting than the idea of it. I think it's the Princess croquettes in particular that cause the disappointment'. Exactly.

The extent to which dark pasts have been foregrounded for tourism remains contentious, but so is selective provision of historical facts in order to satisfy imagined notions of mainstream expectations. To date, however, (historical) cannibalism has been acknowledged but has driven few, if any, (public) culinary touristic strategies as such. Rothenburg, Pakistan, Jamestown, New Zealand and France continue to attract tourists, but are not primarily dark tourist destinations despite their admittedly limited yet mediatised 'dark' pasts.

Kivela and Crotts proposed two possible categories that resonate in the context of this discussion: (a) the *existential* gastronomy tourists, who 'seek food combinations and experiences that foster learning (about gastronomy)'; and (b) the *experimental* gastronomy tourists, who 'keep up-to-date about fashionable foods, ingredients, and recipes. They actively pursue trying out new ingredients and new ways of eating and preparing food' (Kivela & Crotts, 2008: 43–44). No research to date, however, has been reported or published establishing connections between either, or both, categories of gastronomic tourists seeking out, or engaging in, cannibalism, which is not surprising given the extreme consumption involved. Beeton observed that: 'We need to consider what ... people relate to and if it is their empathetic attachment to a story or a place that facilitates tourism' (Beeton, 2005: 237), but such information could also prove to be confronting.

The touristic gaze also frequently seeks out not only familiar sites of interest but also those that may offer a brief frisson counterpointing commodified, legal constructs. Dennis O'Rourke's 1988 *Cannibal Tours* essentially presents a crisis of modernity for both the tourists, who manifest degrees of candour about their expectations – real cannibals! – and the indigenous locals who provide a constructed frisson in order to facilitate the sale of their crafts. Silverman observed that a subtext of the film is 'a dichotomy between the dominant and encompassing tourists ... and the encompassed Sepiks, who typify the dependent "primitive" in ruin' (Silverman, 1999: 53). Not surprisingly, the tourists seek tangible remains of the (imagined) cannibal past and appear content to purchase 'genuine' artefacts whilst simultaneously observing the Sepiks primarily as spectacle. Strain, citing Rony (1996), proposed that the threat of actual cannibalism 'is flattened or disarmed through a fetishizing and objectifying gaze that reduces difference to spectacle, thereby preserving the pleasurable aspect of "fascinating cannibalism"' (Strain, 2003: 105–106). One very vocal local angrily berates the camera with a tirade about the tourists wanting the 'best' price, which, not surprisingly, has nothing to do with the price she is asking; as Silverman (2012: 109) enquired, 'Who can watch this movie and not squirm – even after many viewings?' On the Sepik River, the politics of cannibalism have been reduced to petty squabbling over mementoes evoking a presumably vanished past, annoying tourists notwithstanding.

Consuming cinematic cannibalism

'We were going for blonds, blonds were next on the menu' Catharine says. 'He was famished for blonds, he was fed up with the dark ones and was famished for blonds ... that's how he talked about people, as if they were items on a menu. "That one's delicious-looking, that one is appetizing" or "that one is *not* appetizing" – I think because he was really nearly half-starved from living on pills and salad.' (Spoto, 1997: 212)

So reports soon-to-be lobotomised Catharine of her sexually voracious cousin Sebastian who, it turns out, is himself to be on the menu of crazed beach boys. In Tennessee Williams's overwrought 1958 confessional melodrama *Suddenly Last Summer*, the character of Sebastian Venable is generally acknowledged as a transmutation of Williams's own anguished life. Here, however, it is the drama's consumption motif that is most resonant: not only was Sebastian 'famished' for blonds, his gaze and critique took the form of a de-humanising menu that was, apparently, largely owing to his own limited intake of food, in every sense of the term. The final 'consumption' of Sebastian is, according to Tyler, dramatic and symbolic; he is 'hunted down in the very streets where he has hunted ... his dying flesh devoured by flesh that, in one way or another, he has devoured' (Tyler, 1993: 310). Suddenly, last summer, the tide turned for Sebastian.

The cinematic shocks continued into the early 1960s with *Mondo Cane* (*A Dog's World*) 1962, written and directed by Paolo Cavara, Franco Prosperi and Gualtiero Jacopetti. Employing a documentary format, vignettes provided glimpses of worldwide cultural practices ostensibly intended to inform but with surprising and occasionally shocking subtext. A decade later, cinema returned to the quasi-documentary format and dished up narratives purporting to 'discover' cannibalistic tribes in remote locations. Umberto Lenzi's *The Man from the Deep River* (1972) is considered the first cannibal exploitation film, although it was cannibalism-lite, as actual slaughtering of animals contributed most to its notoriety. The jungle setting is claimed to be Thai, but Thai food as such is not as strong a consumption motif as human flesh.

For the road-trip tourist, the car breakdown on a dark and stormy night apparently in the middle of nowhere is a very creaky horror movie trope. Fortunately for Brad Majors and Janet Weiss there is a light 'over at the Frankenstein place' so all, it seems, is not lost – or is it? Jim Sharman's *The Rocky Horror Picture Show* (1975) has 'sweet transvestite' Dr Frank-N-Furter (Tim Curry) murder motorcycle bad boy Eddie (Meatloaf), then later carve and serve his flesh to unsuspecting dinner guests including lost waifs Brad Majors (Barry Bostwick) and Janet Weiss (Susan Sarandon). Given the intentionally shock-inducing script, cannibalism joins a list of taboos that all tend to blur in the frantic world of the castle that is, according to the criminologist narrator (Charles Gray), 'lost in time, and space, and meaning'.

Deodato's *Cannibal Holocaust* (1980) was promoted in advertising copy as 'the most controversial movie ever made' and was, urban myth-wise, believed to be a 'snuff' film. That same year also saw the release of Margheriti's *Cannibals in the Streets* (1980), also known as *Cannibal Apocalypse*, in which former Vietnam POWs are infected with a condition that compels them to consume human flesh – that of the residents of Atlanta. Wes Craven's *The Hills Have Eyes* series also features cannibal groups who live far from urban settings. Craven's original of 1977 was set in the Nevada desert, while New Mexico was the locale for the 2006 reboot – both popular tourist destinations although hardly culinary capitals in the usual sense. Cannibals, factual and fictional, and their food of preference profoundly trouble traditional consumption preferences and patterns, subverting expectations of both product and practice, not to mention familiar tourist locales.

With Richard Fliescher's *Soylent Green* (1973) it is back to the dystopian future in the year 2022. All of the challenges facing the 20th century at three-quarters time have increased exponentially 47 years later, with the horrific urban exemplar being, not surprisingly, New York City. Overcrowding and infrastructural corruption, as well as rampant systemic collapse and a population of 40 million do not make for easy living. Needless to say, feeding the starving, unemployed masses is not easy either, but the Soylent Corporation manufactures the titular food product in the form of green wafers that are the end-product of processed human corpses. Not surprisingly, the lifestyles of the rich and dishonest continue largely unchanged until challenged by crusader-of-sorts Thorn (Charlton Heston) when he discovers the truth, but 'his hysterical appearance and the chaos around him conspires against him being taken seriously. Closure, then, is achieved through personal knowledge rather than "saving" society for itself ... *Soylent*

Green ... serves as a warning against the negative outcomes of the mass production of modernity, to a point where overconsumption has led to self-consumption' (Forster, 2004: 255).

While cannibalia was far from frequent cinematic content, more familiar and, to a degree, less challenging suburban cannibal contexts began to be served up to cineastes. Paul Bartel's *Eating Raoul* (1982) offers Paul and Mary Bland, who are mortified by life in general, and specifically by the 'swingers' in their apartment block. Their dream is to open a restaurant in the country called either 'Chez Bland' or 'The Country Kitchen', although their critical concern is that they can serve as a signature dish what they consider their specialty: 'the Bland enchilada'. Canby (1982) considered the film 'a very funny comedy about sex, murder and cannibalism, a movie that somehow is never as genteel as Paul and Mary might wish', and Pollock noted that the film is 'so black that it hardly requires the theater lights to be dimmed' (Pollock, 1982).

The 'swingers' become the bane of the Blands' lives, so action is taken and swingers are routinely dispatched by a handy, heavy skillet. Raoul, a local locksmith, becomes enamoured of Mary but also discovers what the Blands have been putting in their garbage compactor. He offers to dispose of the bodies but his interest in Mary continues to grow. Ebert reports that 'Paul grows jealous, especially when he discovers that Raoul has been stealing from them. The next step is perhaps suggested by the title of the movie, or perhaps not' (Ebert, 1982). For Kael, however, viewing was more soporific: '*Eating Raoul* seems sedated. Watching it, I felt as if I were experiencing sensory deprivation' (Kael, 1984: 424).

Cannibalism as black comedy also informed Richardson's *Eat the Rich* (1987), an anarchic British punk version of scandalous goings on and ghastly consumption at the highest levels. The Home Secretary, Nosher, is a vulgar ruffian who swills beer from the can at Royal dinners, then suggests a dalliance to the Queen. Alex, an effete terrorist, takes over 'Bastards' restaurant after being fired, reopening it as 'Eat the Rich', with obnoxious waiters who serve a delicious mincemeat that is the flesh of former patrons murdered during the rebel group's takeover.

Both *Eating Raoul* and *Eat the Rich* struggle somewhat in their attempts to convincingly to deploy the horror of cannibalism within a black comedic revenge paradigm. Each relies heavily on scandalous yet somewhat sophomoric narrative premises to shock, but neither truly fulfils the promise of delivering genuinely subversive polemic. Canby (1982) concludes his review of *Eating Raoul* by describing it as 'an extremely nice comedy about people who know that niceness is next to godliness and that sex is simply disgusting'. Cannibalism, however, does not appear to present any challenge to the Blands' banal yet perverse moral universe.

Similarly, *Eat the Rich* sounds like the opening recommendation of a Swiftian discourse on democratic, if rather dramatic, societal reconfiguration. The narrative attempts to construct cannibalism as a cultural norm, echoing the practices of the Thai jungle dwellers in *The Man from Deep River,* but the latter film, comparatively, manifests a plausible and possibly more convincing anthropological case, that of a cultural norm, than those for whom cannibalism becomes a lifestyle necessity or choice. Armstrong observed that both films, as well as others with similar themes, 'sought to temper the sensationalist horror of their subject with a large measure of surreal comedy' (Armstrong, 2004: 232). Armes wrote of Surrealism that 'many of its key elements are accessible to the cinema: dreams and hallucinations, imagination and the investigation of the unconscious, chance and spontaneity' (Armes, 1974: 185). Despite Surrealism's rich checklist of enthralling elements, few inform, or – apart from the very obvious – operate in *Eating Raoul* or *Eat the Rich.*

London has rarely disappointed the gastronomic tourist. Wiltons, currently at 55 Jermyn St, SW1, has operated since 1742; Simpson's Tavern ('The Oldest Chophouse in London') at Ball Court, 38 1/2 Cornhill, EC3, since 1757; and the Criterion Restaurant since 1873 at 224 Piccadilly, W1. These and many other establishments, have consistently delivered gustatory pleasures as well as a tangible sense of London's rich gastronomic history. A fictional food feast and more, Peter Greenway's magisterial *The Cook, The Thief, His Wife and Her Lover* (1989) runs an elegant gamut from coprophagy to cannibalism within a 'triangular preoccupation with haute cuisine, voyeurism and projected images' (Armstrong, 2004: 221). For the gastronome, the film's *haute cuisine* presented, celebrated and consumed in London's lavishly decorated restaurant Le Hollandais is emblematic of rarefied dining experiences that are the stuff of culinary dreams.

The dreams in this instance, however, are brutally reconfigured through the actions of gangster Albert Spica (Michael Gambon), who manages to perversely enrich the opulent surrounds with his own brand of vivid artistry yet, simultaneously, perpetuate clichéd, compelling criminality. Brinkema meditated on aspic as a filmic device, proposing that 'The crude, violent Spica is a problem for aspic and all that it represents: the restaurant … classical French cuisine, taste as refinement, and the moral qualities ascribed to the aesthetically high' (Brinkema, 2010: 75). Despite the opulence of engagement and consumption, none of the film's resonant historical and artistic framing devices permit narrative escape from Spica's vulgarity and cruelty.

A comeuppance of sorts is Spica's ultimate feast when he is forced to consume some of the cooked corpse of the late Michael, his wife Georgina's bookish lover. He attempts to deploy a pistol but that ends up with Georgina 'who pauses until he has put a forkful of the vile stuff into his mouth and begun to masticate. She then calmly shoots him in the forehead, denouncing him as a "cannibal"' (Armstrong, 2004: 233). Greenaway observed that 'when you've finally devoured everything there is to be eaten, you end up eating one another' (quoted in Siegel, 2000: 59). This reflection may, for all intents, serve as his very particular philosophy of consumption.

Leaving London for South America, whilst the adventure/ecotourist may have to rely on very context-specific foods and liquids, the remote drama and beauty of the Andes, from tropical Colombia and Venezuela to the southern-most regions of Chile and Argentina, tend to offset culinary limitations. Such anticipated limitations, however, can be planned for; the unanticipated, culinary and otherwise, tends to be much more challenging.

On 13 October 1972, Uruguayan Air Force Flight 571, with a Uruguayan rugby team on board, crashed on an uncharted peak in a cloud-covered pass in the Andes Mountains on the border between Chile and Argentina. Piers Paul Read's *Alive: The Story of the Andes Survivors* (1974) detailed the terrible ordeal that faced the survivors. Almost 20 years later, Frank Marshall directed *Alive* (1993), with Read's book providing the basis for the film's screenplay. The fact that the crash took place on a previously uncharted peak immediately foreshadows two critical issues: that rescue is highly unlikely, and what the survivors will eat once the plane's snack food is gone.

The moral dilemma facing the survivors in *Alive* echoes that of the Jamestown settlement in the midst of an extreme winter more than three centuries previously when there was, quite literally, no food at all. Necessity is – well, there is no need for adages when hard decisions have to made, menu-wise, so just get on with it. Maslin (1993) observed that the film's director and writer have 'approached this daunting story with what would have to be called good taste. The cannibalism is dealt with briefly and dis-creetly … It is never gruesome and only occasionally risks becoming silly. (… Nando, the moodiest of the survivors: "You didn't take from my sister, did you? God, she was so beautiful!")'. The temptation here can only be: 'Beauty is in the mouth of the beholder'. The real beauty, however, is that of the spectacular Andean mountain scenery captured by director of pho-tography, Peter James; despite the horror, the touristic gaze cannot be other than dazzled.

Just Desserts

Ridley Scott's *Hannibal* (2001) the sequel to Jonathan Demme's *The Silence of the Lambs* (1991), has Anthony Hopkins reprising the role of urbane psycho-path and noted cannibal Dr Hannibal Lecter, who observed: 'A census taker once tried to test me. I ate his liver with some fava beans and a nice chianti'.

Dr Lecter has been on the run for a decade but is tracked down by one of his victims, wealthy child molester Mason Verger (Gary Oldman), hideously disfigured by Lecter while in therapy and now wanting revenge by first tor-turing and then killing him. FBI agent Clarice Starling (Julianne Moore) is Lecter's nemesis and is determined to get him permanently incarcerated, a wish easier articulated than realised, but Verger informs her that Lecter is in Florence, and so the game begins.

Compelling locations enrich the film's narrative and pictorial momentum, not to mention the promise of Italian food. Florence always delivers, so the Ponte Vecchio and the Duomo are postcard perfect, with the less familiar Palazzo Capponi and Palazzo Vecchio offering new temptations. Lecter blends into local crowds but is recognised by Chief Inspector Pazzi (Giancarlo Giannini) who attempts capture, but becomes yet another victim, hanging eviscerated against a Florentine façade. Lecter flees to the USA where he dispenses with Verger courtesy of a specially bred herd of voracious wild boars originally intended to consume Lecter himself.

The film's most original consumption vignette has Dr Lecter taking Clarice to the secluded lake house of Justice Department's Paul Krendler (Ray Liotta), who has been drugged by Lecter. Clarice awakes sometime later to discover Lecter cooking, with a heavily sedated Krendler in a wheelchair at an elegant table set for dinner. With deft, surgical skill Lecter removes the upper cranium of Krendler's skull, removes a section of his prefrontal cortex, sautés it, and finally feeds it to the sedated Krendler.

Auto-cannibalism, or autosarcophagy, seems a fitting descriptor of the act in this vignette, but as Krendler only consumes the sautéd fragment under heavy sedation – the choice was not his. Libbon *et al.* (2015: 152) noted that 'Only nine previous cases of self- or auto-cannibalism (autosarcophagy) have previously been reported in the literature' and their case study takes the tally to 10. A science-fiction take on auto-cannibalism – yet to be filmed – is explored in *The Savage Mouth*, a short story by Sakyo Komatsu (1978) in which a man disillusioned by life creates a machine that will dismember his body, then cook the parts in a programmed sequence and feed them to him. When the police finally break in to the apartment, all that remain are his insatiable, gnashing teeth, all that cannibalism allows.

Bower identifies cannibalism as a sociocultural disruption and in questioning whether or not it belongs in the genre of food movies concludes that 'whether food is coded negatively or positively ... it is often a major ingredient in the cinematic experience' (Bower, 2004a: 4). No judgement, just insight. And no tasteful fadeout here; let Avramescu (2003: 3) illuminate the conclusion:

In his strangeness, the cannibal is sovereign over a species of freedom. His story is one that casts light on the origins of the modern state and the boundaries of modern civilization, and weighs up their right to existence.

14 The Picnic: Gastronomy *Al Fresco*

Mad Men (Season 2, Episode 7, 2008)

The Draper family picnic is a bucolic idyll pulsing with all the obligatory mid-20th century advertising tropes. Don and Betty, with offspring Sally and Robert, pick at food and loll languidly in a *Saturday Evening Post*-worthy colour-coordinated cloud of red outdoor accessories and Betty's dress fabric of pink summer roses.

The sequence begins with a silent pan across the sweeping chrome dashboard of the Newport Blue and Olympic White 1962 Cadillac Coupe de Ville to the open driver's door framing Don, Betty and daughter Sally relaxing in the sunlight-dappled glade, a tranquil counterpoint to the series' usual Madison Avenue madness. The stillness inspires Betty to reflect that 'We should do this more often', to which Don responds 'We should *only* do this'. Their musings are interrupted by Bobby needing to pee, so he is sent off to find a tree, but when Sally murmurs that she, too, would like to 'tinkle' outside, Don tells a tale of his 'challenging childhood' on the farm, thereby reminding her to be very grateful for indoor plumbing – when available, that is.

Don next observes that 'we should probably get going if we don't want to hit the traffic', so he chugs down the rest of his beer, then pitches the empty can into the distance. Betty, meanwhile, packs up the picnic paraphernalia, blithely shakes the litter off the rug onto the grass, walks back to the car, and the Cadillac is then driven out of the frame, sunlight glinting on the chrome. The static image of the empty picnic site is held for six seconds or so, with the viewer's eye drawn in most cases, presumably, to the litter left behind with such cavalier abandon.

So, the final motif of the Draper picnic, that of the residual refuse, is politically charged, evoking both a culture's partially unconscious contempt for the environment as well as the limited impact of the 'Keep America Beautiful' campaign nine years after it began. The viewer in 2008 was given the opportunity to focus on the ugliness left behind in the glade while the

Drapers rode home in their 'insolent chariot' (Keats, 1958), their dreamy picnic recollections untroubled by pesky social responsibility. 1960s nostalgia for picnics has, however, been permanently sullied by the Drapers, a counterpoint to the more common exclusion of any negativities in fiction set in idyllic rural touristscapes (Frost & Laing, 2014).

Picnic Panorama: Noting the Necessities

Litter notwithstanding, the Draper outing highlights many of the polarities that generate tensions embedded in both the popular cultural construct and the familiar experiential reality of the picnic. Csergo concluded that 'As with many other everyday social practices, picnics have not been recorded in accustomed historical sources' (Csergo, 2003: 139), but noted that sources such as painting and literature result in three observations that create associations: 'picnic' becomes a rustic or rural informal meal on the grass; the protocols of 'picnic' develop; and the term becomes a stimulus for imaginative excitement.

Visser proposed 'that the French may have invented the word picnic, "pique-nique" being found earlier than "pic nic" ... It originally referred to a dinner, usually eaten indoors, to which everyone present had contributed some food, and possibly also a fee to attend' (Visser, 1991: 150). Csergo (2003: 141) offered a detailed overview of pique-nique, dating its first inclusion in the third edition of the *Dictionnaire de l'Academie* in 1740 (2003: 141).

Whilst conceding 'the vagaries of the English climate', Burnett proposed that 'eating in the open has for centuries been a recreational activity of all social classes, whether in domestic gardens, parks and other public places' (Burnett, 2003: 29). Picnic practices may also echo cultural practices and attitudes, such as those of the French having picnics in the Bois de Boulogne who are, according to Wechsburg, 'forming small islands, keeping to themselves, as in their homes. They would keep their shutters closed if they could bring them along' (Wechsberg, 1999: 101). A picnic necessitates relocating not only consumption, but also embedded cultural practices, be they those of individual, family, lovers or the end-of-year office function. Mobility, also by necessity, becomes a critical component of the enterprise, as even the most modest picnic means all that is deemed necessary must be moved to the location despite the picnic taking the form of a lunchtime interlude. Even if the picnic is only a brief encounter with the outdoors for an hour or so, the essential operational form remains remarkably consistent and familiar, one that is widely known and understood, and has usually been experienced through early family outings by the majority of participants.

The childhood literature of many pasts often trumpets a British imperial salute to the anomalously formal, if not essentially para-military, structure of what is intended to be both an informal and a relaxing break from routine.

For many, those books served as early manuals for many of life's processes, and the picnic may well be an exemplar of such instruction. The embedded polarities and protocols of picnics are, however, still remarkably consistent with what must have been the earliest forms of the experience: eating out of doors, usually in a group, and with a more relaxed approach to consumption and – dare it be written – etiquette. The practices of consumption have for many of a certain social strata simply been relocated outdoors with only a nod in the general direction of relaxing fixed behaviours.

Elizabeth David was inspired by Henry James, who had laid down a picnic technique along the lines of: 'not so good as to fail an amusing disorder, not yet so bad as to defeat the proper function of the repasts' (David, 1965: 209; see also pp. 211–217 for David on food for picnics and Oriental picnics). According to Visser, 'We reserve a whole type of eating experience for "out of doors", where for once we eat seated on the ground. We are very self-conscious about picnics, and the freedom we grant ourselves to lounge about on a blanket eating cold food with our hands' (Visser, 1991: 150). Gill also observed that 'eating outside is where everything started … Ideally, everything should be hand-held' (Gill, 2007: 38). The picnic outdoors, it seems, has always provided an opportunity for shrugging off indoor protocols and celebrating freedom in many forms.

The media – never missing an opportunity for both consolidating and validating cultural change in quite specific forms – have been the primary means of recording and then disseminating change, essentially providing the equivalent of (imagined) literary, painterly and filmic how-to manuals in locations both familiar and exotic.

What are perhaps most compelling about the theory and practice of the picnic are polarities that may generate and sustain tension in all that constitutes 'picnic' – formality/informality; private/public; regulated/unregulated; wholesome/decadent; urban/rural – all contributing to what Hartley described as 'part institution, part medium in their own right, part activity and part symbol' (Hartley, 1992: 9). Picnics, it seems, may potentially manifest a political potency that their familiar, innocuously inert surfaces belie.

Picnic Perspectives and the Past

Nostalgic memory is both selective and unreliable, but generally operates in two domains: personal and/or historical nostalgia (Kim, 2005; Stern, 1992). Such selectivity and unreliability may result in recollections that have little to do with actuality, but are consolidated with age, resulting in rose-coloured recollections at the expense of historical accuracy. Margalit proposed that, in a broader sense, nostalgia may distort past reality, idealising an experience or an object while locating it in times characterised mostly by purity and innocence (Margalit, 2011: 273). This is frequently evident when childhood is recalled by a group who shared experiences in a specific context or location, with the 'facts' often varying across individual memories. Leboe and Ansons (2006: 596) noted that 'reflections on the past are accompanied by the sense that past events were happier than those closer to the present ... those were the "good old days"'. They further argued, however, that 'many instances of nostalgic experience represent distorted perception, leading to an appreciation of the past that is more fantasy than reality' (Leboe & Ansons, 2006: 607).

In the case of 'autocamping' in 1920s and 1930s America, the reality of camping became a pragmatic choice for many travellers who eschewed the inflated costs and inferior service of the limited accommodation and food outlets on the rapidly developing highways. Belasco observed that 'A good picnic or camping spot could be found along the road, in a field, or in a schoolyard' (Belasco, 1979: 44). While there is an obvious roadside romanticism that aligns with the innocuous picnic construct operating in this example, the reality was much more the outcome of exploitative operators and the subsequent Wall Street collapse. Such 'good old days', however, may be just as much a distortion of 'the past' as the dangerously fraught present.

Despite the very selective reassurances of *Reader's Digest*'s platitudinous *Good Old Days Good Old Ways: Wisdom of the Past for the Needs of Today* (Healey, 1999) and Oliver's *The Australian Home Beautiful: From Hills Hoist to High Rise* (1999), both briefly discussed picnics in the Australian context, drawing attention to the vicissitudes of extreme weather and all the 'stuff' that has to be transported to the picnic site in order to feed and occupy the happy throng. The picnic is generally characterised as a relaxed, leisure-time activity undertaken away from home in a tranquil natural setting where too much food and beverage are consumed, then some games may be undertaken to both aid digestion and occupy already over-excited picnic participants. Simplicity is, according to Gill, 'the order of the day for a successful picnic. Remember that eating outside is where it all started' (Gill, 2007: 38), but eating outside can take a multiplicity of forms, from modest to very grand.

Elizabeth David recalled a hospitable family from her childhood who were very much given to 'out-of-door entertainments, pageants and picnics' that had a very formal tone, concluding in the picnic, when the meal was 'handed around by the footman, and in composition resembling ... an Edwardian wedding breakfast' (David, 1965: 208). Similarly, the Glyndebourne Opera Festival takes place every summer in Sussex and is where, according to Bailey, the British picnic 'reaches its apotheosis ... Here, in evening dress, opera lovers repair between the acts to the lawns ... for refreshments they may have brought with them or have ordered from a caterer' (Bailey, 1970: 23). Mrs Beeton on picnics seems to have particular resonance for Glyndebourne when she advises 'Take three corkscrews ... and champagne à discretion – water can be obtained, so it is useless to take it' (quoted in National Gallery Women's Association, 1978: 95).

Relocating dining-room grandeur to the outdoors was practised by colonial invaders, such as those in early Federal Washington anxious to enforce the distance between themselves and their indentured workers, with one matron, Mrs Bagot, reductively finding memorable 'the black women cooking our dinner' and 'a group of fishermen [who] collected to see us' (Carson, 1990: 123–124).

The early 20th century saw a rise in automobile production and increasing private car ownership, which made getting away from routine and regulation a reality for those who were newly 'auto' mobile. Sutton observed that 'The great British picnic was all-of-a-fashion for the pre-Second World War family motorist, and weekend exeats to grassy banks and byways were very common. Not only would the car take the family to their picnic place but, judging by the numerous period photographs of such occasions, it also seemed to attend, parked like a patriarch somewhere in the nearby background' (Sutton, 1996: 98).

Sociologists Robert and Helen Lynd undertook a study in the mid-1920s and mid-1930s in Muncie, Indiana which they euphemistically titled *Middletown* (Lynd & Lynd, 1956), noting the profound sociocultural impacts of the new automobility. Focusing on the automobile in 'Middletown', one significant emergent pastime, according to Pettifer and Turner, was the picnic; 'Driving out for a picnic seems to have had an enduring attraction for the motorist – perhaps sustained by the belief that fresh air stimulated the appetite or, in the words of the American Automobile Association guide, "incited the jaded appetite into most unexpected relish of the plainest food and plenty of it"' (Pettifer & Turner, 1984: 87). Hartley also observed, perhaps unnecessarily and via curiously dated terminology, that the 'driving of motor cars is by now an inescapable attribute of picnics' (Hartley, 1992: 57).

The wonderfully peripatetic *Two Fat Ladies* travelled about on Jennifer Patterson's signature Triumph Thunderbird motorcycle with Clarissa Dickson Wright in the Watsonian Jubilee sidecar, extolling on TV the diverse pleasures of gastronomy in general, and picnics in particular, in both formal and informal settings. They brought to the picnic rug, so to speak, a rich feast of personal experience and travel, with Patterson picnicking on 'Frittata with the fishermen at Taormina in Sicily ... diving for sea urchins to eat straight from the rocks, pig-sticking outings with the Hussars in Benghazi, and wontons by the Yangtze in China' (Patterson & Dickson Wright, 1997: 164). Dickson Wright concluded, however, that 'I am not, I think, a picnic person: picnics seem to ... involve carting a lot of food large distances to eat in circumstances and temperatures less pleasant than if one had stayed at home' (Patterson & Dickson Wright, 1997: 165). Dickson Wright identified what can be considered either the fundamental pleasure of the picnic enthusiast or the bane of those coerced into participating. Leaving the comfort of the dining room for the outdoors may pose a significant challenge to polite practices of consumption, not to mention the anticipated vicissitudes of climate and inevitable lack of facilities. The other obvious corollary here is that picnic food constitutes either a reconfiguration of familiar dishes into more portable forms or a simplification of food on offer, thereby facilitating consumption in locations beyond the dining room.

Many adventures associated with travel often begin with gastronomy in the form of national cuisines and the locations in which they are experienced. Writing on the Spanish *paella*, Feibleman observed that the first paellas were cooked outside over open fires, a practice considered by many as the optimal method, as 'Many Spanish picnickers plan a paella as the main feature of their outings' (Feibleman, 1970: 74). In Armenia, the banks of mountain streams frequently provide dramatic picnic settings for large parties of up to 45 people from collective farms, who bring live lambs, plenty of bread, raw vegetables, cheese, as well as home-made vodka, beer and lemonade (Papashvily & Papashvily, 1971: 154). Enjoying a 'pique-nique' in France is the stuff of many touristic dreams – lamb brochettes, 'Tarte a la Tomate', 'fromages' and 'vin blanc' on a hill above the Seine – and closer to gastronomic heaven (Fisher, 1968: 44–49).

The picnic construct is not, however, without challenges to function, form and sociocultural mores, but is widely understood, experienced and currently operationalised as a benign recreational phenomenon that manifests globally. Charles, however, offered an insight into such operationalisation with the observation that the key is 'the democracy of the picnic rug, where ownership is transferred to the group' (Charles, 2010: 14).

So, having considered all of the above, go and get out the tartan rug, make the sandwiches, put the iced sponge in the cake-tin, fill the Thermos, and have an umbrella in the car 'just in case', as the journey to explore the picnic begins. Along the way there will be an interrogation of some of the picnic's representations, 'reality' and locations in three media forms of painting, literature and the cinema, drawn from the respective Western canons. Needless to say, exploring modes and locations, both actual and imagined, will also provide opportunities to investigate possible synergies manifested through the intersection of mediated gastronomic and touristic inspirations and motivations.

Picturing the Picnic: Ravishing Representations

> It is pictures rather than propositions, metaphors rather than statements, which determine most of our philosophical convictions ... the story of the domination of the mind of the West by ocular metaphors. (Rorty, 1980: 12–13)

Rorty's assertion privileged the visual, echoing perhaps the powerful recognition that human sight operates significantly and influentially before the development of both speech and the ability to write. Seeing usually results in believing, but the understanding and 'shaping' of what is encountered and observed contributes to the growth of comprehension and the ability to 'read' increasingly more complex visual contexts. 'Picnic' as a descriptor connotes a range of signifiers that can function as a basic checklist of content and process but is also dynamic yet often context-specific in terms of dress code, location, behaviours, activities, and food and beverages. Each of those signifiers is likely to stimulate a range of visual images experientially embedded in an individual gaze and consolidated by discrete discourses.

'Different gazes are "authorised"', according to Crenshaw and Urry (1997: 176), 'by different discourses such as ... the discourse of education ..., that of health, and ... play ... Different discourses imply different socialities'. It may be that such socialities manifest most readily in the way the picnic as both construct and reality is thought about, discussed and depicted. Looking at images of picnics may inspire a yearning for such a bucolic pleasure, stimulate a desire to understand the social and political experience of a picnic or generate questions about a particular moment captured in a painted or literary or cinematic picnic. The fundamental premise of the picnic embodies informality in terms of consumption and socialising in non-urban spaces, and in doing so briefly rejects most of the practices of formal, urban and regulated consumption. The desire to record such pleasurable moments is evident in extant paintings the world over but the three considered here feature either de facto or dedicated picnics:

- *The Harvesters* (Pieter Bruegel the Elder, 1565), The Metropolitan Museum, New York (this painting can be viewed at http://www. metmuseum.org/toah/works-of-art/19.164);
- *Le déjeuner sur l'herbe* (Edouard Manet, 1863), Musée d'Orsay, Paris (this painting can be viewed at http://www.musee-orsay.fr/index.php?id= 851&L=1&tx_commentaire_pi1%5BshowUid%5D=7123); and
- *The Picnic* (Jeffrey Smart, 1980), private collection (this painting can be viewed at http://www.smhshop.com.au/the-picnic-1980-by-jeffrey-smart).

Burnett (2003: 21) observes that, by necessity, 19th century agricultural labourers 'ate out', irrespective of weather. Given that their working day was from sunrise to sunset, enough food for several meals was needed, the most common being '"doorsteps" of bread, with cheese, an onion and if possible a pint of beer and (they) thought it "a meal fit for a king"' (Burnett, 2003: 23).

The temptation here, and certainly in Bruegel's *The Harvesters*, may be to romanticise what is probably one of very few pauses for the mid-16th century workers from the back-breaking task of manual harvesting. It is tempting to be seduced by the manicured sweep of wheat and the steady progress of the harvesters, and the touristic eye will no doubt be drawn to the numerous charms of the landscape, including the church with steeple and the wonderful vistas. All is orderly progress but, simultaneously, transformative, particularly with regard to the landscape as well as the distant town and ships in the bay indicative of an economy perhaps no longer solely reliant on agriculture. There is much to behold, with the essential dynamic being that of the seasonal reconfigurations of the northern European landscape, but here is a languid summer moment that will be shortly replaced by the necessity of the workers returning to harvesting.

Returning to the 'picnic', a number of familiar tropes are again evident. The group shares the moment with a white cloth on the ground serving as table linen. Most are eating bread or drinking milk in a rustic manner, although some pears are also evident on the cloth. The foregrounded counterpoint to both the workers and the 'picnickers' is one fellow who may have overindulged, or is simply exhausted, sleeping contentedly. Were it not for their turning away from the marvellous vista, and the necessity of the workers' toil, this painted vignette would constitute the essence of a simple summer picnic.

Almost 300 years after Bruegel, Manet's candid *Le déjeuner sur l'herbe* (1863) presents a very different picnic indeed. A bourgeois quartet has located a shady forest glade by a stream for their picnic luncheon on the grass. While one woman wades in the pond in the background, two prosperous gentlemen semi-recline, one gesturing as he makes a point. One discordant element of the composition is the naked woman turning to gaze at the viewer, who may be the artist, or just a passer-by. Her gaze is direct, perhaps even brazen, her nudity apparently incidental, suggesting that the women may be paid companions. Discarded clothes and the unsettling topography of the landscape are disruptive pictorial elements; this picnic is somewhat awry, but all present seem composed and unconcerned that their idyll is being observed. The woman's nudity could also indicate her status as an artist's model, despite the lack of any painterly activity in the glade. Manet may be evoking the nudes of classical antiquity, or just celebrating the female form, but whatever his intention the scene is curiously lacking any sense of the erotic. Manet's is an intimate picnic but devoid of intimacy as such; the only passion appears to be in the gentlemen's polemic, hardly the stuff of an engaging luncheon on any grass.

Brown observed that 'At the time of its "succes de scandale" at the "Salon des refusés" in 1863, one critic admitted that he searched "in vain for the meaning" of it' (Brown, 1999), but the enigma remains. Picnics are generally not expected to be mysterious events, but Manet's, with its mystery intact, is all the richer for it.

Jeffrey Smart's *The Picnic* (1980) also has a mysterious quality, despite two males and a woman sharing what appears to be an innocuous forest picnic. Brown (2012), however, links the arrangement of Smart's picnic trio to an almost identical Renaissance group in Raimondi's *Judgement of Paris* (after Raphael) c. 1475–before 1543. Smart has also updated Manet's grouping and has clothed each in swimming attire, the woman affecting a retro green one-piece and the men in Speedos of sorts, although the man whose gaze is directed at the artist/viewer appears to be wearing more of a loosely fitting nappy. While this is odd, another curiosity manifests in the bisection of the trio by the strong verticality of the portable radio antenna that takes the eye directly upwards above the forest canopy. Modernity, of which the group's radio is an exemplar, is consolidated by a looming candy-striped tower of indeterminate function, an industrial schism in an otherwise familiar picnic grouping. Locating a tranquil and private picnic spot is not always easy, so compromises may have to be made.

Despite the sun shining above the forest canopy, below all is gloom apart from the sunlit trio. There is even a second, lower layer of foliage that adds further mystery to the moment but the natural spotlight illuminates a familiar biblical temptation motif, with the woman in the green one-piece offering an apple in the general direction of the men. Carnality is a counterpoint to the usually wholesome picnic construct, but is a critical undercurrent for both Smart and Manet.

The three painted picnics illuminate locations and quite specific social dynamics of necessity for Bruegel, and somewhat ambiguous pleasure for Manet and Smart. Each of the picnics is restorative, surely both a desirable intent and outcome for any escape from routine, no matter how brief the temporal interlude. Bruegel captures a few brief moments of consumption and repose, but the resumption of harvesting may only be moments away. Manet foregrounds a nod to classicism and a saucy picnic paean to modernism, unshackling the past in order to rebelliously greet 'La Belle Époque'. Smart's emerald clad temptress hosts a picnic in a sunny spotlight, but reminders of both the old world and new frame familiar frolics.

Picnic Prose: Engaging Eating

> At last they could eat chips in the sun! Which, in a way, is Blackpool's great paradox. The idea of a seaside holiday is to lie in the sun, soak up the rays, and then sip something a little stronger. Blackpool's skies are almost permanently leaden. (Black, 2006: 43)

Black's bleak focus on overcast British skies draws attention to absent sunshine that is conducive to eating outdoors and is usually considered the critical prerequisite for a picnic outing.

In the sunny land 'Down Under' Fahey proposed that 'Australians have defined the art of eating outdoors, especially the barbeque and picnic' (Fahey, 2005: 15), an outcome, no doubt, largely attributable to the sun-soaked climate of most of the 'Antipodes'.

In the poem *Aussie Picnic* (Thomas, 1969), the imagery borders on the stereotypical but nevertheless skilfully evokes the essence of the challenging

Australian landscape and climate. This is no European shady glade with its muted light and romantic shadows, nor is there much refinement evident in the food or drink on offer, or in the rustic cooking methods. The charred sausages and chops with tea and beer eschew more epicurean delights, but convincingly connote simple pleasures and hearty appetites. Thomas transmutes the bush barbeque into a quasi-religious ritual, with the 'log table' as high altar and 'White Crow, Heinz's, or Rosella' – each an iconic Australian commercial tomato sauce – which has 'baptised' the rite. The weak, wintry light and austere setting suggest that more traditional picnic pleasures may be in short supply, but the 'charred ... to perfection' sausages and chops, and the warmth of the tea enhance the deftly managed sense of expectation and enjoyment.

Aussie Picnic's setting is the Australian bush, a collective descriptor for the vast grey-green sweep of scraggy undergrowth that disorients the unwary wanderer with its uniform palette and ominous, pervasive silence. To the new Australian settlers of the early 19th century the bush offered very little that seemed familiar or reassuring, and added infernal summer temperatures and the terrible destruction of bushfires, experiences that still pose identical, enduring threats. The Australian bush had none of the soft edges and muted tones of Europe; it was, and is, an uneasy, unfamiliar and foreboding space, one largely of challenges, even to the initiated. As an inspiration in both painting and literature, the bush was reimagined as yet another bucolic idyll, yet its inherent dangers and mystery remained. Being 'lost in the bush' was no picnic, so to speak, more of which anon, but when the bush was the nearest, and only, natural space for recreation, there was no alternative.

Summer in England, on the other hand, is summer flowers, summer holidays, and – hopefully – summer sunshine, all of which make a picnic a very appealing prospect. Ursula and Gudrun, the Brangwen sisters in D.H. Lawrence's *Women in Love* (1921), together enjoy the first vividly evoked picnic in Chapter 14, 'Water-Party'. Fortunately it is a perfect summer's day and, despite the crowds on the Crich estate, they locate a small boat and paddle off to a place where 'a tiny stream flowed into the lake, with reeds and flowery march pink willow and herb' (Lawrence, 1921: 183). They moor the boat ashore, then shed their clothes and bath naked, returning to the grove 'like nymphs', thun ran (naked) amongst the beech-trees 'big and splendid, a steel-grey scaffolding of trunks and boughs' (Lawrence, 1921: 184). After dressing, the sisters enjoy their picnic of tea that is hot and 'aromatic', cucumber and caviar sandwiches, and cakes. The picnic food, however, is given much less address than Lawrence's interrogation of the elemental physical and intellectual forces driving the sisters, the picnic a brief pause only from their intense search for meaning, understanding, validation and acknowledgement. Two tragic deaths at the end of the day profoundly shift the narrative focus, the picnic and its fleeting pleasures all but erased by the hollow horror of life being suddenly snuffed out, candle-like.

The second picnic in Chapter 23, 'Excurse', appears to be more promise than actuality, with Ursula accompanying paramour Rupert as he seeks 'this good immediate darkness' (Lawrence, 1921: 358). They drive, with a brief stop at a post office/shop where he purchases 'bread, and cheese, and raisins, and apples, and hard chocolate' (Lawrence, 1921: 359). Back on the road they run into darkness again and 'She did not ask where they were going, she did not care' (Lawrence, 1921), but Sherwood Forest proves to be their destination. Ghostly trees 'like old priests' stand sentinel as 'She had her desire fulfilled. He had his desire fulfilled' (Lawrence, 1921: 361). As no further mention is made of the food, it may be safe to assume that a picnic is not part of their mutual fulfilment.

For Lawrence, it seems, the usually innocuous picnic becomes a spatial and temporal device for stimulating intellectual interrogations, reactions and behaviours generally uncharacteristic of the phenomenon. Sensuous, remote natural settings away from families and pesky pets seem perfectly suited to picnics plus. No ordinary picnic outings for Lawrence it seems but, then again, where is the guide book of approved, appropriate picnic practices?

Finally, we have two picnic vignettes from volumes written ostensibly for children, but memories of which tend to stay with readers long after childhood: Kenneth Grahame's *The Wind in the Willows* (1908) and Ian Fleming's *Chitty Chitty Bang Bang: The Magical Car* (1964). Each story has a hugely successful picnic in a magical location, the memories of which possibly last a lifetime. For those who were read to about Mole, Rat, Badger, Otter and Toad and those who read for themselves the story of Chitty Chitty Bang Bang, the flying car, the magic endures.

At the beginning of *The Wind in the Willows* Mole stops his spring cleaning and makes his way up his tunnel to the sunlit meadow above his home. Thrilled by the warm sunshine and birdsong, he heads for the river bank where he is 'bewitched, entranced, fascinated' (Grahame, 1908: 8). Water Rat appears, extolling all the pleasures of 'messing-about-in-boats' and promptly produces a very substantial wicker luncheon-basket, containing 'cold chicken … cold tongue cold ham cold beef pickled gherkins salad french rolls cress sandwiches potted meat ginger beer lemonade sodawater' (Grahame, 1908: 11). Their picnic is enjoyed in a pretty glade; Otter and Badger appear, but do not linger, and tales of Toad are told. Mole's enthusiasm to row home, however, results in an upturned boat and a very wet end to the picnic.

Grahame employs instructional picnic tropes such as the counterpointing of domestic obligation with the freedom of the outdoors, the pleasures associated with the relaxed consumption of favourite foods in a pretty natural setting rather the usual more formal constraints of meals indoors, and the lesson that, no matter how carefully detailed the preparation, unforeseen events and annoying interventions may mar the merriment.

Ian Fleming's *Chitty Chitty Bang Bang: The Magical Car* (1964) must be read, not viewed, as the execrable filmic 'musical' adaptation of the novel (directed by Ken Hughes, 1968) is an abomination and to be avoided at all costs.

One hot Saturday in August Commander Potts informs his family – mother Mimsie and eight-year-old twins Jeremy and Jemima – that it is going to be 'a roaster, a scorcher. There's only one thing to do, and that's for us to take a delicious picnic and climb into CHITTY-CHITTY-BANG-BANG and dash off down the Dover road to the sea' (Fleming, 1964: 35). Everyone is delighted until they become stuck in traffic, but the car advises via a red knob to PULL, then PULL IDIOT when Commander Potts hesitates. The big green car becomes an aerocar, and flies into the air above the jammed traffic, circles the tower of Canterbury Cathedral and finally lands on a sandbank in the middle of the English Channel. After they have all swum about, they sit down around 'Mimsie's hamper ... and ate up every single hard-boiled egg, every single cold sausage, and every single strawberry jam puff' (Fleming, 1964: 55). Satiated, the family all doze off, awakening to find that the tide has crept in – with another adventure about to begin.

The Potts' picnic is marvellous and magical, yet practical and pragmatic as well. There is a no-nonsense approach to life in general, with obstacles faced and solutions developed. The wonderful matter-of-fact narrative and tone of address dignify the Potts family's adventures, imbuing them with the amazement of childhood under the watchful eye of empathic adults.

Grahame and Fleming both created worlds of wonder that were ordered and recognisable, with an animal picnic that was a tiny England of ritual anxieties, and a flying car that made imaginations soar en route to a sandbank picnic surrounded by sea.

Picnics at the Pictures: Cinematic Consumption

In Alfred Hitchcock's *To Catch a Thief* (1954) urbane, retired jewel thief John Robie (Cary Grant) finds himself the centre of police attention when a 'cat' burglar is relieving wealthy matrons holidaying on the French Riviera of their fabulous jewels. The burglaries resemble those of Robie's former 'career' and whilst the police have earmarked him for the thefts, they have no hard evidence; the thief vanishes without a trace into the night after every robbery. Elegant, wealthy Frances 'Francie' Stevens (Grace Kelly) and her wise-cracking, nouveau riche mother 'Jessie' (Jessie Royce Landis) display, like many of the hotel's guests, fabulous jewelry and that seems to be attracting Robie's attention.

After a swim the next day Francie offers to drive Robie in her Sunbeam Alpine convertible on an inspection tour of possible rental properties for him, ending up high on the coast road, the famous Grand Corniche between Nice and Monaco. Francie pulls the Sunbeam off the road and stops, overlooking

Monaco and the sparkling Mediterranean beyond. When Robie asks why, she replies 'I thought you said you were hungry', and when this is confirmed, she informs him that there is a picnic hamper in the trunk. The next line of banter is the wonderfully charged: 'Do you want a leg or a breast?' to which he replies 'You make the choice'. The picnic consists only of cold chicken and beer but promises, and delivers, so much more, particularly in terms of ambiance and ambiguity. Bosley Crowther (1955) in *The New York Times* observed that 'If you've never heard double-entendre, you will hear it in this film'. The humble meal evokes Francie's former life before the wealth, that of a common-sense country girl (no pun intended) who is neither dazzled by refracted light, nor about to be duped by a thief, no matter how polished his faceted performance.

The Côte d'Azur's spectacular geography and established reputation as a mid-century jet-set playground give it international tourism cachet, both of which are directly referred to in the following exchange after Francie has been watching John:

> 'You're just not convincing, John. You're like an American character in an English movie – you just don't talk the way an American tourist ought to talk', to which he replies: 'Don't you know that all the guide books say "Don't behave like a tourist"?'

Behaviours preceding and during this picnic exchange are flirtatious yet circumlocutory; there is potential passion in the air, but the elephant in the Sunbeam, so to speak, is Robie's former criminal career resonating with imminent possibilities and probabilities. Despite his protestations, glittering jewels in a range of forms surround him, not the least of which is the jewel (Francie) in the exquisite setting (the Côte d'Azur). Both are tourists but with atypical tourist agendas. Truffaut wrote that *To Catch a Thief* 'is a curious film that both renews Hitchcock and leaves him unchanged, an amusing, interesting film, very wicked about French police and American tourists' (Truffaut, 1978: 82).

The year 1955 saw the release of the cinematic version of *Picnic*, a romantic comedy-drama adaptation directed by Joshua Logan of William Inge's 1953 Pulitzer Prize winning play. The setting is a rural Kansas town in the early 1950s and the narrative action spans only 24 hours. The town is profoundly changed when a stranger, Hal Carter (William Holden), arrives and challenges what have always been considered certainties. There is no longer any excuse for, or tolerance of, complacency; established conventions are challenged and lives disrupted and reconfigured.

The picnic of the title is a traditional element of the town's annual Labor Day celebration, but it is not until Hal and town beauty Madge Owens (Kim Novak) dance together that certainties begin to be challenged. O'Neill (2013: 570) observes that 'Modernism understood individual identity, alone and

isolated, as separated from societal and cultural norms', effectively disman-
tling the (imagined) communitas of small towns, as well as the benign construct that Hollywood had long perpetuated with the likes of Capra's *Mr.
Deeds Goes to Town* (1936), Wood's *Our Town* (1940) and Capra's *It's a Wonderful
Life* (1946). Inge's *Picnic* is less about communal consumption and much more
about catharsis and the inevitability of change, with Hal Carter as its agent;
Logan's film version is true to Inge's dramatic themes and inevitable outcomes. The moral? Always talk to handsome strangers.

A decade later, on an alpine meadow near Salzburg, Austria, a very different picnic was taking place. In Robert Wise's *The Sound of Music* (1965) the
seven von Trapp children, dressed alike in outfits made from curtain fabric,
frolic about, devour luncheon and then launch enthusiastically into
'Do-Re-Mi', accompanied on the guitar by nun-turned-governess (and imminent stepmother) Maria (Julie Andrews), who sews and sings with equal
gusto. The picnic food and drink are almost incidental, as nobody really
cares about the down time between the songs that presumably are intended
to illuminate the already simplistic and predictable narrative. The Austrian
alpine location, however, completely steals the scene, long before any mountains, metaphoric or otherwise, must be climbed.

The final filmic picnic is the most unsettling, despite similar claims having
been made of *The Sound of Music*. Peter Weir's magisterial mystery, *Picnic at
Hanging Rock* (1975), adapted from Joan Lindsay's 1967 novel of the same title,
is the fictional story of three schoolgirls disappearing from a picnic at the
eponymous rock near Woodend, Victoria, on St Valentine's Day, 1900. The
state's name, Victoria, reminds the reader of the era as well as of the deeply
conservative approaches to the education of young ladies in a private college.

There is, however, significant manipulation by Lindsay in her novel to
convince the reader that the narrative is reportage rather than fiction. In the
preface she notes: 'Whether "Picnic at Hanging Rock" is fact or fiction, my
readers must decide for themselves. As the fateful picnic took place in the
year 1900, and all the characters … in this book are long since dead, it hardly
seems important' (quoted in Peary, 1982: 123).

What is possibly most curious about the narrative is why Hanging Rock
was chosen as the picnic site at all. Certainly there was proximity to the
college in Woodend and, apart from the much higher and more imposing
nearby Mt Macedon, Hanging Rock is an interesting geological formation.
Picnics, as has been asserted here, are various in construct, location, inspiration and motivation. Martin (1980: 97) proposes that 'True works of fantasy… are open-ended, suspending themselves between possible explanations'.
This idea serves both novel and film well, despite the temptation to accept
Lindsay's tale as the truth.

One final observation is that the ominous, eerie throb of the heat at the
Rock (and the film soundtrack) invokes the elemental relationship that indigenous Australians have with every part of their existence, biological and

biomorphic. They are 'of' the land, not merely 'on' the land. References to premonitions and supernatural phenomena invest both novel and film, as do evocations of sexuality: the white summer dresses worn when the girls 'enter' the Rock certainly connote virginity, if not virgin sacrifice.

The four filmic picnics range, then, from whimsical, to cathartic, to saccharine and, finally, to possibly sacrificial. The distinctive narrative arc of each film has obvious, embedded leisure tropes that further illuminate and interrogate the picnic construct.

Hitchcock manipulates the viewer with exotic beauty that manifests dualities in almost every frame. The exquisitely sunny Côte d'Azur touristic locations distract the viewer from its darker criminal underbelly which, whilst not exactly played for laughs, rarely presents the handsome players with the risk of real danger. It is the script where the ricochets are most evident, the exemplar being the provocative picnic question of 'breast or leg?' posed by the urbane Francie.

Logan expands Inge's cathartic picnic metaphor, yet also convincingly manages the depiction of the inevitability of change that the small town must face. The traditional constant on the town's calendar has always been the annual Labor Day picnic, but the arrival of Hal and his immediate attraction to, and for, Madge, is a small town dream come true. For many, however, the presence of the interloper creates a schism compounded by Madge's affectionate response to the attractive stranger and the rejection of her former beau. Change has come to town; the picnic is over for another year.

Wise created a saccharine tsunami that, despite the shadows of Nazism creeping across the screenplay, still manages a triumphant alpine ascent into the realm of escape and escapism. The picnic scene, however, playfully manages the script's ponderous polarities: out with uniforms and whistles, in with curtain fabric clothes; reject regulation, embrace emotion; formality out, frolicking in; and 'Do-Re-Mi' provides the final picnic panegyric.

Weir's picnic creates panic when three schoolgirls vanish at the ominous 'Hanging Rock'. No reasons or motives can be ascribed to their disappearance – it is inexplicable, and elemental, like the throbbing grey-green bush that surrounds the rock. The College's St Valentine's Day picnic of February 1900 has become a lament of loss in the heat and searing sunlight of a nightmarish summer Saturday.

Packing up the Picnic

What initially appeared to be an exploration of a familiar, apparently benign opportunity for relaxation and consumption in attractive settings away from home has been reconfigured through the investigation and interrogation of a range of media representations. The picnic has generally been understood and operationalised as an informal leisure adventure, yet while traditional picnic practices and protocols have been consistently paradigmatic, the mediated representations of painted, literary and cinematic picnics discussed here have offered further hopefully engaging, possibly challenging insights into the picnic phenomenon. Gastronomy, in all its multiple forms, has also been shaken up though touristic relocation, particularly when explored in contexts and locations that challenge familiar patterns and places of consumption. Remember, 'If you go down to the woods today, you're sure of a big surprise'.

15 Gastronomic Globalisation

Babette's Feast (1987)

The setting is an isolated coastal village in 19th century Denmark. The Lutheran pastor and his two daughters tend a small community of mainly elderly parishioners. The sisters have opportunities to leave, but choose to stay. When the father dies, they continue his work. Life is simple and austere.

Paris is wracked by revolution. A refugee – Babette – comes to the village. Her husband and child have been killed in the fighting. They have no work for her, but she volunteers to be an unpaid housekeeper. Fourteen years pass. Babette is a hard worker and she has learnt to produce Danish specialities such as dried fish and ale and bread soup. The only concern that the sisters have is that the parishioners are becoming increasingly argumentative and surly. Their father's teaching of tolerance and love seems to be fading.

Babette wins 10,000 francs in the lottery. She asks the sisters for permission to prepare a special French feast. They assume that Babette will now leave and that this will be a going-away party. Babette throws herself into preparations. When her supplies arrive, they include cages of quails, a giant block of ice, many cases of wine and even a live turtle. The sisters become worried that things are getting out of control. Will the feast become a drunken party? They call the parishioners together, warning them that, 'we have exposed ourselves to dangerous, even evil powers … the tongue … has accomplished great and glorious deeds for man, but it is also a source of unleashed evil and deadly poison'. They all promise that, no matter what horrors they are served, they will not say anything about the food or drink, so as to not to upset Babette. They all pledge, 'it will be as if we never had the sense of taste'.

The feast day arrives. The table is set with china, crystal and silver candlesticks. The Lutherans, all dressed in black, are stunned by this excessive display, which contrasts with their usual austerity. They stick to their resolve, saying as Grace, 'may the bread nourish my body, may the body do my soul's bidding' and whispering to each other, 'like the wedding at Cana, the food is of no importance'.

An unexpected guest arrives. It is the General. Years ago he had unsuccessfully courted one of the sisters. Thwarted, he has since focused on his career – although he has doubts as to whether or not this was the right pathway. Distinct from the parishioners owing to his colourful uniform, he is also not privy to the agreement between the other diners. Accordingly, he functions to give voice to the exceptional quality of the meal. First off he proclaims that it is the finest sherry he has ever tasted. Then he declares that it is real turtle soup. 'Blinis Demidoff!', he exclaims. Matched with Veuve Clicquot 1860!

The other diners secretly agree with the General. This is nothing like what they expected. However, they must stick to their promise and not comment on the meal. Instead they search for other topics. They reminisce about the old pastor and what a good influence he was. As they eat and drink, they are buoyed by goodwill and bonhomie. Old scores are settled and slights apologised for.

Out comes *cailles en sacophage* (quail in pastry). The General recalls that he has only ever had this once before, at the famous Café Anglais in Paris. And this is just as good! He remembers it as the best restaurant in Paris – and unusual in that it had a female chef.

The meal is over. All quarrels and feuds are over. The congregation join hands and sing. Never have they had such a magnificent meal. The General confesses to one of the sisters that he has always loved her.

It is revealed that Babette was indeed the former chef of the Café Anglais. It was her whole life before the revolution and the loss of her family. She is going to stay in the village. Anyway, she has spent the whole 10,000 francs on the feast. The sisters exclaim, 'but you'll be poor!' Babette's response is that, 'an artist is never poor'.

This cinematic fairy tale is open to a wide range of interpretations, but for the purposes of this book, we will focus on two key themes. The first is that food is at the centre of the story. The finale of the piece is that Babette is able to concoct the most magnificent feast. Importantly, it is not only central to the plot, but also central to the audience's vision. The courses and the accompanying wines are provided in great detail. The camera lingers on them. The General – as the guide or mediator for both the guests and the audience – explicitly tells all what he is eating and drinking.

Indeed, such is the film's attention to detail that it is possible to reconstruct the feast. Thus in 2009, Per Se, Thomas Keller's New York restaurant, charged diners $3500 per head ($6000 for a booking for two), to see the film, followed by a re-enactment of Babette's meal, complete with matched wines (Macaulay, 2009). Journalist J. Bryan Lowder, associate editor of *Slate* magazine, merely chose to recreate one dish as an experiment: 'today, when caloric abundance is the rule rather than the exception, does a complicated, lovingly prepared meal still have the power to bring people together? To find out, I determined to recreate Babette's *pièce de résistance*, the *cailles en sacophage*, for a group of friends' (Lowder, 2013). The meal was a technical success but the importance in the evening lay in his realisation that:

> the fact that my guests were enjoying themselves – my food and service, as the grist for the gathering, were more important than my constant presence ... Babette's story is an argument for the idea that spending money, time, and energy cooking for friends is the best gift a home cook can give, especially if they enjoy themselves so much that they practically forget who's behind the stove.

He contrasts this with Julie Powell's efforts in *Julie and Julia* – 'she may master French cooking, but in the end, the only guest she's interested in feeding is her ego' (Lowder, 2013).

Lowder recognises that such a gastronomic feast has the potential to be transformative. Before the dinner in *Babette's Feast*, the congregation is bitter and divided, symbolically demonstrated by their eating meals alone. Coming together over this special meal, they are forced to commune and communicate. As they revel in the delicious courses, they reminisce about how special their old pastor was and how silly their petty quarrels really were.

The second issue in *Babette's Feast* is not so obvious. Whilst the village seems to be isolated, it unfolds that it is connected to a greater world. The congregation may be stay-at-homes, but a range of outsiders interact with them. Babette comes from Paris on a boat on which her brother is a sailor and with a letter of introduction from a French singer who stayed in the village years ago. When she plans her feast, she is able to ship in all manner of exotic ingredients and expensive wines. The General is able to act as a sort of narrator for the feast because he has travelled widely. Indeed, it emerges that, not only is he quite familiar with the delights of Parisian cuisine, but he actually once dined at the Café Anglais when Babette was the chef. The action might take place in a small village, but this is a global world.

It is over 25 years since *Babette's Feast* was made. It is now quite a different gastronomic world. Whereas the film contrasted French culinary excellence with an isolated and traditional Danish village, now our views have changed considerably. In 2010, 2011, 2012 and 2014, a Danish restaurant – Noma – won the San Pellegrino/*Restaurant* magazine award for the World's Best Restaurant. Strikingly, the *Thrillist* Top 18 World's Best Food Cities includes Copenhagen, but not Paris (Alexander & Childers, 2014). Nordic – or New Nordic – Cuisine is in vogue.

Setting a Future Research Agenda

We conclude this book in this final chapter with a return to a number of themes developed throughout this book that we believe warrant deeper examination. There are eight key areas that we identify as a potential focus for future research.

Gastronomy in a digital age

Technological developments over the last 20 years have become so embedded in our lives that it is hard to remember life without them or to fully understand just how pervasive their influence has been. We have witnessed the rise of mobile (cell) phones and then smart phones, through which we are connected to the outside world wherever we go, and information is at our fingertips, whether it be the translation of a menu written in a foreign language, a review of a restaurant or the whereabouts of the latest pop-up establishment. This information revolution has been facilitated by new forms of media, notably social media. Twitter, Facebook, Instagram and Pinterest allow opinions and images to go viral, while blogs like *Julie and Julia* create enough hype to attract the attention of Hollywood. Discussion boards such as TripAdvisor and Zomato (formerly Urbanspoon) give the consumer a platform and the power to bring a restaurant or hotel to its knees or to boost patronage. Future studies might explore whether these websites are having a deleterious effect on rating systems such as the Michelin stars, and examine their influence more generally on the selection of places to eat and thus ultimately on sales.

The influence of this new media can also be seen on food etiquette, where photographing dishes, taking selfies and checking messages during a meal are common occurrences. This may be an outcome of less formal styles of dining or in fact be a partial catalyst for this phenomenon. This is again an interesting avenue for research. As we become more self-obsessed, does the food become less important, more a photo opportunity than a gastronomic experience? Cinemas have banned the use of phones, with *Lord of the Rings* actor Elijah Wood commenting: 'A movie theatre is meant to create an immersive experience for the audience, not one in which they can work on their blog' (Brown, 2013b). Is a restaurant experience any different? Similarly, in the theatre, there are examples of the exasperated actors taking matters into their own hands when they see the tell-tale lights of phones lit up in the darkness (Gajanan, 2015). Some restaurant owners have started to ban the use of telephones during service (Fricker, 2012), but given its ubiquity, has this behaviour simply become the new social norm and thus unlikely to change?

Media and trust

Induced and organic image formation are distinguished by levels of trust. Tourists know that marketing produced by destinations and tourism operators will be overwhelmingly positive and they apply the appropriate filters. In contrast, independent sources may have a higher level of trust and accordingly be more persuasive. This then leads to the search for personalities who will feature in the media and come across as independent and trustworthy.

The trick is to create the illusion that the media chef or celebrity is not being paid to promote a destination or product, but rather has somehow casually wandered along like a flaneur and discovered it.

Research into the attributes and effectiveness of this independence has an important commercial dimension. It could tell us more about how tourists and consumers make decisions and how they are influenced. Similarly, research on parasocial connections between the audience and television performers could be extended to media chefs. Chefs like Jamie Oliver, Rick Stein and Alice Waters are not only popular, but they are trusted. Are we able to go deeper into understanding how that relationship with their fans developed and continues to work?

Food-themed tourist experiences

The interest in food-themed tourist experiences is such that even cruise companies such as Oceania Cruises and Silversea are now incorporating on-board cooking schools into their programmes of activities. Picking up on trends in casual dining, P&O Cruises have replaced their buffet with a food court. It comes with eight distinctively themed outlets, offering fare such as curries and fish and chips. There is a rise in food-themed guided tours, such that food becomes the *peak experience* (defined by Quan and Wang (2004) as the main reason for visiting a destination) rather than a mere supporting experience. People on these tours visit the likes of food markets, wineries, artisan food producers and restaurants. For some, trip planning is based around a visit to one of the top restaurants in the world:

> Restaurants like Heston Blumenthal's The Fat Duck in Berkshire and René Redzepi's Noma in Copenhagen are culinary shrines that aficionados have to experience. It becomes an obsession for some; a frenzy of eating at the right places. (Laing & Frost, 2015b: 186)

Others are more interested in going behind the scenes, with restaurant kitchen visits offered by companies such as Tenedor Tours in Spain and Culinary Tours of Charleston in the USA. Some producers are becoming more theatrical – evoking the Experience Economy – creating spectacular performances and displays in their windows to draw in customers. Two examples of chocolatiers taking this approach are shown in Figures 15.1 and 15.2. In Girona, Spain, El Celler de Con Roca was voted the San Pellegrino World's Best Restaurant in 2013 and 2015. Such a prize raises the city's profile amongst tourists, but the restaurant has a four year waiting list for bookings. How to overcome such a disconnection? The solution was for the city authorities to work with the restaurant and other local chefs to create a pop-up restaurant showcasing regional produce. With a changing menu, it allows tourists a taste of what the iconic restaurant has to offer (Figure 15.3).

Figure 15.1 A chocolatier performs in the window of a shop in the tourism precinct of Brussels, Belgium (photo J. Laing)

Figure 15.2 A spectacular Easter display in a chocolatier in Dijon, France (photo W. Frost)

Figure 15.3 Pop-up restaurant showcasing regional produce and chefs in Girona, Spain (photo J. Laing)

Future demand for these types of experiences could be the subject of further study. Does the ultimate foodie trip involve eating in space? What is the latest *must-see* foodie destination? And what do you do with a jaded foodie who has seen and done 'it all'?

Trends in dining

There are two polar opposite trends in dining that bear further examination by researchers. The first is the concern for authenticity, which Laing and Frost (2015b) argue is one of the hallmarks of the *food explorer*. One interesting theoretical framework to use might be Tresidder's (2015: 1) concept of the *terroir restaurant*, 'in which the diner can consume tangible elements of both culture and landscape'. In this way, a concept that is understood in a wine context has been applied to restaurants, which are inextricably attached to the place in which they are located.

The second trend is for fast food to be repositioned as a premium niche in the market. McDonald's now promotes a burger that customers create for themselves. An advertisement they placed in the September 2015 issue of *Marie Claire Australia* refers to one example as a 'gourmet creation' complete with 'a dollop of garlic aioli'. Restaurants advertising *dude food* and food vans and food trucks are essentially often serving variations on burgers and fries, to be eaten with the fingers. Is the fish taco the acceptable face of fast food?

Figure 15.4 Fish and chips, transformed from takeaway to casual gourmet dining, complete with an Heirloom Tomato Caprese Salad (photo W. Frost)

The growing casualisation of dining is thus juxtaposed with the promotion of this food as a form of artisanal fare (see Figure 15.4). Perhaps the nub of the popularity of the food van/food truck is the desire for authenticity, mentioned above?

Children as foodies

A new niche market has been identified – the *child foodie* – who watches *Masterchef* and its derivative television shows, and has an encyclopaedic knowledge about food. Allied to this is the child who has been taught about nutrition by the likes of Jamie Oliver and is thus possibly more discerning about food choices than their parents. A new book by Australian journalist Larissa Dubecki, *Prick with a Fork* (2015), contains a diatribe against what she calls 'an inversion of nature'. In her view: 'fluency in restaurants is something that ought to develop slowly, like a fossil, or a baby elephant, or a taste for prog-rock'. While she is on the surface having a laugh at gastronomic precocity, there is a sharp edge to Dubecki's wit, perhaps the result of too many dinners served as a waitress to picky eaters masquerading as gastronomes. Ozersky (2012), on the other hand, sees a juvenile fascination with food as desirable where it results in a 'trend for getting kids into cooking'.

The question remains as to how this trend will affect travel, with requests made of parents for gastronomic highlights, rather than the standard child's meal. It may force airlines, for example, to re-examine meals designed for children, which are often heavy on sugary snack foods, designed to keep the kids – and thus their parents and other passengers – happy. Restaurants might need to consider providing meals that are just smaller versions of adult fare, rather than a separate children's menu.

This may be a cultural issue, arising from attitudes and expectations in the English-speaking world. In contrast, a range of ethnic cuisines are noted for having a 'family-friendly' culture when it comes to eating. The Chinese and Italians – particularly through restaurants outside of their home country – have a reputation for informal, happy and bustling approaches to meals. Such informal and communal styles of enjoying food are attractive to many in the modern world and these foodways are increasingly crossing cultural boundaries and driving the casualisation of dining (Frost & Laing, 2016, in press; Gabaccia, 1998; Laing & Frost, 2015b; Tuchman & Levine, 1993).

Non-Western trends

This book has been largely Western-centric, reflecting the background of the authors and their current research interests. Nevertheless, we acknowledge that the intersection of gastronomy, tourism and the media also occurs in a non-Western context, including new destinations and cuisines to be discovered and a history of gastronomy that has different roots and influences. There are also different social media platforms such as China's Weibo and WeChat and political and cultural systems that may affect the way that food is perceived and consumed outside the West. There is scope for more research to tease out these issues, particularly in the context of China and India – two countries with large and growing numbers of their population travelling for the first time.

New foodie destinations

The rise of new foodie destinations such as Copenhagen (Tresidder, 2015), San Sebastián and Girona in Spain (Svejenova et al., 2007), Cuba (Bell, 2013) and Peru (García, 2013) has received some attention in the literature to date, but there is potential to extend the work that has been done. Future studies might, for example, consider the role played by food champions in the development of these destinations, for example the clustering of food-related businesses, as well as their promotion to potential visitors.

The media's fascination with lists of best, hottest and rising food destinations is an area that requires investigation. An example is the Thrillist Top 20 World's Best Food Cities for 2014 (Alexander & Childers, 2014). Number one is Bordeaux. The others (in order) are: Bologna, Bombay, London, New

York, Marrakesh, Cartagena, Istanbul, Tokyo, Barcelona, Hong Kong, Copenhagen, Montreal, New Orleans, Buenos Aires, Ho Chi Minh City, Melbourne and George Town (Malaysia). How are such lists constructed? How important is provocation and being different? To what extent are they influenced by the advertising budgets of destinations? Finally, are they trusted and relied upon by tourists?

Placeless gastronomy

It is axiomatic that gastronomic tourism is based on place and that concepts like terroir and authenticity are critical for destinations. Nonetheless, there is still a counter trend, one that returns us to the fictional Accidental Tourist Guides (Tyler, 1985) that we started this book with. Some researchers are beginning to look at the phenomenon of tourists in popular destinations eating in placeless restaurants. Falconer (2013) interviewed backpackers who travelled around Asia with the best intentions of immersing themselves in local cuisines and cultures. While they did this, they also found themselves drawn to cafés and restaurants that offered international cuisine – such as pizza and English roasts in India. Similarly, Nepal (2015) found a trend towards globalised food outlets in Nepal. Examples from the Khumbu region included an Irish Pub and a faux Starbucks. Clearly, the trend towards distinctive regional food cultures and experiences is not universal. That the tourists in these studies wanted both regional and globalised cuisines leaves us with much more to investigate regarding the links between tourism, gastronomy and the media.

References

Adams, T. (2015) The Stein family saga: 40 years of the Seafood Restaurant. *The Guardian*, 19 April. See http://www.theguardian.com/lifeandstyle/2015/apr/19/rick-stein-family-saga-40-years-seafood-restaurant-padstow (accessed 5 July 2015).

Adema, P. (2000) Vicarious consumption: Food, television and the ambiguity of modernity. *Journal of American and Comparative Cultures* 23 (3), 113–123.

Age, The (2015) Explore Dublin, an ancient city of myths and mysteries. *The Saturday Age*, Travel, 4 July, p. 20.

Agel, J. (1970) *The Making of Kubrick's 2001*. USA: New American Library.

Albala, K. (2011) The historical models of food and power in European courts of the nineteenth century: An exposition essay and prologue. In D. De Vooght (ed.) *Royal Taste: Food, Power and Status at the European Courts After 1789* (pp. 13–29). Farnham: Ashgate.

Alexander, K. and Childers, L. (2014) *The World's 18 Best Food Cities*. See www.thrillist.com/eat/nation/the-world-s-best-food-cities (accessed 10 September 2015).

Alexander, S. (2002) *Cooking & Travelling in South-West France*. Melbourne: Penguin.

Alexander, S. (2009) *Stephanie Alexander's Kitchen Garden Companion*. Melbourne: Penguin.

Alexander, S. (2014) Stephanie Alexander. See http://www.stephaniealexander.com.au (accessed 13 November 2014).

Annas, J. (1987) Epicurus on pleasure and happiness. *Philosophical Topics* 15 (2), 5–21.

Armes, R. (1974) *Film and Reality: An Historical Survey*. Harmondsworth: Penguin.

Armstrong, R. (2004) All-consuming passions: Peter Greenaway's The Cook, the Thief, His Wife and Her Lover. In A. Bower (ed.) *Reel Food: Essays on Food and Film* (pp. 219–234). London: Routledge.

Associated Press (2013) Fake Mars mission fuelled by chocolate. *The Age*, 15 August, p. 17.

Australian Farmers' Market Association (2014) What is AFMA? See http://www.farmersmarkets.org.au/about (accessed 12 August 2015).

Australian Foreign Press (2008) Mousse murderer gets 20 years, 28 February. See http://www.abc.net.au/news/2008-02-27/mousse-murdered-gets-20-years/1055408 (accessed 26 February 2015).

Australian Technology Park (2015) Kylie Kwong launches new cookbook at Everleigh Farmers' Market. See www.atp.com.au/News—Resources/Latest-news/Kylie-Kwong-launches-new-cookbook-at-Eveleigh-Farmers–Market (accessed 1 February 2015).

Avramescu, C. (2003) *An Intellectual History of Cannibalism*. Princeton, NJ: Princeton University Press [reprinted 2011].

Ay, C., Aytekin, P. and Nardali, S. (2010) Guerrilla marketing communication tools and ethical problems in guerrilla advertising. *American Journal of Economics and Business Administration* 2 (3), 280.

Baber, L.M. and Frongillo, E.A. (2003) Farmer and seller interactions in farmers' markets in upstate New York. *American Journal of Alternate Agriculture* 18 (2), 87–94.

Bailey, A. (1970) *The Cooking of the British Isles.* New York: Little Brown.

Bainger, F. (2013) Van Go – Perth's new mobile food trend. *Perth Now Sunday Times,* 24 June. See http://www.perthnow.com.au/news/western-australia/van-go-perths-new-mobile-food-trend/story-fnhocxo3-1226668882083 (accessed 10 October 2013).

Baker, W. (1999) The sign of the cannibal: Melville and the making of a postcolonial reader. *Reference Reviews* 13 (8), 24.

Baker, D., Hamshaw, K. and Kolodinsky, J. (2009) Who shops at the market? Using consumer surveys to grow farmers' markets: Findings from a regional market in northwestern Vermont. *Journal of Extension* 47 (6), 1–9.

Banivanua-Mar, T. (2010) Cannibalism and colonialism: Charting colonies and frontiers in nineteenth century Fiji. *Comparative Studies in Society and History* 52 (2), 255–281.

Barber, E.W. (2013) *Dancing Goddesses: Folklore, Archaeology, and the Origins of European Dance.* London and New York: Norton.

Baron, C. (2006) Dinner and a movie. *Food, Culture & Society* 9 (1), 93–117.

Barthel, S., Parker, J. and Ernstson, H. (2013) Food and green space in cities: A resilience lens on gardens and urban environmental movements. *Urban Studies* 52 (7), 1321–1338.

Basil, M. (2012) A history of farmers' markets in Canada. *Journal of Historical Research in Marketing* 4 (9), 397–407.

Bauman, Z. (2007) *Liquid Times: Living in an Age of Uncertainty.* Cambridge: Polity Press.

Beardsworth, A. and Keil, T. (1997) *Sociology on the Menu.* London and New York: Routledge.

Becker, H., Naaman, M. and Gravano, L. (2009) Event identification in social media. *Twelfth International Workshop on the Web and Databases,* 28 June 2009, Providence, RI.

Becker, H., Iter, D., Naaman, M. and Gravano, L. (2012) Identifying content for planned events across social media sites. *Association for Computing Machinery in Web Search and Data Mining Conference Proceedings,* 8–12 February 2012, Seattle, WA.

Beer, S., Edwards, J., Fernanades, C. and Sampaio, F. (2002) Regional food cultures: Integral to the rural tourism product? In A.-M. Hjalager and G. Richards (eds) *Tourism and Gastronomy* (pp. 207–223). London and New York: Routledge.

Beeton, S. (2005) *Film-Induced Tourism.* Clevedon: Channel View Publications.

Belasco, W. (1979) *Americans on the Road: From Autocamp to Motel.* Baltimore, MD: The Johns Hopkins Press.

Bell, L. (2013) Viva a Food Revolution. *The Saturday Age,* Travel, 16 March. See http://www.theage.com.au/travel/activity/food-and-wine/viva-a-food-revolution-20130314-2g2js.html (accessed 22 March 2013).

Bergqvist, A. and Leinoff, L. (2011) Once you pop your customer will shop: A study about pop-up stores. Unpublished Masters thesis, Linnaeus University.

Berry, B. (2011) *Health and Wellness Trends for Canada and the World. Agriculture and Agri-Food.* Canada: The Government of Canada.

Bhattacharyya, D. (1997) Mediating India: An analysis of a guidebook. *Annals of Tourism Research* 29 (2), 371–389.

Black, W. (2006) *The Land that Thyme Forgot.* London: Corgi.

Block, K., Gibbs, L., Staiger, P.K., Gold, L., Johnson, B., Macfarlane, S., Long, C. and Townsend, M. (2012) Growing community: The impact of the Stephanie Alexander Kitchen Garden Program on the social and learning environment in primary schools. *Health Education and Behaviour* 39 (4), 419–432.

Blumenthal, H. (2010) *Heston's Fantastical Feasts.* London: Bloomsbury.

Boniface, P. (2003) *Tasting Tourism: Travelling for Food and Drink.* Aldershot and Burlington, VT: Ashgate.

Bourland, T. (1993) The development of food systems for space. *Trends in Food Science and Technology* 4 (9), 271–276.

Bower, A. (2004a) Watching food: The production of food, film and values. In A. Bower (ed.) *Reel Food: Essays on Food and Film* (pp. 1–13). London: Routledge.

Bower, A.L. (2004b) Romanced by cookbooks. *Gastronomica* 4 (2), 35–42.

Boyce, B. (2011) To boldly go where no food has gone before. *Journal of the American Dietetic Association* 111 (1), 45–49.

Boyd, S.W. (2016) Reflections on Slow Food: From 'movement' to an emergent research field. In D. Timothy (ed.) *Heritage Cuisines: Traditions, Identities and Tourism* (pp. 166–179). London and New York: Routledge.

Boyne, S., Williams, F. and Hall, D. (2002) On the trail of regional success: Tourism, food production and the Isle of Arran Taste Trail. In A.-M. Hjalager and G. Richards (eds) *Tourism and Gastronomy* (pp. 101–114). London and New York: Routledge.

Brandes, S. (1997) Sugar, colonialism and death: On the origins of Mexico's Day of the Dead. *Comparative Studies in Society and History* 39 (2), 270–299.

Brennan, I. (2015) Pete Evans' co-authored Paleo Diet cookbook for babies under investigation. *ABC News*, 12 March. See http://www.abc.net.au/news/2015-03-12/paleo-diet-cookbook-for-babies-under-investigation-pete-evans/6309452 (accessed 12 July 2015).

Brennan-Horley, C., Connell, J. and Gibson, C. (2007) The Parkes Elvis Revival Festival: Economic development and contested place identities in rural Australia. *Geographical Research* 45 (1), 71–84.

Brillat-Savarin, J. (1825) *The Philosophy of Taste*. London: Folio Society [reprinted 2008].

Brinkema, E. (2010) Rot's Progress: Gastronomy according to Peter Greenaway. *Differences* 21 (3), 73–96.

Brown, A. (2002) Farmers' market research 1940–2000: An inventory and review. *American Journal of Alternate Agriculture* 17 (4), 167–176.

Brown, C. and Miller, S.M. (2008) The impacts of local markets: A review of research on farmers' markets and community supported agriculture. *American Journal of Agricultural Economics* 90 (5), 1298–1302.

Brown, C., Miller, S.M., Boone, D.A., Boone H.N. Jr, Gartin, S.A. and McConnell, T.R. (2006) The importance of farmers' markets for West Virginia direct marketers. *Renewable Agriculture and Food Systems* 22 (1), 20–29.

Brown, D. (1969) *The Cooking of Scandinavia*. New York: Little Brown.

Brown, D. (2013a) Skeleton of teenage girl confirms cannibalism at Jamestown colony. *The Washington Post* online, May 1, http://www.washingtonpost.com/national/health-science/skeleton-of-teenage-girl-confirms-cannibalism-at-jamestown-colony/2013/05/01/story.html (accessed 20 January 2015).

Brown, J. (2013b) Is it rude to use your smart phone during screenings? Cinema etiquette debate rages in the US. *The Independent*, 14 August. See http://www.independent.co.uk/arts-entertainment/films/news/is-it-rude-to-use-your-smart-phone-during-screenings-cinema-etiquette-debate-rages-in-us-8762147.html (accessed 13 September 2015).

Brown, K.H. and Jameton, A.L. (2000) Public health implications of urban agriculture. *Journal of Public Health Policy* 21 (1), 20–39.

Brown, M. (1999) Manet's Le Dejeuner sur L'Herbe, *CAA Reviews*, May.

Brown, M. (2012) Levelling time: The figurative painting of Rick Amor, Eolo Paul Bottaro and Jeffrey Smart. Unpublished Masters thesis, The University of Melbourne.

Brownlie, D., Hewer, P. and Horne, S. (2005) Culinary tourism: An exploratory reading of contemporary representations of cooking. *Consumption, Markets and Culture* 8 (1), 7–26.

Bruwer, J. (2002) Wine and food events: A golden opportunity to learn more about wine consumers. *The Australian and New Zealand Wine Industry Journal* 17 (3), 92–99.

Bryant, N. (2014) Slow mo food. *The Age*, Good Weekend magazine, 1 November, pp. 24–27.

Bryson, B. (1995) *Notes from a Small Island*. New York: Harper.

Buchmann, A., Moore, K. and Fisher, D. (2010) Experiencing film tourism: Authenticity and fellowship. *Annals of Tourism Research* 37 (1), 229–248.

Bukszpan, D. (2015) 6 celebrity endorsements that enraged consumers. *Fortune*, 19 April. See http://fortune.com/2015/04/19/celebrity-endorsements-gone-wrong/ (accessed 2 September 2015).

Buman, M.P., Bertmann, F., Heckler, E.B., Winter, S.J., Sheats, J.L., King, A.C. and Wharton, C.M. (2014) A qualitative study of shopper experiences at an urban farmers' market using the Stanford Healthy Neighborhood Discovery Tool. *Public Health Nutrition* 18 (6), 994–100.

Burnaby, F. (1877) *A Ride to Khiva: Travels and Adventures in Central Asia*. London: Century [reprinted 1983].

Burnett, J. (2003) Eating in the open air in England, 1830–1914. In M. Jacobs and P. Scholliers (eds) *Eating Out in Europe: Picnics, Gourmet Dining and Snacks since the Late Eighteenth Century* (pp. 21–37). Oxford: Berg.

Busby, G. Huang, R. and Jarman, R. (2013) The Stein effect: An alternative film-induced tourism perspective. *International Journal of Tourism Research* 15 (6), 570–582.

Byker, C., Shanks, J., Misyak, S. and Serrano, E. (2012) Characterising farmers' market shoppers: A literature review. *Journal of Hunger and Environmental Nutrition* 7 (1), 38–52.

Byrne, A., Whitehead, M. and Breen, S. (2003) The naked truth of celebrity endorsement. *British Food Journal* 105 (4/5), 288–296.

Canby, V. (1982) Eating Raoul Comedy with an offbeat couple. *The New York Times*, 25 September, A1, p. 1.

Carl, D., Kindon, S. and Smith, K. (2007) Tourists experiences on film locations: New Zealand as Middle Earth. *Tourism Geographies* 9 (1), 49–63.

Carluccio, A. (2012) *A Recipe for Life*. London and Melbourne: Hardie Grant Books.

Carroll, M., Hadley, D. and Willmott, H. (2005) Introduction: Setting the table. In M. Carroll, D. Hadley and H. Willmott (eds) *Consuming Passions: Dining from antiquity to the eighteenth century* (pp. 11–21). Stroud: Tempus.

Carson, B. (1990) *Ambitious Appetites: Dining, Behaviour and Patterns of Consumption in Federal Washington*. Washington, DC: The American Institute of Architects Press.

Carter, B. (2013a) Mobile food trucks have unfair advantages, say Adelaide restaurateurs. *Hospitality Magazine*, 20 March. See http://www.hospitalitymagazine.com.au/food/news/mobile-food-vans-have-unfair-advantage-say-adelaide (accessed 13 July 2015).

Carter, B. (2013b) Perth embraces the food truck craze. *Hospitality Magazine*, 25 June. See http://www.hospitalitymagazine.com.au/food/news/perth-embraces-the-food-truck-craze (accessed 26 June 2015).

Carter, B. (2014) Council trials food trucks in Melbourne CBD. *Hospitality Magazine*, 3 June. See http://www.hospitalitymagazine.com.au/food/news/city-of-melbourne-trials-food-trucks-in-cbd (accessed 13 July 2015).

Carter, S.L. (1998) *Civility: Manners, Morals and the Etiquette of Democracy*. New York: Basic Books.

Castro, D.C., Samuels, M. and Harman, A.E. (2013) A community garden based obesity prevention program. *American Journal of Preventative Medicine* 44 (33), 193–199.

Castronovo, C. and Huang, L. (2012) Social media in an alternative marketing communication model. *Journal of Marketing Development and Competitiveness* 6 (1), 117–134.

Caton, K. and Santos, C.A. (2007) Heritage tourism on Route 66: Deconstructing nostalgia. *Journal of Travel Research* 45 (4), 371–386.

Cavicchi, A. and Santini, C. (eds) (2014) *Food and Wine Events in Europe*. London and New York: Routledge.

Chaney, L. (1998) *Elizabeth David: A Biography*. London: Macmillan.

Charles, E. (2010) Survival guide to eating alfresco. *The Age*, Melbourne, 12 January, p. 14.

Charsley, S.R. (1992) *Wedding Cakes and Cultural History.* New York: Routledge.

Cherro Osorio, S. (2013) Peruvian gastronomy: Influences of culinary brokers on the overall tourist experience in Peru. Conference presentation at the *3rd Australasian Food Cultures and Networks Conference*, Southern Cross University, 29–31 October, Daylesford, Victoria.

Cherro Osorio, S.G. and Best, G. (2015) A case study on culture brokers and their role in tourism management in the indigenous community of Taquile Island in Puno, Peru. *International Journal of Tourism Research* 17 (4), 347–355.

Cherry-Garrard, A. (1922) *The Worst Journey in the World.* 2010 reprint. London: Vintage Books.

Child, J. with Prud'homme, A. (2006) *My Life in France.* New York: Anchor.

City of Melbourne (2012) City Research Branch, Census of Land Use and Employment (CLUE), 2012 update. See http://www.melbourne.vic.gov.au/AboutMelbourne/Statistics/Pages/MelbourneSnapshot.aspx (accessed 18 June 2015).

City of Melbourne (2015) Melbourne's multicultural history. See https://www.melbourne.vic.gov.au/AboutMelbourne/History/Pages/multiculturalhistory.aspx (accessed 18 June 2015).

Civitello, L. (2004) *Cuisine and Culture: A History of Food and People.* Hoboken, NJ: Wiley.

Clark, P. (1975) Thoughts for food II: Culinary culture in contemporary France. *The French Review* 49 (2), 198–205.

Clarke, A. (2014) Culture and authenticity in food and wine events. In A. Cavicchi and C. Santini (eds) *Food and Wine Events in Europe* (pp. 45–57). London and New York: Routledge.

Clawson, T. (2010) *The Unauthorized Guide to Doing Business the Jamie Oliver Way: 10 Secrets of the Irrepressible One-Man Brand.* Brisbane: Wiley.

Cockell, C.S. (2007) *Space on Earth: Saving Our World By Seeking Others.* Houndmills: Macmillan.

Cohen, E. (2004) *Contemporary Tourism: Diversity and Change.* Kidlington: Elsevier.

Cohen, E. and Avieli, N. (2004) Food in tourism: Attraction and impediment. *Annals of Tourism Research* 31 (4), 755–778.

Connell, J. (2012) Film tourism: Evolution, progress and prospects. *Tourism Management* 33 (5), 1007–1029.

Connell, J. (2014) Soft country? Rural and regional Australia in *Country Style*. In R. Duffy-Jones and J. Connell (eds) *Rural Change in Australia* (pp. 211–234). Aldershot: Ashgate.

Conner, D., Colasanti, K., Ross, R. and Smalley, S. (2010) Locally grown food and farmers' markets: Consumer attitudes and behaviours. *Sustainability* 2 (3), 742–756.

Cooper E. (1986) Chinese table manners: You are *how* you eat. *Human Organism* 45 (2), 179–184.

Cooper, M., Douglas, G. and Perchonok, M. (2011) Developing the NASA food system for long-duration missions. *Journal of Food Science* 76 (2), 40–48.

Cordon Bleu (2015) *Cordon Bleu.* See http://www.lecordonbleu.com.au/about/en (accessed 15 August 2015).

Cornish, R. (2015) Food fraud angers farmers. *The Age*, 11 July, p. 16.

Coster, M. and Kennon, N. (2005) New generations farmers' markets in rural communities. Rural Industries Research and Development Corporation, 1–42.

Cousins, J., O'Gorman, K. and Stierand, M. (2010) Molecular gastronomy: Cuisine innovation or modern-day alchemy? *International Journal of Contemporary Hospitality Management* 22 (3), 399–415.

Crawford, S. (2015) Drug-dealing socialite Lisa Danielle Stockbridge says jail food sent her bald. *The Daily Telegraph*, 17 July. See http://www.dailytelegraph.com.au/news/nsw/drug-dealing-socialite-lisa-danielle-stockbridge-says-jail-food-sent-her-bald/story-fni0cx12-1227444848668 (accessed 2 September 2015).

Creasy, R. (2013) *The Edible Flower Garden*. Singapore: Tuttle.

Crenshaw, C. and Urry, J. (1997) Tourism and the photographic eye. In C. Rojek and J. Urry (eds) *Touring Cultures: Transformations of Travel and Theory* (pp. 176–195). London: Routledge.

Crouch, G. (2013) *Homo sapiens* on vacation: What can we learn from Darwin? *Journal of Travel Research* 52 (5), 575–590.

Crouch, G.I. (2001) The market for space tourism: Early indications. *Journal of Travel Research* 40 (2), 222–228.

Crowther, B. (1955) Screen: Cat man out 'To Catch a Thief'; Grant is ex-burglar in Hitchcock thriller. *The New York Times*, 5 August, p. 14.

Csergo, J. (2003) The picnic in nineteenth-century France. A social event involving food: Both a necessity and a form of entertainment. In M. Jacobs and P. Scholliers (eds) *Eating Out in Europe: Picnics, Gourmet Dining and Snacks since the Late Eighteenth Century* (pp. 139–159). Oxford: Berg.

Curtis, J. (2011) Hugh Fearnley-Whittingstall reveals his Hampshire restaurant plans. *Southern Daily Echo*, 14 July. See http://www.dailyecho.co.uk/news/10546975.Hugh_Fearnley_Whittingstall__reveals_his_Hampshire_restaurant_plans/?ref=rss (accessed 2 February 2015).

Danhi, R. (2003) What is your country's culinary identity? *Culinology Currents* (Winter), 4–5.

David, E. (1951) *A Book of Mediterranean Food*. 2007 edition. London: Folio Society.

David, E. (1951) *French Country Cooking*. London: Folio Society [reprinted 2008].

David, E. (1954) *Italian Food*. London: Folio Books [reprinted 2006].

David, E. (1965) *Summer Cooking*. New York: New York Review Books.

Davidson, K. (2001) 2001 No Space Odyssey – Famous year in fiction is here, but scientists are left to marvel only at movie. *San Francisco Chronicle*, 1 January, A8.

Defoe, D. (1719) *Robinson Crusoe*. London: Penguin [reprinted 2003].

DeJean, J. (2005) *The Essence of Style. How the French Invented High Fashion, Fine Food, Chic Cafés, Style, Sophistication and Glamour*. New York: Free Press.

Derham, J. (2013) The challenges of managing adverse food reactions: 2000 years and counting. Unpublished paper. CAUTHE Conference, Lincoln University, New Zealand, 11–14 February 2013.

De Solier, I. (2005) TV dinners: Culinary television, education and distinction. *Continuum: Journal of Media & Cultural Studies* 19 (4), 465–481.

De Vooght, D. (ed.) (2011) *Royal Taste: Food, Power and Status at the European Courts after 1789*. Farnham: Ashgate.

De Vooght, D. and Scholliers, P. (2011) Introduction. Food and power: Studying food at (modern) courts. In D. De Vooght (ed.) *Royal Taste: Food, Power and Status at the European Courts after 1789* (pp. 1–12). Farnham: Ashgate.

Dickie, J. (2008) *Delizia! The Epic History of the Italians and Their Food*. New York: Simon & Schuster.

Dickinson, J. and Lumsdon, L. (2010) *Slow Travel and Tourism*. London: Earthscan.

Dicum, G. (2010) At pop-ups, chefs take chances with little risk. *The New York Times*, 12 February. See http://www.nytimes.com/2010/02/12/dining/12sfdine.html?_r=0 (accessed 11 June 2015).

Dieticians Association of Australia (2015) *Media alert: Bubba Yum Yum*, 13 March. See http://daa.asn.au/wp-content/uploads/2015/03/Media-alert-Bubba-Yum-Yum_FINAL.pdf (accessed 13 July 2015).

Dietler, M. (2001) Theorizing the feast: Rituals of consumption, commensal politics, and power in African contexts. In M. Dietler and B. Hayden (eds) *Feasts: Archaeological and Ethnographic Perspectives on Food, Politics and Power* (pp. 65–114). Washington, DC and London: Smithsonian Institution Press.

Dietler, M. and Hayden, B. (2001) Digesting the feast: Good to eat, good to drink, good to think: An introduction. In M. Dietler and B. Hayden (eds) *Feasts: Archaeological and Ethnographic Perspectives on Food, Politics and Power* (pp. 1–20). Washington, DC and London: Smithsonian Institution Press.

Diski, J. (2009) All eat all. *London Review of Books* 31 (15), 21–23.

Dixon, R. (2008) Blumenthal finds perfection at the Fat Duck. *The Guardian*, 15 August. See http://www.theguardian.com/lifeandstyle/2008/aug/15/heston.blumenthal (accessed 15 August 2015).

Donelly, B. and Toscano, N. (2015) Cancer faker turns over finance data. *The Age*, 11 July, p. 12.

Drake, L. and Lawson, L.J. (2014) Validating verdancy or vacancy? The relationship of community gardens and vacant lands in the US. *Cities* 40, 133–142.

Dubecki, L. (2015) *Prick with a Fork: The World's Worst Waitress Spills the Beans*. Sydney: Allen & Unwin.

Duff, J. (2004) Setting the menu: Dietary guidelines, corporate interests, and nutrition policy. In J. Germov and L.Williams (eds) *A Sociology of Food and Nutrition. The Social Appetite*. Melbourne: Oxford University Press.

Dupertuis, Y.M., Kossovsky, M.P., Kyle, U.G., Raguso, C.A., Genton L. and Pichard, C. (2003) Food intake in 1707 hospitalised patients: A prospective comprehensive hospital survey. *Clinical Nutrition* 22 (2), 115–123.

Duram, L. and Cawley, M. (2012) Irish chefs and restaurants in the geography of 'local' food value chains. *The Open Geography Journal* 5 (1), 16–25.

Du Rand, G.E. and Heath, E. (2006) Towards a framework for food tourism as an element of destination marketing. *Current Issues in Tourism* 9 (3), 206–234.

Ebert, R. (1982) *Eating Raoul*, 1 January. See http://www.rogerebert.com/reviews/eating-raoul-1982 (accessed 8 March 2015).

Edible Wild Food (2015) *Foraging for food in the wild*. See http://www.ediblewildfood.com/foraging-for-food.aspx (accessed 11 March 2015).

Edge, J.T. (2011) Let us now praise famous cooks. Introduction. In E.M. Mickler, *White Trash Cooking* (pp. x–xii). Berkeley, CA: Ten Speed Press.

Elepua, G., Mazzocco, M. and Goldsmith, P. (2010) Consumer segments in urban and suburban farmers markets. *International Food Agribusiness Management Review* 13 (2), 3–14.

Evert, S. (2013) Europe's hypocritical history of cannibalism. *Smithsonian.com*, 24 April. See http://www.smithsonianmag.com/history/europes-hypocritical-history-of-cannibalism-42642371/?1=&page=2/ (accessed 1 March 2015).

Eves, A. and Gesch, B. (2003) Food provision and the nutritional implications of food choices made by young adult males, in a young offenders' institution. *Journal of Human Nutrition and Dietetics* 16 (3), 167–179.

Fahey, W. (2005) *Tucker Track: The Curious History of Food in Australia*. Sydney: ABC Books.

Falassi, A. (1987) Festival: Definition and morphology. In A. Falassi (ed.) *Time Out of Time: Essays on the festival* (pp. 1–10). Albuquerque, NM: University of New Mexico Press.

Falconer, E. (2013) Transformations of the backpacking food tourist: Emotions and conflict. *Tourist Studies* 13 (1), 21–35.

Farmers' Markets New Zealand (2014) *About FMNZ*. See http://www farmersmarkets.org.nz (accessed 1 August 2015).

Fat Duck, The (2015) *The Fat Duck*. See http://www.thefatduck.co.uk/ (accessed 15 July 2015).

Feibleman, P. (1970) *The Cooking of Spain and Portugal*. New York: Little Brown.

Festing, H. (1998) *Farmers' Markets: An American Success Story*. Bath: Ecologic Books.

Fields, K. (2002) Demand for the gastronomy tourism product: Motivational factors. In A.-M. Hjalager and G. Richards (eds) *Tourism and Gastronomy* (pp. 36–50). London and New York: Routledge.

Fischler, C. (1981) Food preferences, nutritional wisdom, and sociocultural evaluation. In D.N. Walcher and N. Kretchmer (eds) *Food, Nutrition and Evolution. Food as a Factor in the Genesis of Human Variability*. USA: Mason.

Fisher, M. (2013) The cannibals of North Korea, *The Washington Post*, 5 February. See https://www.washingtonpost.com/news/worldviews/wp/2013/02/05/the-cannibals-of-north-korea (accessed 27 January 2015).

Fisher, M.F.K. (1968) *The Cooking of Provincial France*. New York: Little Brown.

Flandrin, J.-L. (2007) *Arranging the Meal: A History of Table Service in France*. Berkeley, CA: University of California Press.

Fleming, I. (1964) *Chitty Chitty Bang Bang: The Magical Car*. Somervill, MA: Candlewick [reprinted 2014].

Florida, R. (2002) *The Rise of the Creative Class: And How It's Transforming Work, Leisure, Community and Everyday Life*. Cambridge, MA: Basic Books.

Florida, R. (2005) *Cities and the Creative Classes*. London and New York: Routledge.

Foden, B. (2015) Bluff Oyster Festival: How $10 helped make the world Bluff's oyster. *Stuff.co.nz*, 23 May. See http://www.stuff.co.nz/life-style/food-wine/68759987/Bluff-Oyster-Festival-How-10-helped-make-the-world-Bluffs-oyster (accessed 13 September 2015).

Forster, L. (2004) Futuristic foodways: The metaphorical meaning of food in science fiction film. In A.L. Bower (ed.) *Reel Food: Essays on Food and Film* (pp. 251–265). Routledge: New York.

Fox, J. (2011) Risk preference and food consumption. In J. Lusk, J. Roosen and J. Shogren (eds) *The Oxford Handbook of the Economics of Food and Consumption Policy*. Oxford: Oxford University Press.

Fox, R. (2014) *Food and Eating: An Anthropological Perspective*. Oxford: Social Issues Research Centre. See http://www.sirc.org/publik/foxfood.pdf (accessed 15 September 2014).

Freedman, P. (2011) American restaurants and cuisine in the mid-nineteenth century. *The New England Quarterly* LXXXIV (1), 5–59.

Fricker, M. (2012) Keep your phones off the dinner table: Top chef so fed up with diners texting and checking Facebook that he's banned mobiles. *The Mirror*, 13 July. See http://www.mirror.co.uk/news/uk-news/birmingham-restaurant-bans-mobile-phones-1142451 (accessed 13 September 2015).

Frochot, I. (2003) An analysis of regional positioning and its associated food images in French tourism regional brochures. *Journal of Travel & Tourism Marketing* 14 (3–4), 77–96.

Frost, W. (2002) Powerhouse economies of the Pacific: A comparative study of gold and wheat in nineteenth century Victoria and California. In D.O. Flynn, A. Giráldez and J. Sobredo (eds) *Studies in Pacific History: Economics, Politics, and Migration* (pp. 61–74). Aldershot and Burlington, VT: Ashgate.

Frost, W. (2010) Life-changing experiences: Film and tourists in the Australian Outback. *Annals of Tourism Research* 37 (3), 707–726.

Frost, W. and Laing, J. (2011) *Strategic Management of Festivals and Events*. Melbourne: Cengage.

Frost, W. and Laing, J. (2013) Communicating persuasive messages through slow food festivals. *Journal of Vacation Marketing* 19 (1), 67–74.

Frost, W. and Laing, J. (2014) Fictional media and imagining escape to rural villages. *Tourism Geographies* 16 (2), 207–220.

Frost, W. and Laing, J. (2015a) Ritual structure and traditions of events. In J. Laing and W. Frost (eds) *Rituals and Traditional Events in a Modern World* (pp. 1–19). London: Routledge.

Frost, W. and Laing, J. (2015b) Avoiding burnout: The succession planning, governance and resourcing of rural tourism festivals. *Journal of Sustainable Tourism* 23 (8/9), 1298–1317.

Frost, W. and Laing, J. (2016) Cuisine, migration, colonialism and diasporic identity. In D. Timothy (ed.) *Heritage Cuisines: Traditions, Identities and Tourism* (pp. 37–52). London and New York: Routledge.

Frost, W. and Laing, J. (in press) The food revolution in Melbourne, 1980–2015. In M. Sahakian, C. Saloma and S. Erkman (eds) *Food Consumption in the City: Practices and Patterns in Urban Asia and the Pacific*. London: Routledge.

Frost, W., Laing, J., Wheeler, F. and Reeves, K. (2010) Coffee culture, heritage and destination image: Melbourne and the Italian model. In L. Jolliffe (ed.) *Coffee Culture, Destinations and Tourism* (pp. 99–110). Bristol: Channel View Publications.

Gabaccia, D.R. (1998) *We Are What We Eat: Ethnic Food and the Making of Americans*. Cambridge, MA: Harvard University Press.

Gajanan, M. (2015) Patti Lupone snatches phone from texter during Shows for Days play. *The Guardian*, 10 July. See http://www.theguardian.com/stage/2015/jul/09/patti-lupone-takes-phone-texting-shows-for-days-theater (accessed 13 September 2015).

Galway International Oyster and Seafood Festival (2015) *History of The Galway International Oyster & Seafood Festival*. See http://galwayoysterfestival.com/index.php/history-of-the-galway-international-oyster-seafood-festival/ (accessed 20 July 2015).

García, M.E. (2013) The taste of conquest: Colonialism, cosmopolitics, and the dark side of Peru's gastronomic boom. *The Journal of Latin American and Caribbean Anthropology* 18 (3), 505–524.

Getz, D. and Brown, G. (2004) Critical success factors for wine tourism regions: A demand analysis. *Tourism Management* 27 (1), 146–158.

Getz, D., Robinson, R., Andersson, T. and Vujicic, S. (2014) *Foodies and Food Tourism*. Oxford: Goodfellow.

Gibbs, L., Staiger, P.K., Johnson, B., Block, K., Macfarlane, S., Gold, L., Kulas, J., Townsend, M., Long, C. and Ukoumunne, O. (2013) Expanding children's food experiences: The impact of a school-based kitchen garden program. *Journal of Nutrition Education and Behaviour* 45 (2), 137–146.

Gilbert, E. (2006) *Eat Pray Love*. London: Bloomsbury.

Gill, A.A. (2007) *Table Talk: Sweet and Sour, Salt and Bitter*. London: Phoenix.

Gill, A.A. (2010) Italy Inc. *Gourmet Traveller*, May, pp. 115–117.

Gillespie, D. (2008) *Sweet Poison: Why Sugar Makes Us Fat*. Melbourne: Penguin.

Goldman, A., Krider, R. and Ramaswami, S. (1999) The persistent competitive advantage of traditional food retails in Asia: Wet markets continued dominance in Hong Kong. *Journal of Macromarketing* 19 (2), 126–129.

Gomes, T. (2005) *Flavours of Portugal*. San Diego, CA: Thunder Bay Press.

Gormley, T.T., Downey, G. and O'Beirne, D. (1987) *Food, Health and the Consumer*. Essex: Elsevier.

Gössling, S. and Hall, C.M. (2013) Sustainable culinary systems: An introduction. In C.M. Hall and S. Gössling (eds) *Sustainable Culinary Systems: Local Foods, Innovation, Tourism and Hospitality* (pp. 1–39). London and New York: Routledge.

Gould, M.R. (2015) Punishment and the rite of purification at the Angola Prison Rodeo, Louisiana, USA. In J. Laing and W. Frost (eds) *Rituals and Traditional Events in the Modern World* (pp. 173–185). London and New York: Routledge.

Govindasamy, R., Italia, J., Zurbriggen, M. and Hossain, F. (2003) Producer satisfaction with returns from farmers' market related activity. *American Journal of Alternative Agriculture* 18 (2), 80–86.

Grahame, K. (1908) *The Wind in the Willows*. London: Borders Press/The Templar Company [reprinted 2000].

Green, M. (2015) There's no such thing as too much garlic. *The Age*, 11 April, p. 22.

Grescoe, T. (2005) *The Devil's Picnic: Around the World in Pursuit of Forbidden Fruit*. New York: Bloomsbury.

Griffin, M.R. and Frongillo, E.A (2003) Experiences and perspectives of farmers from Upstate New York farmers' markets. *Agriculture and Human Values* 20 (2), 189–203.

Griffenhagen, G.B. (1992) The materia medica of Christopher Columbus. *Pharmacy in History* 34 (3), 131–145.

Grundy, R. (2015) Stefano de Pieri returns to the Grand Hotel, Mildura. *Good Food*, 19 February. See http://www.goodfood.com.au/good-food/food-news/stefano-de-pieri-returns-to-the-grand-hotel-mildura-20150219-13j0uk.html (accessed 20 April 2015).

Guthrie, J., Guthrie, A., Lawson, R. and Cameron, A. (2006) Farmers' markets: The small business counter-revolution in food production and retailing. *British Food Journal* 108 (7), 560 – 573.

Hadley, D. (2005) Dining in disharmony in the later Middle Ages. In M. Carroll, D. Hadley and H. Willmott (eds) *Consuming Passions: Dining From Antiquity to the Eighteenth Century* (pp. 101–119). Stroud: Tempus.

Hall, C.M. (1992) *Hallmark Tourist Events: Impacts, Management and Planning*. London: Belhaven Press.

Hall, C.M. (2012) The Contradictions and paradoxes of slow food: Environmental change, sustainability and the conservation of taste. In S. Fullagar, K. Markwell and E. Wilson (eds) *Slow Tourism: Experiences and Mobilities* (pp. 53–68). Bristol: Channel View Publications.

Hall, C.M. (2013) The local in farmers' markets in New Zealand. In C.M. Hall and S. Gössling (eds) *Sustainable Culinary Systems: Local Foods, Innovation, Tourism and Hospitality* (pp. 99–121). London and New York: Routledge.

Hall, C.M. and Mitchell, R. (2002a) Tourism as a force for gastronomic globalization and localization. In A.-M. Hjalager and G. Richards (eds) *Tourism and Gastronomy* (pp. 71–87). London and New York: Routledge.

Hall, C.M. and Mitchell, R. (2002b) The changing nature of the relationship between cuisines and tourism in Australia and New Zealand. In A.-M. Hjalager and G. Richards (eds) *Tourism and Gastronomy* (pp. 186–206). London and New York: Routledge.

Hall, C.M. and Sharples, L. (2008) Food events, festivals and farmers' markets: An introduction. In C.M. Hall and L. Sharples (eds) *Food and Wine Festivals and Events around the World* (pp. 3–23). Oxford: Elsevier.

Halliwell, E. (2011) 'Try my burgers first,' celebrity chef Darren Simpson tells KFC critics. *The Sunday Telegraph*, 21 August. See http://www.news.com.au/entertainment/tv/try-my-burgers-first-celebrity-chef-darren-simpson-tells-kfc-critics/story-e6frfmyi-1226118866955 (accessed 2 September 2015).

Hartley, J. (1992) *The Politics of Pictures: The Creation of the Public in the Age of Popular Media*. London: Routledge.

Harvey, D.C. (2001) Heritage pasts and heritage presents: Temporality, meaning and the scope of heritage studies. *International Journal of Heritage Studies* 7 (4), 319–338.

Haverluk, T.W. (2003) Mex-America: From margin to mainstream. In G.J. Hausladen (ed.) *Western Places, American Myths: How we Think about the West* (pp. 166–183). Reno and Las Vegas, NV: University of Nevada Press.

Hawthorne, M. and Wright, J. (2014) Scalpers scam bookings for the Fat Duck. *The Sydney Morning Herald*, 18 November. See http://www.goodfood.com.au/good-food/food-news/table-scalpers-target-heston-blumenthals-the-fat-duck-20141117-11oerh.html (accessed 15 July 2015).

Hays, S., Page, S.J. and Buhalis, D. (2013) Social media as a destination marketing tool: Its use by national tourism organisations. *Current Issues in Tourism* 16 (3), 211–239.

Healey, J. (1999) (ed.) *Good Old Days, Good Old Ways: Wisdom of the Past for the Needs of Today*. Sydney: Reader's Digest.

Hede, A.-M. and Stokes, R. (2009) Network analysis of tourism events: An approach to improve marketing practices for sustainable tourism. *Journal of Travel and Tourism Marketing* 26 (7), 656–669.

Hegarty, J. A. and O'Mahony, G.B. (2001) Gastronomy: A phenomenon of cultural expressionism and an aesthetic for living. *Hospitality Management* 20 (1), 3–13.

Henderson, J. (2009) Food tourism reviewed. *British Food Journal* 11 (4), 317–326.

Hertzmann, P. (2010) Recipe structure: An historical survey. In R. Hosking (ed.) *Food and Language: Proceedings of the Oxford Symposium on Food and Cooking 2009.* Totnes, Devon: Prospect Books.

Hewison, R. (1987) *The Heritage Industry: Britain in a Climate of Decline.* London: Metheun.

Higham, J. and Ritchie, B. (2001) The evolution of festivals and other events in rural Southern New Zealand. *Event Management* 7 (1), 39–49.

Hobsbawm, E. and Ranger, T. (1983) *The Invention of Tradition.* Cambridge: Cambridge University Press.

Holden, M. and Scerri, A. (2012) More than this: Liveable Melbourne meets liveable Vancouver. *Cities* 31, 444–453.

Hollows, J. and Jones, S. (2010) At least he's doing something: Moral entrepreneurship and individual responsibility in Jamie's Ministry of Food. *European Journal of Cultural Studies* 13 (3), 307–322.

Hollows, J., Jones, S., Taylor, B. and Dowthwaite (2014) Making sense of urban food festivals: Cultural regeneration, disorder and hospitable cities. *Journal of Policy Research in Tourism, Leisure & Events* 6 (1), 1–14.

Hooper, B. (2010) Food and travel. *Reference & User Services Quarterly* 50 (2), 122–125.

Howard, P. (2003) *Heritage: Management, Interpretation, Identity.* London and New York: Continuum.

Humble N. (2002) Little Swans with Luxette and Loved Boy Pudding: Changing fashions in cookery books. *Women: A Cultural Review* 13 (3), 322–338.

Hunt, A.R. (2007) Consumer interactions and influences on farmers' market vendors. *Renewable Agriculture and Food Systems* 22 (1), 54–66.

Hutter, K. and Hoffmann, S. (2011) Guerrilla marketing: The nature of the concept and propositions for further research. *Asian Journal of Marketing* 5 (2), 39–54.

Ignatov, E. and Smith, S. (2006) Segmenting Canadian culinary tourists. *Current Issues in Tourism* 9 (3), 235–255.

Iorio, M. and Wall, G. (2015) Beyond the masks: Continuity and change in a Sardinian rite. In J. Laing and W. Frost (eds) *Rituals and Traditional Events in a Modern World* (pp. 126–140). London: Routledge.

Jackson, J. (2010) *Year in the Life of Padstow, Polzeath and Rock.* London: Frances Lincoln.

Jackson, S. (2012) *Death by Chocolate: The Serial Poisoning of Victorian Brighton.* Stroud: Fonthill Media.

Jaine, T. (2008) Introduction. In J. Brillat-Savarin, *The Philosophy of Taste,* 2008 edition. London: Folio Society [originally published 1825].

Jamie's Ministry of Food (2012). Our story. Jamie's Ministry of Food. See http://www.jamieoliver.com/jamies-ministry-of-food-australia/about.php (accessed 2 September 2015).

Janiskee, B. (1980) South Carolina's harvest festivals: Rural delights for day tripping urbanites. *Journal of Cultural Geography* 1 (1), 96–104.

Jolliffe, L. (2007) Tea and travel: Transforming the material culture of tea. In L. Jolliffe (ed.) *Tea and Tourism: Tourists, Traditions and Transformations* (pp. 38–52). Clevedon: Channel View Publications.

Jolliffe, L. (2008) Connecting farmers' markets and tourists in New Brunswick, Canada. In C.M. Hall and L. Sharples (eds) *Food and Wine Festivals and Events Around the World* (pp. 232–248). Oxford and Burlington, MA: Butterworth-Heinemann.

Jones, A. and Jenkins, I. (2002) A Taste of Wales – Blas Ar Gymru: Institutional malaise in promoting Welsh food tourism products. In A.-M. Hjalager and G. Richards (eds) *Tourism and Gastronomy* (pp. 115–131). London and New York: Routledge.

Jones, P., Hillier, D. and Comfort, D. (2007) Changing times and changing places for market halls and covered markets. *International Journal of Retail and Distribution Management* 35 (3), 200–209.

Jones, S. and Taylor, B. (2001) Food writing and food cultures: The case of Elizabeth David and Jane Grigson. *European Journal of Cultural Studies* 4 (2), 171–188.

Jones, S. and Taylor, B. (2013) Food journalism. In B. Turner and R. Orange (eds) *Specialist Journalism*. Abingdon and New York: Routledge.

Kael, P. (1984) *Taking It All In*. New York: Holt, Rinehart and Winston.

Keats, J. (1958) *The Insolent Chariots*. Philadelphia, PA: J.B. Lippincott.

Keen, L. and Gardner, J. (2014) Heston Blumenthal moves Fat Duck to Melbourne. *Australian Financial Review*, 13 March. See http://www.afr.com/business/retail/fmcg/heston-blumenthal-moves-fat-duck-to-melbourne-20140331-ix9mx (accessed 13 July 2015).

Kelly, I. (2003) *Cooking for Kings: The Life of Antonin Carême: The First Celebrity Chef*. London: Short Books.

Kelly Oysters (2015) *Welcome to Kelly Oysters*. See http://www.kellyoysters.com/ (accessed 14 September 2015).

Kerwin, J. and Seddon, R. (2002) Eating in space – From an astronaut's perspective. *Nutrition* 18 (10), 921–925.

Ketchum, C. (2005) The essence of cooking shows: How the food network constructs consumer fantasies. *Journal of Communication Inquiry* 29 (3), 217–234.

Khoo, R. (2012) *The Little Paris Kitchen*. London: Penguin.

Kim, H. (2005) Nostalgia and tourism. *Tourism Analysis* 10, 85–88.

Kim, H., Fiore, A.M., Niehm, L.S. and Jeong, M. (2010) Psychographic characteristics affecting behavioral intentions towards pop-up retail. *International Journal of Retail & Distribution Management* 38 (2), 133–154.

Kim, S. (2012) Audience involvement and film tourism experiences: Emotional places, emotional experiences. *Tourism Management* 33 (2), 387–396.

Kim, S. and Ellis, A. (2015) Noodle production and consumption: From agriculture to food tourism in Japan. *Tourism Geographies* 17 (1), 151–167.

Kitson, M. (2015) How this lettuce may unlock the future of space travel. *News.com.au*, 1 September. See http://www.news.com.au/technology/science/how-this-lettuce-may-unlock-the-future-of-space-travel/story-fnjwlcze-1227507856460 (accessed 2 September 2015).

Kivela, J. and Crotts, J.C. (2006) Tourism and gastronomy: Gastronomy's influence on how tourists experience a destination. *Journal of Hospitality and Tourism Research* 30 (3), 354–377.

Kivela, J. and Crotts, J. (2008) Gastronomy tourism. *Journal of Culinary Science and Technology* 4 (2/3), 39–55.

Koerth-Baker, M. (2013) Are we there yet? Good Weekend magazine, *The Age*, 10 August, p. 11.

Kohlstedt, S.G. (1997) Nature study in North America and Australasia, 1890–1945: International connections and local implications. *Historical Records of Australian Science* 11 (3), 439–454.

Komatsu, S. (1978) The savage mouth. In L. Harding (ed.) *Rooms of Paradise*. Melbourne: Quartet.

Kondrup, J., Johansen, N., Plum, L.M., Bak, L., Hojlund Larsen, I., Martinsen, A., Anderson, J.R., Baernthesen, H., Bunch, E. and Lauesen, N. (2002) Incidence of nutritional risk and causes of inadequate nutritional care in hospitals. *Clinical Nutrition* 21 (6), 461–468.

Kwong, K. (2003) *Heart and Soul*. Melbourne: Penguin.

Kwong, K. (2004) *George Negus Tonight*, Broadcast 11 November. See http://www.abc.net.au/gnt/profiles/Transcripts/s1242188.htm (accessed 15 January 2015).

Lade, C. and Jackson, J. (2004) Key success factors in regional festivals: Some Australian experiences. *Event Management* 9 (1/2), 1–11.

Laing, J. and Frost, W. (2012) *Books and Travel: Inspiration, Quests and Transformation.* Bristol: Channel View.

Laing, J. and Frost, W. (2013) Food, wine ... heritage, identity? Two case studies of Italian diaspora festivals in regional Victoria. *Tourism Analysis* 18 (3), 323–334.

Laing, J. and Frost, W. (2014) *Explorer Travellers and Adventure Tourism.* Bristol: Channel View Publications.

Laing, J. and Frost, W. (2015a) Christmas traditions: Pagan roots, invented rites. In J. Laing and W. Frost (eds) *Rituals and Traditional Events in a Modern World* (pp. 103–125). London: Routledge.

Laing, J. and Frost, W. (2015b) The new food explorer: Beyond the Experience Economy. In I. Yeoman, U. McMahon-Beattie, K. Fields, J. Albrecht and K. Meethan (eds) *The Future of Food Tourism: Foodies, Experiences, Exclusivity, Visions and Political Capital* (pp. 177–193). Bristol: Channel View Publications.

Laing, J. and Mair, J. (2015) Music festivals and social inclusion: The festival organizers' perspective. *Leisure Sciences* 37 (3), 252–268.

Lair, A. (2011) The ceremony of dining at Napoleon III's court between 1852 and 1870. In D. De Vooght (ed.) *Royal Taste: Food, Power and Status at the European Courts after 1789* (pp. 143–169). Farnham: Ashgate.

Lane, C. (2013) Taste makers in the 'fine dining' restaurant industry: The attribution of aesthetic and economic value by gastronomic guides. *Poetics* 41, 342–365.

Langbein, A. (2015) Annabel's story. See http://www.annabel-langbein.com/annabel/about/ (accessed 19 March 2015).

Lawrence, D.H (1921) *Women in Love.* Harmondsworth: Penguin [reprinted 1967].

Leboe, J. and Ansons, T. (2006) On misattributing good remembering to a happy past: An investigation into the cognitive roots of nostalgia. *Emotion* 6 (4), 596–610.

Lee, I. and Arcodia, C. (2011) The role of regional food festivals for destination branding. *International Journal of Tourism Research* 13 (4), 355–367.

Lee, W., Xiong, L. and Hu, C. (2012) The effect of Facebook users' arousal and valence on intention to go to the festival: Applying an extension of the technology acceptance model. *International Journal of Hospitality Management* 31, 819–827.

Levinson, J.C. (1984) *Guerilla Marketing: How to Make Big Profits in Your Small Business.* new York: Houghton Mifflin.

Levy, P. and Barr, A. (1984) *The Official Foodie Handbook.* London: Ebury Press.

Lewis, G.H. (1997) Celebrating asparagus: Community and the rationally constructed food festival. *Journal of American Culture* 20 (4), 73–78.

Lewis, S. (2013) Cafes' new sources have rich local flavour. *The Age*, 1 June, p. 7.

Libbon, R., Hamalian, G. and Yager, J. (2015) Self-cannibalism (autosarcophagy) in psychosis: A case report. *The Journal of Nervous and Mental Disease* 293 (2), 152–153.

Lim, Y., Chung, Y. and Weaver, P.A. (2012) The impact of social media on destination branding: Consumer-generated videos versus destination marketer-generated videos. *Journal of Vacation Marketing* 18 (3), 197–206.

Lindsay, J. (1967) *Picnic at Hanging Rock.* (1970 edn) Melbourne: Penguin.

Lowder, J.B. (2013) Cooking with Babette – I made the richest, most expensive dish from the best food movie of all time. *Slate*, 31 July. See http://www.slate.com/articles/life/food/2013/07/cailles_en_sarcophage_babette_s_feast_s_richest_most_expensive_dish_made.html (accessed 13 September 2015).

Lummis, T. (2005) *Pacific Paradises: The Discovery of Tahiti & Hawaii.* Stroud: Sutton.

Lynd, R.S. and Lynd, H.M. (1956) *Middletown: A Study in American Culture.* New York: Harcourt, Brace & World.

Macaulay, S. (2009) Dinner and a movie? *Filmmaking*, 8 January. See https://filmmaker-magazine.com/3890-dinner-and-a-movie/ (accessed 13 September 2015).

MacCannell, D. (1992) *Empty Meeting Grounds: The Tourist Papers*. London: Routledge.

Macionis, N. and Sparks, B. (2009) Film-induced tourism: An incidental experience. *Tourism Review International* 13 (2), 93–102.

Mackenzie, S. (2011) Celebrity farmers and A-list ingredients, *Hampshire Chronicle*, 1 November. See http://www.theguardian.com/lifeandstyle/wordofmouth/2011/nov/01/celebrity-farmers-a-list-ingredients (accessed 2 February 2015).

Maddocks, C. (2014) Fresh thinking. *The Sydney Morning Herald*, 12 April. See http://smh.domain.com.au/design-and-living/fresh-thinking-20140414-36nan.html (accessed 22 March 2015).

Mair, J. and Laing, J. (2012) The greening of music festivals: Motivations, barriers and outcomes. Applying the Mair and Jago Model. *Journal of Sustainable Tourism* 20 (5), 683–700.

Malm, S. (2014) Pakistan to bring in anti-cannibalism law after gruesome case of two brothers who had been digging up corpses and using them to make curry. *Daily Mail*, http://www.dailymail.co.uk/news/article-2806203/Pakistan-bring-anti-cannibalism-law-gruesome-case-two-brothers-digging-corpses-using-make-stews.html/(accessed 25 February 2015).

Mangold, W.G. and Faulds, D.J. (2009) Social media: The new hybrid element of the promotion mix. *Business Horizons* 52, 357–365.

Månsson, M. (2011) Mediatized tourism. *Annals of Tourism Research* 38 (4), 1634–1652.

Margalit, A. (2011) Nostalgia. *Psychoanalytic Dialogues* 21 (3), 271–280.

Mariani-Costantini, A. and Ligabue, G. (1992) Did Columbus also open the exploration of the modern diet? *Nutrition Reviews* 50 (11), 313–318.

Martin, A. (1980) Fantasy. In S. Murray (ed.) *The New Australian Cinema* (pp. 97–102). Melbourne: Nelson.

Maruyama, M. and Trung, L.V. (2006) Supermarkets in Vietnam: Opportunities and obstacles. *Asian Economic Journal* 21 (1), 19–46.

Maslin, J. (1993) Tasteful cannibalism as upbeat viewing, *The New York Times*, 15 January. See http://www.nytimes.com/1993/01/15/movies/reviews-film-tasteful-cannibalism-as-upbeat-viewing.html (accessed 29 January 2015).

Mathewson, K. (2000) Cultural Landscapes and Ecology III: Foraging/farming, food, festivities. *Progress in Human Geography* 24 (3), 457–474.

Mayfield, T.L. and Crompton, J.L. (1995) The status of the marketing concept among festival organisers. *Journal of Travel Research* 33, 14–22.

McCabe, C. (2012) Full forage ahead. *The Weekend Australian*, 5–6 May, p. 6.

McCabe, C. (2015) Upwardly mobile. *The Weekend Australian*, 18–18 July, p. 10.

McKelvey, S. and Grady, J. (2008) Sponsorship program protection strategies for special sport events: Are event organizers outmaneuvering ambush marketers. *Journal of Sport Management* 22 (5), 550–586.

McLaughlin, K. (2009) Food truck nation. *The Wall Street Journal*, 5 June. See http://www.wsj.com/articles/SB10001424052970204456604574201934018170554 (accessed 17 August 2015).

Melbourne Food and Wine Festival (2015) MFWF 2015 highlights. See www.melbourne-foodandwine.com.au (accessed 20 July 2015).

Memmott, M. (2013) Now he tells us: 'Tang sucks,' says Apollo 11's Buzz Aldrin. NPR, 13 June. See http://www.npr.org/sections/thetwo-way/2013/06/13/191271824/now-he-tells-us-tang-sucks-says-apollo-11s-buzz-aldrin (accessed 2 September 2015).

Mennell, S. (1985) *All Manners of Food: Eating and Taste in England and France from the Middle Ages to the Present*. Oxford: Blackwell.

Mennell, S. (2003) Eating in the public sphere in the nineteenth and twentieth centuries. In M. Jacobs and P. Scholliers (eds) *Eating Out in Europe: Picnics, Gourmet Dining and Snacks Since the Late Eighteenth Century*. Oxford; New York: Berg.

Mercille, J. (2005) Media effects on image: The case of Tibet. *Annals of Tourism Research* 32 (4), 1039–1055.

Meryment, E. (2011) New lingo on the tips of our tongues. *The Daily Mail*, 25 January. See http://www.dailytelegraph.com.au/new-lingo-on-the-tips-of-our-tongues/story-fn6bm6am-1225993766983 (accessed 15 July 2015).

Micheelsen, A., Havn, L., Poulsen, S., Larsen, T. and Holm, L. (2014) The acceptability of the New Nordic Diet by participants in a controlled six-month dietary intervention. *Food Quality and Preference* 36, 20–26.

Mickler, E.M. (1986) *White Trash Cooking*. Berkeley, CA: Ten Speed Press [reprinted 2011].

Miklavcic, A. and LeBlanc, M.N. (2014) Culture brokers, clinically applied ethnography, and cultural mediation. In L. Kirmayer, J. Guzder and C. Rousseau (eds) *Cultural Consultation: Encountering the Other in Mental Health Care* (pp. 115–137). New York: Springer.

Minor Hotel Group (2014) Imaginative dining. *Footprints*, 6, p. 11.

Mintz, S.W. and Du Bois, C.M. (2002) The anthropology of food and eating. *Annual Review of Anthropology* 31, 99–119.

Mitchell, J.T. (2006) Conflicting threat perceptions at a rural agricultural fair. *Tourism Management* 27 (6), 1298–1307.

Mitchell, R. and Hall, C.M. (2003) Consuming tourists: Food tourism consumer behaviour. In C.M. Hall, L. Sharples, R. Mitchell, N. Macionis and B. Cambourne (eds) *Food Tourism Around the World: Development, Management and Markets* (pp. 60–80). Oxford and Burlington MA: Butterworth Heinemann.

Money, L. (2012) Food for thought brings festival to life. *The Sydney Morning Herald*, 1 March. See http://www.smh.com.au/national/melbourne-life/food-for-thought-brings-festival-to-life-20120229-1u31l.html (accessed 20 July 2015).

Moore, T. (2006) *Death by Chocolate*. Harmondsworth: Penguin.

Morales, A. and Kettles, G. (2009) Healthy food outside: Farmers' markets, taco trucks, and sidewalk fruit vendors. *Journal of Contemporary Health Law and Policy* 26 (1), 20–48.

Mulvihill, K. (2010) Pop-up stores become popular for New York landlords. *The New York Times*, 22 June. See http://www.nytimes.com/2010/06/23/realestate/commercial/23popup.html (accessed 13 July 2015).

Murphy, A.J. (2011) Farmers' markets as retail spaces. *International Journal of Retail and Distribution Management* 39 (9), 582–597.

Murphy, G. (2010) *Mars: A Survival Guide*. Sydney: HarperCollins.

Murphy, J.M. (2003) *Education for Sustainability: Findings from the Evaluation Study of the Edible Schoolyard*. Berkeley, CA: Center for Ecoliteracy.

Mykletun, R. and Gyimóthy, S. (2010) Beyond the renaissance of the traditional Voss sheep's-head meal: Tradition, culinary art, scariness and entrepreneurship. *Tourism Management* 31 (3), 434–446.

National Farmers' Retail and Markets Association (2014) Who is FARMA? See www.farma.org.uk (accessed 1 August 2014).

National Gallery Women's Association (1978) *A Cook's Tour of the National Gallery of Victoria*. Melbourne: Hyland House.

Nepal, S.K. (2015) Irish pubs and dream cafes: Tourism, tradition and modernity in Nepal's Khumbu (Everest) region. *Tourism Recreation Research* 40 (2), 248–261.

Neuhaus, J. (1999) The way to a man's heart: Gender roles, domestic ideology, and cookbooks in the 1950s. *Journal of Social History* 32 (3), 529–555.

Nicholson, R.E. and Pearce, D.G. (2001) Why do people attend events: A comparative analysis of visitor motivations at four South Island events. *Journal of Travel Research* 39 (4), 449–460.

Niehm, L.S., Fiore, A.M. Jeong, M. and Kim, H. (2007) Pop-up retail's acceptability as an innovative business strategy and enhancer of the consumer shopping experience. *Journal of Shopping Center Research* 13 (2), 1–26.

Niland, J. (1995) Food gardens in South Africa. *City Farmer.* See http://www.cityfarmer.org/s.africa.html (accessed 12 January 2015).

Nolan, A. (2011) *Death by Chocolate.* Dublin: O'Brien.

NZPA (2007) Bluff keeps oyster festival after community rallies. *NZ Herald*, 13 December. See http://www.nzherald.co.nz/food-wine/news/article.cfm?c_id=206&objectid=10482182 (accessed 8 September 2015).

O'Dell, T. (2005) Experiencescapes: blurring borders and testing connections. In T. O'Dell and P. Billing (eds) *Experiencescapes: Tourism, Culture and Economy* (pp. 11–33). Copenhagen: Copenhagen Business School Press.

Ohnuki-Tierney, E. (1997) McDonald's in Japan: Changing manners and etiquette. In J.L. Watson (ed.) *Golden Arches East* (pp. 161–182). Redwood City, CA: Stanford University Press.

Oliver, J. (1999) *The Australian Home Beautiful: From Hills Hoist to High Rise.* Sydney: Home Beautiful.

Oliver, J. (2005) *Jamie's Italy.* London: Penguin.

Oliver, J. (2009) *Jamie's America.* London: Penguin.

Oliver, J. (2010) *Jamie does Spain, Italy, Sweden, Morocco, Greece and France.* London: Penguin.

Oliver, J. (2014) Jamie Oliver. See http://www.jamieoliverfoodfoundation.org.uk/jamies_big_vision (accessed 12 November 2014).

Oliver, J. (2015) Jamie Oliver, biography. See http://www.jamieoliver.com/about/jamie-oliver-biog/#5EAthZSDvOVHX3iA (accessed 17 February 2015).

O'Neill, M. (2013) Golden Boy by Clifford Odets, and: Picnic by William Inge (review). *Theatre Journal* 65 (4), 568–571.

Ooi, C-S. (2005) A theory of tourist experiences: The management of attention. In T. O'Dell and P. Billing (eds) *Experiencescapes: Tourism, Culture and Economy* (pp. 51–68). Copenhagen: Copenhagen Business School Press.

Ozersky, J. (2012) Are foodie kids the sign of end times? *Time*, 4 April. See http://ideas.time.com/2012/04/04/are-foodie-kids-the-sign-of-end-times/ (accessed 13 September 2015).

Panelli, R., Allen, D., Ellison, B., Kelly, A., John, A. and Tipa, G. (2008) Beyond Bluff oysters? Place identity and ethnicity in a peripheral coastal setting. *Journal of Rural Studies* 24 (1), 41–55.

Papashvily, H. and Papashvily, G. (1971) *The Cooking of Russia.* New York: Little Brown.

Parasecoli, F. and de Abreu e Lima, P. (2012) Eat your way through culture: Gastronomic tourism as performance and bodily experience. In S. Fullagar, K. Markwell and E. Wilson (eds) *Slow Tourism Experiences and Mobilities* (pp. 69–83). Bristol: Channel View Publications.

Park, K-S., Resinger, Y. and Kang, H.-J. (2008) Visitors' motivation for attending the South Beach Wine and Food Festival, Miami Beach, Florida. *Journal of Travel & Tourism Marketing* 25 (2), 161–181.

Parkhurst Ferguson, P. (1998) A culinary field in the making: Gastronomy in 19th century France. *American Journal of Sociology* 104 (3), 597–641.

Patterson, J. and Dickson Wright, C. (1998) *Two Fat Ladies Ride Again.* Sydney: ABC Books.

Pearce, P., Filep, S. and Ross, G. (2010) *Tourists, Tourism and the Good Life.* London: Routledge.

Peary, D. (1982) *Cult Movies: A Hundred Ways to Find the Reel Thing.* London: Vermillion.

Perchonok, M. and Bourland, C. (2002) NASA food systems: Past, present, and future. *Nutrition* 18 (10), 913–920.

Perry, C. (1989) Restaurant review: Grill Rises from Ashes of Les Anges. *Los Angeles Times*, 1 December, METRO, p. 1.

Pettifer, J. and Turner, N. (1984) *Automania: Man and the Motorcar*. London: Collins.

Pilcher, S.M. (2006) *Food in World History*. New York and Oxford: Routledge.

Pine, B.J. and Gilmore, J.H. (1999) *The Experience Economy: Work is Theatre & Every Business a Stage*. Harvard, MA: Harvard Business School Press.

Plummer, R., Telfer, D., Hashimoto, A. and Summers, R. (2005) Beer tourism in Canada along the Waterloo-Wellington Ale Trail. *Tourism Management* 25 (3), 447–458.

Pollan, M. (2006) *The Omnivore's Dilemma: The Search for a Perfect Meal in a Fast-Food World*. London: Bloomsbury.

Pollock, D. (1982) Having dessert after Eating Raoul. *The Los Angeles Times*, 1 November, Part VI, p. 4.

Powell, J. (2005) *Julie and Julia: My Year of Cooking Dangerously*. New York: Bay Back Books.

Pratt, S. and Matthews, K. (2004) *Superfoods. Fourteen Foods That Will Change Your Life*. New York: Harper Collins.

Prosterman, L. (1981) Food and alliance at the county fair. *Western Folklore* 40 (1), 81–90.

Quan, S. and Wang, N. (2004) Towards a structural model of the tourist experience: An illustration from food experiences in tourism. *Tourism Management* 25 (3), 297–305.

Quinn, B. (2006) Problematising 'festival tourism': Arts festivals and sustainable development in Ireland. *Journal of Sustainable Tourism* 14 (3), 288–306.

Ramshaw, G. (2016) Food, heritage and nationalism. In D. Timothy (ed.) *Heritage Cuisines* (pp. 53–64). London and New York: Routledge.

Ravenscroft, N. and Matteucci, X. (2003) The festival as carnivalesque: Social governance and control at Pamplona's San Fermin Fiesta. *Tourism, Culture and Communication* 4 (1), 1–15.

Reese, R. (2014) Seeds of Change offers $190,000 in funding to help support school gardens, community gardens and farms. PR Newswire (US), 3 March. See http://www.prnewswire.com/news-releases/seeds-of-change-offers-190000-in-funding-to-help-support-school-gardens-community-gardens-and-farms-248177641.html (accessed 25 March 2015).

Rehm, Z. (2014) A new study of urban farming in Los Angeles, USA. *Resource Magazine* 21 (2), 6–8.

Reijnders, S. (2011) Stalking the Count: Dracula, fandom and tourism. *Annals of Tourism Research* 38 (1), 231–248.

Reimer, G.D. (1990) Packaging dreams: Canadian tour operators at work. *Annals of Tourism Research* 17 (4), 501–512.

Richards, G. (2002) Gastronomy: An essential ingredient in tourism production and consumption? In A.-M. Hjalager and G. Richards (eds) *Tourism and Gastronomy* (pp. 3–20). London and New York: Routledge.

Rigby, M. (2013) Urban foraging: Uncovering the secret fruits of the city. *The Guardian*, 12 September. See http://www.theguardian.com/lifeandstyle/australia-food-blog/2013/sep/12/urban-foraging-food-city (accessed 10 February 2015).

Riley Fitch, N. (1997) *Appetite for Life: The Biography of Julia Child*. New York: First Anchor Books.

Roberts, A. (2014) Jamie Oliver studying for a degree so he has 'proper knowledge'. *The Telegraph*, 21 December. See http://www.telegraph.co.uk/news/celebritynews/11306602/Jamie-Oliver-studying-for-a-degree-so-he-has-proper-knowledge.html (accessed 20 September 2015).

Robinson, R. and Clifford, C. (2012) Authenticity and festival foodservice experiences. *Annals of Tourism Research* 39 (2), 571–600.

Robinson, T. (n.d.) Urban food foraging. Coming to a city near you! See http://permaculture.com.au/urban-food-foraging-coming-to-a-city-near-you (accessed 4 July 2015).

Roesch, S. (2009) *The Experiences of Film Location Tourists.* Bristol: Channel View Publications.

Rogers, D. (2011) Babylonstoren. See http://www.travelandleisure.com/travel-guide/south-african-winelands/hotels/babylonstoren (accessed 17 March 2015).

Rogers, P. and Anastasiadou, C. (2011) Community involvement in festivals: Exploring ways of increasing local participation. *Event Management* 15, 387–399.

Rony, F.T. (1996) *The Third Eye: Race, Cinema, and Ethnographic Spectacle.* Durham: Duke University Press.

Rorty, R. (1980) *Philosophy and the Mirror of Nature.* Oxford: Blackwell.

Rusher, K. (2003) The Bluff Oyster Festival and regional economic development: Festivals as culture commodified. In C.M. Hall, B. Cambourne, L. Sharples, N. Macionis and R. Mitchell (eds) *Food Tourism Around the World: Development, Management and Markets* (pp. 192–205). Amsterdam: Butterworth Heinemann.

Russell, S.A. (2013) Southbank's pop up plantation. *Broadsheet Media,* 4 March. See http://www.broadsheet.com.au/melbourne/food-and-drink/article/southbanks-pop-plan-tation (accessed 15 May 2015).

Ryan, R.M. and Deci, E.L. (2001) On happiness and human potentials: A review of research on hedonic and eudaimonic well-being. *Annual Review of Psychology* 52 (1), 141–166.

Sage, C. (2014) *Making and Un-making Meat: Cultural Boundaries, Environmental Thresholds and Dietary Transgressions. Food Transgressions: Making Sense of Contemporary Food Politics.* Farnham: Ashgate.

Sage, L. (1999) *The Cambridge Guide to Women's Writing in English.* Cambridge: Cambridge University Press.

Salkeld, L. (2007) The battle of 'Padstein': TV chef Rick Stein at war with the locals. *The Daily Mail,* 7 June. See http://www.dailymail.co.uk/news/article-460297/The-battle-Padstein-TV-chef-Rick-Stein-war-locals.html (accessed 29 June 2015).

Santich, B. (2004) The study of gastronomy and its relevance to hospitality education and training. *Hospitality Management* 23 (1), 15–24.

Santini, C., Cavicchi, A. and Belletti, E. (2013) Preserving the authenticity of food and wine festivals: The case of Italy. *Il Capitale Culturale* VIII, 251–271.

Santos, C.A. (2004) Framing Portugal: Representational dynamics. *Annals of Tourism Research* 31 (1), 122–138.

SBS (2015a) *Heston's Feasts, About the Show.* See http://www.sbs.com.au/shows/hestons-feasts/about/page/i/1/h/About/ (accessed 15 July 2015).

SBS (2015b) *Heston's Feasts, Roman.* See http://www.sbs.com.au/shows/hestonsfeasts/episodes/detail/episode/2317/season/1 (accessed 15 July 2015).

Scarpato, R. (2002a) Gastronomy as a tourist product: The perspective of gastronomy studies. In A.M. Hjalager and G. Richards (eds) *Tourism and Gastronomy* (pp. 51–70). London and New York: Routledge.

Scarpato, R. (2002b) Sustainable gastronomy as a tourist product. In A.-M. Hjalager and G. Richards (eds) *Tourism and Gastronomy* (pp. 132–152). London and New York: Routledge.

Schlosser, E. (2001) *Fast Food Nation: The Dark Side of the All-American Meal.* Boston, MA: Houghton Mifflin.

Schnell, S.M. (2007) Food with a farmer's face: Community-supported agriculture in the United States. *Geographical Review* 97 (4), 550–564.

Schnell, S.M. (2011) The Local traveller: Farming, food and place in state and provincial tourism guides, 1993–2008. *Journal of Cultural Geography* 28 (8), 281–309.

Schult, G. (2014) Nebraska looking at ways to grow urban agriculture. Associated Press Newswires, 31 May. See http://www.washingtontimes.com/news/2014/may/31/nebraska-looking-at-ways-to-grow-urban-agriculture/?page=all (accessed 26 February 2015).

Scrinis, G. (2013) *Nutritionalism. The Science and Politics of Dietary Advice*. Australia: Allen and Unwin.

Sharpe, E.K. (2008) Festivals and social change: Intersections of pleasure and politics at a community music festival. *Leisure Sciences* 30 (3), 217–234.

Shaw, N.S., Rutherdale, M. and Kenny, J. (2008) Eating more and enjoying it less: U.S. prison diets for women. *Women and Health* 10 (1), 39–57.

Shuman, A. (1981) The rhetoric of portions. *Western Folklore* 40 (1), 72–80.

Sidali, K.L., Kastenholz, E. and Bianchi, R. (2015) Food tourism, niche markets and products in rural markets: Combining the intimacy model and the experience economy as a rural development strategy. *Journal of Sustainable Tourism* 23 (8/9), 1179–1197.

Siefert, C.J., Kothuri, R., Jacobs, D.B., Levine, B., Plummer, J. and Marci, C.D. (2009) Winning the Super 'Buzz' Bowl: How biometrically-based emotional engagement correlates with online views and comments for Super Bowl advertisements. *Journal of Advertising Research* 49 (3), 293–303.

Siegel, J. (2000) Greenaway by the numbers. In M. Gras and V. Gras (eds) *Peter Greenaway: Interviews. Conversations with Filmmakers Series* (pp. 66–90). Jackson, MS: University Press of Mississippi.

Silkes, C.A., Cai, L.A. and Lehto, X.Y. (2013) Marketing to the culinary tourist. *Journal of Travel and Tourism Marketing* 30, 335–349.

Silverman, E. (1999) Tourist art as the crafting of identity in the Sepik River (Papua New Guinea). In R.B. Phillips and C.B. Steiner (eds) *Unpacking Culture: Art and Commodity in Colonial and Postcolonial Worlds* (pp. 51–66). Berkeley, CA: University of California Press.

Silverman, E. (2012) From *Cannibal Tours* to cargo cult: On the aftermath of tourism in the Sepik River, Papua New Guinea. *Tourist Studies* 12 (2), 109–130.

Sims, R. (2009) Food, place and authenticity: Local food and the sustainable tourism experience. *Journal of Sustainable Tourism* 17 (3), 321–336.

Smith, S.L.J. and Xiao, H. (2008) Culinary tourism supply chains: A preliminary examination. *Journal of Travel Research* 46, 289–299.

Spang, R.L. (2000) *The Invention of the Restaurant: Paris and Modern Gastronomic Culture*. Cambridge, MA: Harvard University Press.

Speed, A. (2014) Kitchen Gardens. *Weekend Australian*, Weekend A Plus, 22–23 February, pp. 2–3.

Spitz, B. (2012) *Dearie: The Remarkable Life of Julia Child*. New York: Alfred A. Knopf.

Spoto, D. (1997) *The Kindness of Strangers: The Life of Tennessee Williams*. New York: Da Capo Press.

Stebbins, R.A. (1992) *Amateurs, Professionals and Serious Leisure*. Montreal: McGill-Queen's University Press.

Stein, R. (2013) *Under a Mackerel Sky: A Memoir*. London: Ebury Press.

Stern, B. (1992) Historical and personal nostalgia in advertising text: The fin de siecle effect. *Journal of Advertising* 31 (4), 11–22.

Strain, E. (2003) *Public Places, Private Journeys: Ethnography, Entertainment and the Tourist Gaze*. New Brunswick, NJ: Rutgers University Press.

Strand, O. (2010) London's pop-up restaurants let rising chefs shine. *The New York Times*, 5 October. See http://www.nytimes.com/2010/10/06/dining/06london.html (accessed 11 June 2015).

Strickland, P., Williams, K., Laing, J. and Frost, W. (2016) The use of social media in the wine event industry: A case study of the High Country Harvest in Australia. In G. Szolnoki, L. Thach and D. Kolb (eds) *Successful Social Media & Ecommerce Strategies in the Wine Industry* (pp. 74–92). New York: Palgrave Macmillan.

Stringfellow, L., MacLaren, A., Maclean, M. and O'Gorman, K. (2013) Conceptualizing taste: Food, culture and celebrities. *Tourism Management* 37, 77–85.

Strong, J. (2006) The modern offal eaters. *Gastronomica: The Journal of Food and Culture* 6 (2), 30–39.

Strong, R. (2002) *Feasts: A History of Grand Eating.* London: Jonathan Cape.

Surchi, M. (2011) The temporary store: A new marketing tool for fashion brands. *Journal of Fashion Marketing and Management* 15 (2), 257–270.

Sutherland-Smith, B. (2015) *The Famous Edible Garden.* See http://www.beverleysutherlandsmith.com.au/a/Services/The-Edible-Garden (accessed 6 July 2015).

Sutton, R. (1996) *Motor Mania: A Hundred Years of Motoring.* London: Collins and Brown.

Svejenova, S., Mazza, C. and Planellas, M. (2007) Cooking up change in haute cuisine: Ferran Adrià as an institutional entrepreneur. *Journal of Organizational Behavior* 28 (5), 539–561.

Symons, M. (1999) Gastronomic authenticity and sense of place. In *CAUTHE 1999: Delighting the Senses; Proceedings from the Ninth Australian Tourism and Hospitality Research Conference.* Canberra: Bureau of Tourism Research.

Syrovatkova, M., Hrabak, J. and Spilkova, J. (2014) Farmers' markets' locavore challenge: The potential of local food production for newly emerged farmers' markets in Czechia. *Renewable Agriculture and Food Systems,* 1–13.

Tapsell, L. (ed.) (2013) *Food, Nutrition and Health.* Melbourne: Oxford University Press.

Templeton, A. (2015) Expansion of pop-up bars during Fringe and Festival hurting city pubs and clubs, say traders. *The Advertiser,* 7 March. See http://www.adelaidenow.com.au/entertainment/adelaide-fringe/expansion-of-pop-up-bars-during-fringe-and-festival-hurting-city-pubs-and-clubs-say-traders/story-fnintxwl-1227253060970 (accessed 13 July 2015).

Thomas, S. (1969) Aussie picnic. *Southerly* 29 (3), 210.

Timothy, D. and Boyd, S. (2003) *Heritage Tourism.* Harlow: Prentice Hall.

Timothy, D. and Pena, M. (2016) Food festivals and heritage awareness. In D. Timothy (ed.) *Heritage Cuisines: Traditions, Identities and Tourism* (pp. 148–165). London and New York: Routledge.

Timothy, D.J. and Ron, A.S. (2013a) Heritage cuisines, regional identity and sustainable tourism. In C.M. Hall and S. Gössling (eds) *Sustainable Culinary Systems: Local Foods, Innovation, Tourism and Hospitality* (pp. 275–290). London and New York: Routledge.

Timothy, D.J. and Ron, A.S. (2013b) Understanding heritage cuisines and tourism: Identity, image, authenticity, and change. *Journal of Heritage Tourism* 8 (2–3), 99–104.

Tobias, S.M. (1998) Early American cookbooks as cultural artifacts. *Papers on Language and Literature* 34 (1), 3–18.

Toensmeier, E. (2013) *Paradise Lot: Two Plant Geeks, One-tenth of an Acre, and the Making of an Edible Garden Oasis in the City.* White River Junction, VT: Chelsea Green.

Tong, L. Yu, X. and Liu, H. (2011) Insect for astronauts: Gas exchange in silkworms fed on mulberry and lettuce and the nutritional value of these insects for human consumption during deep space flights. *Bulletin of Entomological Research* 101 (5), 613–622.

Tourism Australia (2014) New tourism campaign puts focus on food and wine experiences. See http://www.tourism.australia.com/news/news-Restaurant-Australia-Launch.aspx (accessed 10 May 2015).

Travelmail Reporter (2014) The Tenthouse Suite! Inside Glastonbury's lavish pop-up hotel … complete with spa, butler service and exclusive restaurant (but you'll need £8,950 if you want the true VIP treatment). *Daily Mail Australia,* 23 June. See www.dailymail.co.uk/travel/article-2665684/Inside-Glastonburys-luxury-pop-hotel-expensive-room-costs-8-950.html (accessed 5 June 2015).

Tresidder, R. (2015) Eating ants: Understanding the terroir restaurant as a form of destination tourism. *Journal of Tourism and Cultural Change* 3 (4), 344–360.

Trexler, M.L. and Sargent, R. (1993) Assessment of nutrition risk knowledge and its relationship to dietary practices of adolescents. *Society for Nutrition Education* 25 (6), 337–344.

Truffaut, F. (1978) *The Films in My Life*. New York: Simon and Schuster.

Tuchman, G. and Levine, H.G. (1993) New York Jews and Chinese food: The social construction of an ethnic pattern. *Journal of Contemporary Ethnography* 22 (3), 382–407.

Turner, B. and Henryks, J. (2012) A study of the demand for community gardens and their benefits for the ACT community. Report Prepared for The Environment and Sustainable Development Directorate ACT. See http://www.actpla.act.gov.au/__data/assets/pdf_file/0017/34145/20130402_Community_Gardens_ACT_-_University_of_Canberra_-_Final_Report.pdf (accessed 11 January 2015).

Tyler, A. (1985) *The Accidental Tourist*. London: Chatto & Windus.

Tyler, A. (2009) Everyone back to mine: Pop-up restaurants in private homes are the latest foodie fad. *The Independent*, 4 June. See http://www.independent.co.uk/life-style/food-and-drink/features/everyone-back-to-mine-popup-restaurants-in-private-homes-are-the-latest-foodie-fad-1696262.html (accessed 13 July 2015).

Tyler, P. (1993) *Screening the Sexes: Homosexuality in the Movies*. New York: Da Capo Press.

Tyrrell, I. (1999) *True Gardens of the Gods: Californian–Australian Environmental Reform, 1860–1930*. Berkeley, CA: University of California Press.

United States Department of Agriculture (USDA) (2014) *Census of Agriculture*. Washington, DC: National Agriculture Statistical Service, US Department of Agriculture. See www.usda.gov (accessed 15 July 2015).

Unruh, D.R. (1979) Characteristics and types of participation in Social Worlds. *Symbolic Interaction* 2 (2), 115–130.

Urde, M., Greyser, S. and Balmer, J.M.T. (2007) Corporate brands with a heritage. *Brand Management* 15 (1), 4–19.

Van der Lans, R., Van Bruggen, G., Eliashberg, J. and Wierenga, B. (2010) A viral branching model for predicting the spread of electronic word of mouth. *Marketing Science* 29 (2), 348–365.

Victorian Farmers' Market Association (2014) *About the VFMA*. See www.vicfarmersmarkets.org.au (accessed 16 July 2015).

Visser, M. (1991) *The Rituals of Dinner: The Origins, Evolution, Eccentricities, and Meaning of Table Manners*. New York: Penguin.

Wang, N. (1999) Rethinking authenticity in tourism experiences. *Annals of Tourism Research* 26 (2), 349–370.

Warhust, M. (2015) Heston's Fat Duck: At $525 per head does it really qualify as a 'pop-up' restaurant? *The Guardian*, 4 February. See http://www.theguardian.com/lifeandstyle/2015/feb/04/hestons-fat-duck-at-525-per-head-does-it-really-qualify-as-a-pop-up-restaurant (accessed 14 May 2015).

Warin, M. (2011) Foucault's progeny: Jamie Oliver and the art of governing obesity. *Social Theory and Health* 9 (1), 24–40.

Waters, A. (2007) *The Art of Simple Food*. New York: Clarkson Potter.

Watson, J.L. and Caldwell, M.L. (eds) (2005) *The Cultural Politics of Food and Eating*. Malden, MA: Blackwell.

Weaver, D.B. and Fennell, D.A. (1997) The vacation farm sector in Sashkatchewan: A profile of operations. *Tourism Management* 18 (6), 357–365.

Webster, K. (2014) Creating wow in the fashion industry: Reflecting on the experience of Melbourne Fashion Festival. In K. Williams, J. Laing and W. Frost (eds) *Fashion, Design and Events* (pp. 118–130). London and New York: Routledge.

Wechsberg, J. (1999) The Bois de Boulogne. In D. Morowitz (ed.) *Trifles Make Perfection: The Selected Essays of Joseph Wechsberg*. Boston, MA: David R. Godine.

Wenande, C. (2014) Stegt Flæsk is Denmark's new national dish. *The Copenhagen Post*, 20 November. See http://cphpost.dk/news/stegt-flaesk-is-denmarks-new-national-dish.11700.html/ (accessed 18 February 2015).

Wessel, G. (2012) From place to nonplace: A case study of social media and contemporary food trucks. *Journal of Urban Design* 17 (4), 511–531.

White, L. and Leung, D. (2015) Wishing you good health, prosperity and happiness: Exploring the rituals and traditions of Chinese New Year. In J. Laing and W. Frost (eds) *Rituals and Traditional Events in a Modern World* (pp. 78–89). London: Routledge.

White, R.J. and Averner, M. (2001) Humans in space. *Nature* 409 (22 February), 1115–1118.

Whyte, W. (1980) *The Social Life of Small Urban Places*. New York: Project for Public Spaces.

Wild Food UK (2015) *Meet Eric*. See http://www.wildfooduk.com/about-us/ (accessed 12 February 2015).

Wilmoth, P. (2015) Kitchen Khoo, *The Weekly Review*, 1 July. See http://www.theweeklyreview.com.au/meet/rachel-khoo-comes-to-melbourne/ (accessed 13 July 2015).

Wilson, S. (2012) *I Quit Sugar: Your Complete 8-week Detox Program and Cookbook*. London: Pan Macmillan.

Wolf, M., Spittler, A. and Ahern, J. (2005) A profile of farmers' markets consumers and the perceived advantages of produce sold at farmers' markets. *Journal of Food Distribution Research* 36 (1), 192–201.

Wood, R. (1991) The shock of the new: A sociology of nouvelle cuisine. *Journal of Consumer Studies and Home Economics* 15 (4), 327–338.

Wood, S. (2015) Dairy made. *The Age*, Good Weekend, 25 July, pp. 18–19.

Woodburn, V. (2014) *Understanding the Characteristics of Australian Farmers' Markets*. Rural Industries Research and Development Corporation (RIRDC) Publication14/040. See http://rirdc.infoservices.com.au/items/14-040 (accessed 4 November 2014).

Yeoman, I. and McMahon-Beattie, U. (2015) The future of food tourism: The Star Trek replicator and exclusivity. In I. Yeoman, U. McMahon-Beattie, K. Fields, J.N. Albrecht and K. Meethan (eds) *The Future of Food Tourism: Foodies, Experiences, Exclusivity, Visions and Political Capital* (pp. 23–48). Bristol: Channel View Publications.

Yeow, P.L. (2010) *Poh's Kitchen: My Cooking Adventures*. Sydney: Harper Collins.

Yonan, J. (2010) Blue Hill Restaurant in Tarrytown, N.Y., sparkles in winter. *Washington Post*, 25 February. See http://www.washingtonpost.com/wp-dyn/content/article/2010/02/25/AR2010022505311.html (accessed 28 February 2015).

Yuan, J.J., Cai, L.A., Morrison, A.M. and Linton, S. (2005) An analysis of wine festival attendees' motivations: A synergy of wine, travel and special events? *Journal of Vacation Marketing* 11 (1), 41–58.

Zaalberg, A., Nijman, H., Bulten, E., Stroosma, L. and van der Staak, C. (2010) Effects of nutritional supplements on aggression, rule-breaking, and psychopathology among young adult prisoners. *Aggressive Behaviour* 36 (2), 117–126.

Ziakas, V. (2013) *Event Portfolio Planning and Management: A Holistic Approach*. London and New York: Routledge.

Zubrin, R. (1996) *The Case for Mars: The Plan to Settle the Red Planet and Why We Must*. New York: Touchstone.

Index

For Product Safety Concerns and Information please contact our EU Authorised
Representative:

Easy Access System Europe

Mustamäe tee 50

10621 Tallinn

Estonia

gpsr.requests@easproject.com

www.ingramcontent.com/pod-product-compliance
Lightning Source LLC
Chambersburg PA
CBHW071417290326
41932CB00046B/1912